BOOKS BY Ira Berkow

The Man Who Robbed the Pierre:
The Story of Bobby Comfort
Red: A Biography of Red Smith
Carew (with Rod Carew)
The DuSable Panthers
Maxwell Street
Beyond the Dream
Rockin' Steady (with Walt Frazier)
Oscar Robertson: The Golden Year

THE MAN WHO ROBBED
The Pierre

THE
MAN
WHO
ROBBED
The Pierre

The Story of Bobby Comfort

IRA BERKOW

NEW YORK *Atheneum* 1987

Library of Congress Cataloging in Publication Data

Berkow, Ira.
The man who robbed the Pierre.

1. Comfort, Robert Anthony, 1932–　. 2. Brigands
and robbers—New York (State)—Biography. I. Title.
HV6653.C65B47　1987　364.1′552′0924 {B}　86–47950
ISBN 0–689–11918–6

Published simultaneously in Canada by Collier Macmillan Canada, Inc.
Composition by Heritage Printers, Inc., Charlotte, North Carolina
Manufactured by Fairfield Graphics, Fairfield, Pennsylvania
Designed by Cathryn S. Aison

FIRST EDITION

ACKNOWLEDGMENTS

By far the single most important source for this book was Bobby Comfort. Over the nearly three years during which this volume was researched and written, I spent many hours tape-recording Comfort at his home in upstate New York, as well as at my own home in New York City. At other times we spoke frequently by telephone.

Comfort's recall of events, dates, incidents, and conversations would prove remarkably accurate. By the time Comfort and I met, in 1978, the statute of limitations had expired on his crimes; he now considered himself "retired," and so felt free to talk of his past life. In the book the clandestine conversations with his partners, particularly Sammy Nalo, are represented as Comfort recalled them. When I met Nalo on Riker's Island—he was being held on charges of another jewel robbery—he refused to give any information regarding his association with Comfort and denied involvement in some of the crimes. It was imperative, however, to check and confirm through other sources as many facts and details as possible. The sources included interviews, records from FBI and police files, as well as material from New York City and Rochester library and newspaper files.

Interviews were conducted with more than one hundred persons. I appreciate the cooperation of all of them. Some conversations were conducted in person, others by phone. Many of those interviewed are mentioned in the text, others are not. I will not attempt a roll call of all who assisted, but I wish to express gratitude to certain individuals for their contributions: Louis Rabon, of the Pierre; Albert Seedman, former chief of detectives, New York Police Department; Detective Lieutenant Edward J. O'Connor, former commander of the Manhattan Robbery Squad; former New York City Detective George Bermudez; FBI agent Joe Holliday; former Manhattan Assistant District Attorney Richard Lowe; Lieutenant Richard Maroney, former prison guard, Attica; Harold J. Smith, former warden of Attica; John Willmarth, parole officer in Rochester; and James B. White, president, Jewelers' Security Alliance in Manhattan.

In some cases one person remembered an incident somewhat differently from another. The version that seemed most plausible to the author was used.

When tape-recorded conversations were used, an attempt was made to keep them as pure as possible, though I did take minor liberties by occasionally filling in an ellipsis, deleting repetition, and transposing a word or sentence to adjust to the requirement of the printed page.

In some instances the names and identifying details of particular individuals were changed to protect their privacy. Some false names were used for Comfort's accomplices in hotel robberies. In these instances Comfort has never revealed their true identities, in order, he says, "to protect the guilty."

Of those who were asked to read and comment on this manuscript I gratefully acknowledge Dolly Case, my wife, and Phil Berger, Richard Close, Richard Fields, Deborah Grody, Ernestine Guglielmo, Virginia Hoitsma Fox, Richard Huttner, Larry Klein, Ted Ravinett, and Joe Wander.

I reserve a special appreciation for Sayre Ross, who was the inspiration, the catalyst, and the primary support for the entire project.

I.B.

THE MAN WHO ROBBED
The Pierre

PROLOGUE

November 14, 1971, Rochester, New York

To a casual eye Bobby Comfort seemed the conventional suburban dweller. He lived with his wife, baby daughter, and mother-in-law in a split-level house on a quiet cul-de-sac in Fairport, New York, twenty miles southeast of Rochester: two cars were in his garage, and he had a spacious front lawn and a backyard complete with a stone barbecue pit and a swimming pool.

The lone discordant note in the neat, shrub-lined backyard was the clothesline that extended between two sycamore trees. Comfort's mother-in-law insisted that her granddaughter's clothes be sun-dried, to insure freshness.

Behind the home were thirty acres of woods that afforded relative privacy—that is, except for an occasional unexpected visitor. Sometimes, Comfort would turn from his cup of coffee in the breakfast room and come face-to-face with a deer staring at him through the window.

The Comforts were private people—cordial, but not overly friendly to the neighbors, and the neighbors respected their privacy and understood that they had their own set of friends. Because Comfort was away a lot, the neighbors assumed he was a traveling salesman of some kind. He was quiet but never failed to wave hello when coming out of the driveway. The last thing they would have imagined was that Mr. Comfort was the most widely sought jewel thief in the country.

The weather had been unusually mild for late autumn and the soft, hilly land, with leaves still clinging to the trees, was dappled various shades of red and brown. Although close to industrial Rochester, the Fairport area was extensively cultivated. Just beyond the community of suburban homes were farmhouses and silos; cornfields and apple orchards dotted the landscape, dairy cows grazed, and mounds of new-mown hay were spread out on the vista Bobby Comfort saw—but didn't really notice—as he wheeled his black Thunderbird along his street and onto Pittsford Road. He had something other than scenery on his mind.

It was mid-morning, the air was nippy, but the sun felt good and strong as it came through the car window and reflected on his sunglasses.

He snapped on the radio to the news. More American bombing raids on North Vietnam; an early-season snowstorm had hit the upper Midwest and might be headed toward Rochester. In the local news a police captain had been indicted on charges of corruption and was turning informant against several colleagues. As if to retreat from thoughts of the police, Comfort pressed another button and heard music.

That's better, he mused.

Shortly, he arrived at the shopping-center parking lot, whisked into the supermarket, picked up two cartons of cigarettes, hurried back to the car, and pulled back onto the road.

The morning traffic noises seemed distant and dreamy. His thoughts returned to the problem.

It was exactly one year ago that he and his partner had pulled their last hotel heist. The robberies they had committed in Manhattan since then were at Sophia Loren's penthouse and an apartment at One Sutton Place, and, although not hotels, the attendant

4

publicity forced them to "semiretire" for a period of time. But he was determined to pull one last job that would net him at least a couple of million dollars—the amount he decided could set him up for life. One more job was all he needed. He knew what it would be.

Absently, he turned onto the expressway, heading in the opposite direction from home. He saw himself in the hotel, the safe-deposit boxes being emptied. A roomful of diamonds. It was beautiful to contemplate. He'd have to balance the odds of the haul with that of being caught and, as a multiple offender, sent back to prison—possibly for the rest of his life.

"Plymouth Avenue," read a sign on the highway. "Jeezus, I'm in *Rochester*," he muttered. He had missed one cutoff. Softly cursing, he swung around onto the next cloverleaf to head back home, nearly a half-hour away.

When he walked into the house, his wife, in low-cut housecoat, was at the kitchen table sipping coffee. A strand of her black hair had fallen across her forehead, and she looked up, eyes large and questioning.

"What happened to you?" she asked.

He kissed her. "I just got carried away with an idea I had, and wound up in Rochester," he said.

"I couldn't imagine . . ."

He placed one carton of cigarettes on the counter, walked into the living room with a lively step, picked up the phone, and dialed a number in New York.

A man's voice answered. "Hello?"

"Can you meet me at the fountain tomorrow at noon?" Comfort asked.

"I'll be there."

Click.

November 15, 1971, New York City

At the Pulitzer Fountain in the Grand Army Plaza at Fifty-ninth Street and Fifth Avenue, which marks the southernmost entrance to Central Park, Bobby Comfort sat and waited on one of the benches. He checked his watch: ten minutes past noon. Sammy was late. It wasn't like him. Comfort stood up and looked around.

The sunlight on this warm day revealed him to be a man of medium build, with broad shoulders tapering to a narrow waist. He was a man in his late thirties with dark hair and fashionably long sideburns. His face had solid features, high cheekbones, a strong chin. He looked out at the scene around him through lightly tinted, metal-framed sunglasses.

Except for his casual attire, he could have been a successful business executive. Today, however, in a honey-colored leather jacket over a beige sport shirt, open at the neck, and a brown cashmere sweater, tailored cord slacks and burgundy Bally loafers, he epitomized the sporty New Yorker.

Upon closer scrutiny, however, a noticeable scar around his mouth and another etched above his right eyebrow signaled yet another occupation, more turbulent and unrefined than anything his appearance portrayed.

Comfort glanced around the plaza, and his eyes came to rest on the activity at the outer edge of the Central Park entrance. Lining the curb were several hansom cabs, the symbol of romance in the big city. Comfort noticed a young couple step into the first open-top carriage. The coachman, in his worn, dented black opera hat, accepted his fee from the young man as the couple settled down for their ride through the park. The driver tugged at the reins and the chestnut horse began its familiar journey through the park, a funny red plume bobbing on its aged head.

Comfort looked toward the Plaza Hotel and saw Sammy the Arab, his partner, walking rapidly toward him. Although he looked serious and determined, his wobbly stride made him appear slightly comical to Comfort.

Sammy Nalo, five feet four, and conscious of his short stature, attempted to overcome what he considered a physical deficiency by wearing elevator shoes. This made him appear taller, but it also made walking quickly troublesome. As usual, he was dressed meticulously, in a gray topcoat, blue pin-striped suit, and what to Comfort appeared to be a new black hairpiece covering Sammy's bald head.

Watching him draw closer, Comfort thought how strange that nature could provide so well for Sammy's chosen profession. He was a superb thief, and his assortment of disguises helped in confusing possible witnesses: Sammy could be five four to five seven, bald or curly-haired; he was dark-complexioned, and could grow a true mustache in less than a week. He sometimes seemed to be not one person but a composite.

Now he sat down next to Bobby without saying a word and looked around. When he felt sure that they weren't being watched, he turned to his bench mate. His deep-set black eyes shone.

"Bobby, I just saw something that would make your mouth water," he said.

"Hello," Comfort said.

Sammy didn't smile. "You know I meant hello," he said. "Does someone have to *say* it?"

"It is proper, isn't it? It's just a little social amenity," said Comfort.

"Social amenity! Okay, how are you? How's your mother-in-law? Your hemorrhoids? How's your dog Buttons? What did I leave out? Look, Bobby, I just came across something important. Jesus Christ! I thought you came down to talk business."

"Okay, Sammy, relax," Comfort said, laughing. "What's getting you so excited today—besides me?"

Sammy ignored the remark. He said softly, with a nod of his head, "Over there, the Plaza. I was just walking through and passed the door next to the cashier. You can see directly into the safety-box room. I saw a guest deposit her diamond necklace into the safety box. Had to be worth half a million dollars." He smiled. "And that's just one box, Bob, can you imagine the stuff in the rest of 'em?"

"Sounds good," said Comfort.

"It *looks* good," Sammy said.

"Sammy, we've both talked about doing one last big score, then quitting."

"And?"

"And if we're going to do it, we've got to do it right—the right place, the right time. If it's going to be big, it has to be the biggest."

"Right. What are you getting at?"

7

A pretzel vendor trundled his cart past the two seated men. Comfort looked up. "You want one?"

"No," said Sammy impatiently.

"Pretzel, mister," said Comfort.

He bit into the pretzel. "Good. Nice and warm. Want a bite?"

"No," said Sammy. "All I want is for you to get to the point."

Comfort rose and motioned Sammy to follow him. He fell in step with Comfort and they walked toward the hansom cab station.

"Let's take a ride," said Comfort. "We can talk better—more private—and I think better when I'm moving."

Comfort selected a closed cab, ensuring the privacy of their discussion.

He said to the driver, "Buddy, up through the park to Seventy-second Street, then turn down Fifth."

"Yes, sir."

Comfort slipped a twenty-dollar bill into the coachman's gloved hand, closed the door of the cabriolet, and settled back on the red tufted seat cushions.

Above the rhythmic clop of the horse's hooves, Comfort said, "I don't want you to take offense, but I've discounted the Plaza. It's not first-rate anymore."

"Rich people still stay at the joint all the time," countered Sammy. "You know that."

"Not like they used to," said Comfort. "It's mostly transient. They even have offices in some of the suites. Nowadays the wealthiest people there are usually the General Motors crowd visiting the new headquarters across the street, and most of those guys sleep with their watches on."

"Hey, Bob, there's still more than enough big stuff in the safe-deposit boxes."

"And there are also three sets of elevator banks, and nine staircases that lead up or down to the lobby, and restaurants that are open at all hours, and people always roaming the lobby. We couldn't cover it unless we came in with an army."

The carriage jostled them as it rolled up the right side of the road that cuts through the park.

"So?" asked Sammy.

Comfort took another bite of his pretzel.

"What about the Waldorf?" Sammy asked.

"That one's even more spread out than the Plaza."

Sammy gave his partner an odd, probing look.

"You got something on your mind. Knock off the bullshit. What is it?"

"I know one place in this city that can give us a complete retirement plan. It's got all the things we've been looking for for a perfect job. It's small enough for maybe four or five guys, only two entrances, and almost no traffic after two in the morning, especially on the day I've chosen. It has seven hundred rooms and suites, three hundred of which are apartments owned by the cream of New York—wealthy widows and business tycoons, with a few dukes and Arab sheiks thrown in. It's the richest hotel in town. And they all keep their jewels in the big vault room behind the cashier's desk."

"Where is this place?"

The cab had come out of the park and was now heading south down Fifth Avenue. Comfort glanced out the window of the hansom, knocked on the roof of the cab, and called to the driver to stop on the west side of Fifth Avenue. They were now at the corner of Sixty-first Street.

The cab stopped, and the partners climbed down.

"Right there," said Comfort, motioning to the hotel directly across the street.

Sammy looked. The canopy read The Pierre.

◆ 1 ◆

Robert Anthony Comfort was born to Joe and Peggy Comfort on October 26, 1932, the second of six children. The family lived on the southeast side of Rochester, in a predominantly Italian section which included smaller groups of Irish, Bohemians, and Germans among their neighbors.

"Comperchio" had been the family name, but Bobby's grandfather, Paolo Comperchio, changed it. He and a brother had come to America from Naples, Italy, hoping to fill their pockets with the gold they had been told lined the streets of America. Naples, in contrast, was dirty, the people poor, and life in the crowded streets seemed hopeless. Paolo's father, a cobbler, had expected that his sons, in true European tradition, would join their father's trade, but neither Paolo nor Giuseppe relished the thought of spending their lives hammering nails into boots in a grimy shop overflowing with leather scraps.

Through relatives living in Wilkes-Barre, Pennsylvania, the Comperchio brothers arranged passage to America. Landing on the shores of their newly adopted country, their joy was tremendous. Not until they arrived in Wilkes-Barre was their ardor dampened, for their relatives had secured jobs for them in the coal mines. They quickly discovered that the life of a poor Naples cobbler was almost glorious compared to that of chipping out a livelihood in a dark, foul-aired, wet tunnel thousands of feet below the surface of the earth.

Eventually, Paolo learned that the railroads needed "gandy dancers," and he happily climbed out of the deep black coal mine to pound rail spikes in the great outdoors. But even laying tracks in a section gang was back-breaking work, and the hours endless. Paolo Comperchio was perceptive and ambitious. He observed that the heavy sledgehammer roadwork was always performed by the immigrant Italians and Poles, while the Irish invariably were the foremen and bosses. If he were to prosper in America, he reasoned, he would have to learn to speak English well. He and his Italian-born wife were soon studiously reading the local newspaper aloud to each other in order to better grasp this new language.

When Paolo Comperchio heard that better railroad jobs were available in Rochester, New York, he moved there with his wife and young brood and made yet another important change. Paolo changed his surname to "Comfort," which sounded more American. He also insisted on being called "Paul." By this time, his English had improved considerably; and when a foreman's job opened on the New York Central Railroad, Paul Comfort got it. The year was 1904.

By the turn of the century, many Italians had moved to Rochester. Jobs were plentiful; the city was flourishing with shoe and clothing factories, the famous Kodak company, flour mills, and the railroad. In the ten years from 1900 to 1910, the Italians increased to over one-fourth of the city's population. And almost all of the immigrants lived along the Genesee River, in crowded tenements infested by rats and overflowing with garbage. It was known as "Poison Row."

The firmly established Irish ran the city. They dominated the police force, held all the political offices, and were the landlords of the tenement slums.

12

The Italians, virtually powerless in the social order, took their frustrations out with violence.

Smoldering beneath the surface was the Black Hand, or Mafia, a legacy of the old *padrone* system of Sicily. Many Italians denied that it existed at all in Rochester, but the authorities were convinced otherwise. There was little doubt that this terrorist organization developed in those early years as a means of gaining community power and economic strength in the city.

As the Italians began to make inroads in the city power structure, they were predictably opposed by the Irish, who were tenacious in maintaining their power base.

Earning a foreman's pay now, Paul Comfort moved his family to a substantially better neighborhood, near the Irish. Two of his sons, convinced that work on the railroad was a reliable source of income, and that smart young men could advance, followed him into jobs with the New York Central. The third son, Joe, took a different route entirely.

Young Joe, like Paul Comfort before him, wanted to do better than his father. It was apparent from his observations in the little world around him that bigger and easier money was available in the gambling parlors around town. Joe took a job in one of the larger bookmaking establishments that operated openly in Rochester by virtue of "the wink" and the cops' greased palms.

Gambling paid off well enough for him to afford the flashiest clothes and the prettiest girls in town. Joe was a dark-haired *bon vivant* who enjoyed his reputation as a ladies' man, and earned the nickname "Joe Gash."

When Peggy O'Horgan, an Irish girl, met him for the first time in a speakeasy, she was struck by his stylish dress and good looks. She was particularly impressed by his manicured fingernails, very unusual in a workingman's town.

To Joe Comfort, Peggy was something different. She was strong-willed and opinionated, and he found her entertaining. Even more intriguing were her large blue eyes and long lustrous hair. She was a tall, pretty girl. And Irish: he found that sinfully delicious. The Irish and the Italians had no love for each other. The Irish viewed the Italians as smelly "greaseballs"; the Italians, who

13

loved their opera and honored the memory of Dante and Michelangelo, snubbed the Irish as uncultured louts with only pretensions of gentility.

The O'Horgans indeed saw themselves as cosmopolites. Frank O'Horgan, Peggy's father, had been the owner of a large sawmill in the *city* of Cork. "County Cork," he would distinguish, "was where the peasants lived and where they spoke with a brogue. We lived in the city of Cork and had a big house and servants and we spoke a fine English."

Frank O'Horgan had spent some time in America visiting relatives who had fled Ireland during the potato famine in the 1840s. Those relatives had settled in Rochester. O'Horgan quickly saw the opportunities America offered, and on his return to Cork he consolidated his holdings, sold part of his property, and booked passage to the new country for himself and his family.

The O'Horgans, with Peggy, age eleven, and Jimmy, age nine, and all their possessions, sailed across the Atlantic in the spring of 1913. They arrived in Rochester and began the process of assimilating to their new surroundings.

Impetuously, without seeking professional advice, Frank O'Horgan invested and eventually lost most of the family fortune in the stock market. The sudden comedown stunned and humiliated him, and it became necessary for O'Horgan to accept a job as a clerk with the railroad.

He rose rapidly with the Central, and was able to retain his bungalow-style house in the better part of the city. Once again O'Horgan was the proud Irishman. A tall, thin, high-cheekboned man, he wore the traditional starched white collar and suit with vest, the status symbol of the executive. His home was kept immaculately clean, with the proverbial lace curtains on all the windows. In the living room sat his proudest possession, the family organ.

Peggy O'Horgan was raised and taught in a strict Catholic manner, but also had to face the reality of coping with life in the tough street she was forced early on to grow up in. Her father, upon learning that his daughter was dating a "wop," was stunned; when she became engaged, he was horrified. He tried to reason with his stubborn daughter about Italians, but to no avail.

14

The Comforts were equally upset with Joe's choice of the Irish colleen.

The attitudes of both families notwithstanding, the banns were published, the wedding date set, and there was no choice but to accept the decision of the headstrong young couple.

After the church ceremony, a huge reception was held in a banquet hall of a prominent Rochester club. The tension between the families remained submerged by the gaiety of the affair, the drinking, the eating, the laughter. The high point was reached when, with the appropriate fanfare from the orchestra, tuxedoed waiters rolled in a cart piled high with hundreds of bananas. Attached to each banana, resembling a leaf, was a hundred-dollar bill. No one was quite sure what this "banana delight" symbolized until the bridegroom opened the accompanying envelope to read it aloud to the assembled guests. "To my new brother-in-law, in recognition of all your people who came over here from the old country in banana boats." It was signed Jimmy O'Horgan. The message was greeted first by silence, the Irish waiting for the reaction of the Italians, the Italians letting the message sink in. Then, slowly, the Italians began to laugh, and then the Irish began to laugh. Soon the room was in an uproar. In fact, peace between the families prevailed until the end of the evening when the effects of the heavy drinking became apparent. Words and curses flew from the Irish side of the room to the Italian, and back again. Punches were thrown and a free-for-all erupted. The chandeliered hall was in the process of being demolished when the newlyweds, gifts under arms, fled out the door, pushing the banana cart ahead of them.

From the beginning of their marriage, Joe and Peggy Comfort picked up where the wedding reception left off. Bobby grew up to the sound of voices raised in argument, particularly his mother's. She complained that Joe never spent enough time at home. Competing with smoke-filled gambling rooms was not her idea of conjugal bliss. Just the sight of Joe Comfort waking at noon and descending the staircase in pajamas with a steamy cigar in his mouth would set off her Irish temper.

Although Joe's earnings bought a sixteen-room wood-framed, two-family house in a clean working-class East Side neighborhood,

Peggy Comfort pleaded with her husband to get a conventional nine-to-five job. She begged him to quit the gambling parlor. It was a bad influence on the children, she argued; Joe was nine and Bobby seven, impressionable ages, and there was a younger son and two younger daughters (and another son would soon be on the way). His job also upset her sense of security—he could be put out of work by the cops in a minute.

With great reluctance he eventually agreed, and secured a job in a factory. This proved to be a short-lived experiment. Joe was summarily fired for organizing crap games instead of tending to his work.

◆ 2 ◆

Spring 1939, Rochester

Bobby longed to skip school this morning and go swimming. But as he stood looking out the picture window in the living room of his parents' house, hands in his pockets, he realized it would be school and not the river. He thought with pleasure of the Genesee River with its exciting, swift currents cascading down the waterfall near the big smoky brewery. Even at age seven, Bobby Comfort had a strong-enough breaststroke to challenge the river that cut and dipped through the length of Rochester. Once or twice a year a youth who couldn't handle the fast waters drowned, the body washing up on the river bank. Bobby was not frightened off by that.

He now breathed the fresh air that blew in the open window and stirred the lace curtains. Outside, the morning sun shone through the trees, and an intricate pattern of lights and shadows fell across the green lawn and the red cobblestones of Scio Street, and upon his father's big blue Packard parked at the curb.

"Bobby, come here, son." The sound of his mother's call interrupted his thoughts.

"Bobby . . ." There it was again. His mother's voice sounded unusually low.

"Okay, Mom," he called back. With a sigh he picked up his schoolbooks from the couch. He walked past the large coffee table with lion's paw legs, and past the floor-model Philco radio.

Mrs. Comfort was standing at the foot of the stairs in the center hall. She wore a lavender housecoat, and her smoothly combed jet-black hair fell almost to her waist.

With a firm hand she cupped her son's chin and said in a conspiratorial tone, "Bobby, I know you can keep a secret, so I'm going to ask you to do a special favor for me."

Bobby, looking at his mother, nodded.

"I want you to go to Pa's room," she continued, "and get something for me."

"Sure, Mom."

"Do you know where Pa keeps his roll of money?"

"I've seen him tuck it under his pillow when he goes to sleep. He has a fat rubber band around it."

"Well, I want you to go upstairs very quietly so you don't wake him, and put your hand under the pillow and slip the money out and take two ten-dollar bills for me, then put the roll back under the pillow."

"I'll get it for you, Ma," Bobby whispered.

It was a very quiet time of day. His older brother was already at school. The other children were playing outside in the yard, and Joe Comfort was sound asleep, having retired only two hours before.

Mrs. Comfort took the schoolbooks from under her son's arm, and then he silently tiptoed up the stairs. By the time he reached the top, he could feel his heart pounding.

Through a crack in the bedroom door, Bobby watched his father's chest rhythmically rise and fall under the blanket. He could hear his heavy breathing.

Fearing the slightest sound might wake his father, Bobby slowly inched the door open and slipped into the room. The room

18

was dark except for a little morning light seeping through the side of the drawn window shade. Bobby gradually adjusted his eyes to the darkness, and after a moment he could make out the framed picture of Jesus hanging on the wall above his parents' bed.

At the bedside Bobby paused and held his breath. He dropped to one knee, then reached cautiously under the pillow—and stopped suddenly as his father moved. When his father grew still again, Bobby edged his small hand farther under the pillow and felt the money roll, touched it, then deftly pulled it out.

He moved toward the thin beam of light filtering through the window, removed the rubber band, extracted the two tens, and put them in his pocket. He banded and returned the roll under the pillow, then padded gingerly across the room and out the door.

Down at the bottom of the stairs, his mother waited. He hand her the money. She smiled, pocketed the bills, and sent him off to school with a kiss.

This scene would be repeated weekly. Sometimes his mother would ask Bobby to snatch twenty-five, fifty, even a hundred dollars from his father's cache.

Feeling that some explanation was necessary, Mrs. Comfort told Bobby that she was worried his father might lose all his money at work, and she wanted enough to feed the family—just in case.

Bobby accepted this, although with difficulty. After all, his father always brought home little surprises—like jelly doughnuts and candies, and frequently left dimes and nickels on the table for the children.

Although Bobby felt that sneaking the money from his father was somehow wrong, on balance he was happy to please his mother, and he did thrill to the challenge.

Sometimes his mother gave Bobby a dollar or two as a reward. Bobby eventually realized that he could do better. Now when he made his periodic forays into his parents' bedroom, he peeled off several bills for himself, leaving his mother none the wiser.

When he was ten, Bobby began spending his time with some of the older "toughs" in the neighborhood, much to his mother's

19

distress. By the time he was eleven, he was robbing something from someone every day or every night.

He found that Davey Nelson was willing to take chances with him. Davey, a hollow-cheeked blond friend who lived nearby in a basement apartment with his mother and third stepfather, was happy to follow Bobby's lead. Their favorite target was supermarkets. Hiding behind big cereal cartons, the boys would wait for closing time. In the dark store they'd load up on fruit cakes and Hershey bars, open a rear window, and sneak out. Occasionally, they were lucky and hit a cash register still filled with money.

On Saturdays he and his friends would bike eight miles to Sea Breeze Amusement Park, where Bobby would pay for a full day of rides and cotton candy.

He was pleased with himself and recognized the power of money, of how his friends deferred to him, of how important it made him feel.

One evening two watches disappeared from a black satchel Bobby's father kept hidden in a downstairs closet. The watches were owned by railroad workers who used them as collateral for their gambling debts until their next payday. Joe Comfort discovered the two watches missing at a time when his wife was in the hospital giving birth to their sixth child, Paul. While visiting her, Joe had angrily accused Mrs. Franklin, the woman Peggy had hired to care for the children, of stealing the watches.

Peggy rallied in support of the trusted housekeeper. Peggy Comfort was convinced that Bobby was the culprit. Her husband refused to believe it was Bobby, stubbornly rejecting the idea that one of his sons would steal from him, but he nevertheless moved the black satchel to his store for safekeeping. Peggy vowed to resolve the matter on her return home.

She recalled, "I came home with the baby, but I was full of thoughts about Bobby. He was going wrong and I didn't know why. He had this thing in him—I don't know what it was. Some kind of devil streak. I knew he was stealing, so I decided to make him tell the truth. I was so distracted and crazy that I didn't know what to do. I got Bobby and I said, 'C'mon up to the attic.' On the way, I stopped at the pantry door and grabbed a big butcher knife.

"There was a table in the attic, and I put Bobby's head down on it. I put the big knife right down to his neck. I said, 'Now Bobby, you're going to tell me the truth. Did you take those watches from that black satchel? If you tell me you didn't take them, I'm gonna cut your throat from ear to ear and I'm gonna let your head hang over. You won't be dead, but you're gonna be suffering.' He got the shivers so bad, he was shivering and shivering. He said, 'I didn't take them.' I said, 'You didn't? Now you got the last time to tell me the truth.'

"He said, 'Kill me then, 'cause I didn't do it!' He said it over and over again. I finally let him go. But I knew damn well he did it."

Eventually, the Comforts learned that the Milani brothers, owners of the meat market on Main Street, had bought the watches from Bobby for five dollars apiece—considerably less than their value. When Joe Comfort attempted to retrieve the watches, the Milanis refused to sell. Joe Comfort made good the losses, and Mrs. Comfort set an 8 P.M. curfew for her son. When he ignored the time, she put the strap to him.

"I could never explain why I did what I did, but I knew that I didn't want anyone telling me what to do," Bobby Comfort said years later. "I liked being independent, and I thought there was something better in life than what I had, and I was going to get it. Sure I had a lot. I had my own room in a big house, yet I'd run away and sleep on park benches. Other times I stayed with friends. But when I'd bring friends home, they thought I lived in a castle. They came from the slums, homes without love. In my house my mother was doing all she could for the family. She was always at the stove cooking. One of my friends thought she had a skillet permanently attached to her arm. She would even cut our meat for us. We'd sit with the steak on our plates and wait until she actually cut it up for us. In winter she carried the coal buckets to the basement and stoked the furnace."

But Joe Comfort, the patriarch, rarely lifted a finger to assist his wife. He firmly adhered to the old-world practice that the head of the house delivered the money—and the woman in the house was responsible for everything else.

◆ 3 ◆

By the age of twelve Bobby Comfort was burglarizing homes throughout Rochester, including some of the so-called burglarproof mansions along East Avenue. He was "hitting" department stores and candy stores indiscriminately—any place that would net him a good take.

These sorties came to an abrupt halt when, at thirteen, he was caught burglarizing a closed gas station and was sent to the state industrial school for delinquents to serve a ten-month sentence. It was there that Bobby experienced his first institutionalized whippings at the hands of the cottage "housefather."

During that period he learned from more hardened kids about "cowboy" crimes—walking straight into an open store with a gun and demanding everything in the cash register.

Shortly after he was released from the industrial school, Bobby found a .38 revolver in a home he was robbing. Until then he'd had little aptitude for, or interest in, any mechanical devices, including guns. Besides, he considered himself a tough kid, someone who could engage in a fight without resorting to the use of any weapon other than his fists. However, he knew the presence of a gun was frightening for victims, and it would expedite matters in a holdup. He never intended to fire a gun at anyone.

In broad daylight, with guns drawn, he and two friends entered a large junkyard, lined up twenty people, employees and customers alike, and demanded that the safe be opened. The thieves took thirteen thousand dollars. This was by far the biggest robbery of the many Comfort—often alone—had committed during that period.

"The Hatless Bandit" was the name the Rochester newspapers dubbed the unknown young hoodlum.

He prided himself on his fearlessness. "Nerve" and "guts" were cherished words of praise from his peers. He relished the image of being fearless.

"I lived in a rough Italian neighborhood," Comfort later recalled, "and you were recognized by how tough you were. Nobody really recognized school intelligence. If you were tough, you were the boss—the leader.

"My mother impressed upon me from the very first day I went to school—'Never take anything from anybody,' she said. To her, 'tough' was important. She made me think it was more important than anything else. When I'd go off to school, she'd tell me to 'put your hands like this.' She made a fist with each hand and extended the middle knuckle. 'And go right for the eyes.' "

Mrs. Comfort attempted this indoctrination with her other sons, but they rebuffed her. She called Bobby her only true Irish boy. And he had an excellent example to follow. His mother loved to tell of her own fights with neighbors. Bobby had the same quick-trigger temper.

"Even though kids were tougher and bigger, they were scared of me," he said. "But I wasn't a bully. No one respects you going after someone smaller, and I didn't. I thought it was low-grade. I always defended smaller kids, weaker kids. Maybe in some crude way I was trying to be like one of the heroes in the fairy tales and books I used to read."

Bobby had learned to read at age four, and remembered, "I must have read a million fairy tales. And when you're a little kid, you always think you're the hero. You're always the good guy. I remember Tom Sawyer, and how he was always running away from home and going someplace. He was like a legend to me, a hero. He did a little stealing and fighting, too."

Westerns fascinated Bobby, and he delighted in the tales of Wild Bill Hickok ("Before I knew that he turned into a cop") and Jesse James ("They made him look like a hero, too, didn't they?").

Comfort dealt with another legend around his home, that of his mother's brother, Jimmy O'Horgan.

Uncle Jimmy had moved to Detroit and became associated with the notorious Purple Gang. There he was supposed to have originated the cocaine trade, taking trips to China and returning with great caches of drugs, and sometimes with beautiful Oriental women in his entourage.

On one visit to Rochester, he arrived with the then-heavyweight boxing champion of the world, Primo Carnera. They rode through the Italian section in Jimmy's Packard limousine to the joy of the crowds, who jumped on the car's running boards.

The police were less than thrilled with Jimmy O'Horgan. They allowed him in town for only three days at a stretch; for whenever O'Horgan was in Rochester, someone mysteriously fell out of a three-story window.

Although Jimmy O'Horgan died when Bobby was an infant, this legend was kept alive for him by Bobby's mother and his father.

In the family album Peggy kept a photograph of her brother. It showed him wearing a light-colored hat tilted rakishly to one side—like his smile—and an attractive woman hooked onto each arm.

One day Jimmy O'Horgan, out in his flashy Cord touring car with a Hollywood starlet, was forced off a road by another car and plummeted from a steep cliff. O'Horgan and the girl were killed instantly. The circumstances were believed to be "gang-related."

Nevertheless, Peggy Comfort revered her brother's memory and prayed for his soul to find peace. She attended church regularly and brought her children with her. Her husband would never be up in time for church—nor did he have the inclination to attend.

24

Bobby would listen attentively to the sermon and believed God punished evildoers.

"I never thought it related to me because I never was hurting anybody," said Comfort. "I never thought I was doing evil. When I fought, it was because I thought I was right. I honestly never thought I started a fight, but when I look back, I see how I sometimes *forced* people into fights."

Stealing wasn't wrong, in his opinion; it was simply a way of life. He saw no difference between his stealing a bike and his mother helping him repaint it—which she did; he saw no difference between stealing a hundred-dollar watch, and the local butcher buying it for five dollars; he saw no difference between his father running a gambling joint and the cops accepting—demanding!—a payoff to keep it open.

And to whom did young Bobby sell his stolen wares? To the "honest" businessmen in the neighborhood. They were his first fences, and they were cheating him, he soon discovered, paying him as little as they could get away with. He was forced to learn the value of the stolen goods—from radios to diamond rings.

"I was raised as a Catholic, to love and to fear God," he said. "And that's what I believed. I thought that the only reason most people didn't rob was that they were either afraid of jail or afraid of the hereafter. I wasn't afraid of either."

During his stay in industrial school, church attendance had been mandatory. When a call went out for altar boys, Comfort volunteered.

The young bandit, his hair slicked back, wearing the gown of the church, carried the candles and followed the priest in prayer.

"I thought it was a good chance to learn Latin," he recalled. "Since I was forced to go to church, I might as well learn what they were talking about. I hated to be ignorant. It was a lot of mumbo jumbo if you didn't know the Latin. Having read a lot as a kid, I thought Latin would help me with words I didn't know in English. I thought it might one day come in handy. And I got pretty good at it."

Occasionally, Bobby visited his father's cigar store in a two-story wooden building on North Street. The cigars and candy bars in the dirty glass cases looked old and stale and dusty. In the rear there was one large card table in the center of the room, with one bright bulb topped by a tin light fixture. The dealer, with his green eyeshade, kept the game moving. A ticker in one corner rattled and spewed out the racing and baseball results. The wall paint was peeling, the floor dusty, and the smoke from burning cigarettes and cheap cigars hung in the windowless room like a fog. But the gamblers were oblivious to their surroundings, their thoughts centering strictly on their bets. Joe Comfort minded least of all; he just sat there and raked off a percentage of every game.

Bobby remembered his father: stocky, dark-complexioned, with bright green eyes, the front brim of his fedora always flattened back, and never without a wreath of smoke from his black Italian cigar.

"I respected my father," Bobby said. "Everybody in the family did, including my mother. He was a nice, likeable guy, good to everybody. Generous. He supported the whole family. He did better than all his brothers who worked on the railroad.

"No one ever felt my father was doing wrong operating a gambling joint. And I knew he was doing right. He was earning a living. It was hard to make a living in those days."

Bobby also remembered the advice his father had offered him: "Because he knew I was stealing, he told me, 'Never admit anything to the cops. Always deny everything, no matter what promises they make to you.'

"He did urge me not to steal. He said it was stupid. He insisted there were other ways to make a buck. He told me about cards and how a good card cheat could make big money. Later on, I took his advice."

By the time he was fourteen, Bobby's parents had absolutely no control over him. Once, when his father hollered at him for stealing, Bobby railed back at him. The argument grew into a vicious shouting match. Before he knew it, he had his father by the throat and had wrestled him to the ground. Suddenly, frightened by his mounting rage and violent impulses, he jumped up and ran off, with his mother's screams echoing in his ears.

"They both became scared of me after that," said Bobby. "And they had no choice but to leave me alone.

"But I tried to do right by my family, and I brought presents home for my brothers and sisters—clothes and bikes—and I'd always bring home a quart of beer for my mother. She liked that." He could afford it. By his fifteenth birthday in 1947, he was making about $250 a week, and was the proud owner of a green 1940 Pontiac coupe.

Although teachers had long tried to impress upon him that, with his intelligence, he had a bright future if he applied himself, school didn't bring him the heady satisfaction he received from stealing.

One morning, when Bobby was sixteen, two policemen appeared at the Comforts' house on Joslyn Street and asked for him. When Bobby came to the door, he was shocked to see the policemen accompanied by a local grocer, an elderly Jewish man, one of his recent "cowboy" victims.

"That's him, officer," said the grocer, pointing a short, stubby finger at Bobby. Comfort was arrested on the spot. Finally, the "Hatless Bandit" had been positively identified.

Judge William O'Connor was a small-boned man who ruled sternly in the Monroe County Criminal Court. He believed intensely that children should be seen and not heard—and for children to commit armed robbery was a sin of the greatest magnitude; it struck at the base of civilization, at the very foundation of a great and free society.

From his lofty position the austere black-robed judge looked down at the smooth-skinned teenager with the neat pompadour and the unremorseful eyes. The grocer had come forth, identified Bobby Comfort, and advised the judge that two other youths were involved. The judge demanded that Bobby reveal the names of his accomplices.

"You have committed a very serious crime," said the judge to Bobby. "Sentencing can be between five years and thirty years. If you cooperate with the court, we will make the sentence as light as possible."

Comfort stared at the judge.

"Who were they?" the judge asked.

"I don't know," said Comfort. "I didn't commit the crime."

The Irish judge flushed with rage.

"You are going to get thirty years if you don't tell me right now!" said the judge.

"I don't know," replied Comfort.

With the bang of his gavel, the judge rasped, "Zero to thirty years!"

Bobby's lawyer jumped up, attempting to save the situation.

"Judge," he said, "this boy—"

"This grown man," the judge shot back.

There was a wail from the seats in the rear, and a tall black-haired woman rushed forward to the bench.

"Oh, Judge, have mercy—don't take my boy away from me." Peggy Comfort looked up at the judge, her eyes filled with tears. "I have ten of 'em at home and I can't afford to lose a one. Not a one."

She often said that she was raising ten children, when in fact she had had six children and four miscarriages. Everything counted when you pleaded for mercy.

"I sympathize with you, Mrs. Comfort," said the judge. "But I have no choice, given the reactions of your son. I see he is a stoic personality. His record indicates to me that he is an incorrigible. It is in the best interests of society that he serve this sentence."

Mrs. Comfort left the courtroom weeping. Bobby's face never changed expression as he was led out of the courtroom.

In Bobby Comfort's adopted moral code, there was nothing lower than a "stool pigeon." It was the rule of the streets in which he lived, starting with the scorned "tattletales," but it was also the code glamorized in the popular gangster motion pictures of the 1930s and 1940s of Comfort's youth. He envisioned himself as an Edward G. Robinson, a James Cagney, a Humphrey Bogart, portraying the "stand-up" image he so admired.

Comfort's court-appointed attorney had pleaded with Bobby to reveal the names of his accomplices. "What difference does it make?" he asked.

Comfort replied, "It makes a difference to me—I don't want anyone thinking that he's forced me to talk."

"Do you know what a thirty-year prison sentence is, Bob?"

"Looks like I'll find out."

◆ 4 ◆

Heavy snows blanketed the farmlands of upstate New York. Snow hung from the branches of trees like exquisite lace, and cars bore crowns of snow. Whiteness was everywhere, and it shrouded the land with a sense of unreality.

Bobby Comfort was on his way to the New York State Vocational Institution at Coxsackie, a prison. He sat on the hard wooden bench in the back of a prison van, looking out the Cyclone-wire window. Except for the jolting motion of the van and the muffled noise of the motor, everything appeared serene.

Bobby himself was outwardly calm, but churning inside with fears about what lay ahead. He had heard stories about Coxsackie—the fights, the homosexuals, the knifings.

The vehicle carrying the prisoners passed through the small snow-covered town of Coxsackie, along the frozen Hudson River, then wound its way out of town and, after a short distance, reached the forbidding gray reformatory which held, inside its thirty-foot-high walls, five hundred boys ages sixteen to nineteen.

Bobby was delivered to the Receiving Room for New Inmates,

interviewed briefly, examined for social diseases and lice, and given a short, curt lecture relative to the behavior expected from him during his imprisonment.

The processing completed, he was sent temporarily into the prison yard to await the results of his tests and ultimate assignment into the prison population.

He stood alone for a few minutes, when suddenly a bell rang and a horde of boys spilled out of the building and filled the yard. Comfort stood, hands in the pockets of his fur-collared leather jacket, watching the noisy exodus. Shortly, he was approached by a stocky boy whose black curly hair glistened from the falling snow. He was taller and much broader than the slight five-foot-seven, 130-pound Comfort.

"You new here, ain't ya?" the boy asked.

"Yeah, I am."

"Where you from?"

"Rochester."

"Well, Rochester, you see that line on the wall there?"

"The red line?"

"Yeah."

"I see it."

"Well, you gotta stand on the other side of that line. You can't stand here."

Assuming that this was some kind of a prison rule, Comfort started to the other side, then hesitated. He said to the boy, "Why do I stand over there?"

"The guys from New York City—the guys from the Jolly Boys, the Scorpions, and the Cobras and clubs like that—we stand here," he answered. As he spoke, several boys came up and stood behind him. He continued, "And guys from Rochester, Syracuse, Buffalo—places like that—they're creeps and punks and they gotta stand on the other side of the line. That's where you go." Waiting with head cocked, the New York City kid glared at Comfort.

"Well," said Comfort softly, "I *was* going there nice, but since that's the reason they stand there, I ain't going."

Without another word the boy leaped at Comfort. The two went sprawling in the snow, swinging and kicking and biting. Sev-

30

eral guards hurriedly broke through the crowd, jumped in, and hauled the fighters apart.

Both boys were dragged by four burly guards to an isolated cell block in the bowels of the prison basement.

"Take off your clothes," one of the guards shouted at Comfort.

"I'm not takin' off my clothes."

Comfort thrust his arm above his head just in time to ward off the blow of a heavy club aimed at his head. The full power of the blow paralyzed his arm. His clothes were ripped off and he was pounded again and again. The intolerable pain tore through Comfort's young body. He remembered the world in his head turning bright orange.

When he awoke—he had no idea how long he had been out—every part of his body throbbed with pain. His arms felt limp and his body constrained. He discovered he was in a straitjacket, lying on the cement floor of a small dark cell.

Later that day the straitjacket was removed. But the beating had been so ferocious it would be a week before Comfort could straighten his body in order to stand fully upright.

For the next sixty days Comfort remained isolated and naked in that cell. The lone barred window high on the wall had been intentionally broken by a guard to let in the cold winter air. At night a small blanket was tossed into his cell. The blanket was only large enough either to cover him or to lie on, to protect his body from the cold stone floor. To keep from freezing, he continually rotated the placement of the blanket. Also in the cell was a metal bucket—" 'Shit bucket,' we called it," said Comfort.

A prisoner in the isolation cell or "strip cell," as it is known, was given a daily ration of bread and water—except for every third day, when he received a bowl of thin vegetable soup. Once a week Comfort was allowed a shower. Otherwise he was totally confined to that bare, frigid room with gray stone walls and heavy steel door.

As part of his punishment, once a day he was wrapped in a straitjacket and guards pummeled him with clubs. They beat Comfort until he was too weak to control his bowels. "You couldn't keep it in," recalled Comfort. "The guards enjoyed beating you until they saw the shit coming out. I hated their guts."

31

Upon release from solitary confinement, he was returned to "population." Comfort, like the other prisoners, continued to be whipped into line by the guards. A suicide, or a suicide attempt, occurred periodically. One morning a seventeen-year-old prisoner was found hanging by his belt from a pipe in his cell. Another young convict slit his wrist with a razor blade stolen from the barber shop.

"A lot of kids were tough when they went in and then got beaten down," Comfort recalled. "I knew one kid named Williams, a black kid, who had nothing else in his life except the respect he got for being tough. He couldn't take it at Coxsackie. The beatings made him delirious. He was in the cell next to mine. He tried killing himself, but the guards caught him and dragged him out by his feet. He was cryin', 'Mama, mama, I don't wanna live here no more.' It was horrible. Everybody heard him. We knew it wasn't bullshit. We never saw him again."

Four of the guards were particularly notorious and were known to the prisoners as *Wild Bill* O'Brien, *Madman* Lynch, *Bone Crusher* Gerwin, and Jorin the Nazi.

Looking at them, Comfort saw petty men who took their greatest pleasure in beating the young prisoners. The guards knew they were despised but acted as though they didn't care.

For various small rule infractions—sometimes just talking in chow line, sometimes answering a guard's question with profanity—Comfort would be returned to the "strip cell" again, and the beatings resumed.

He dreamed of killing the guards, especially O'Brien. O'Brien used to laugh when he hit Comfort. Bobby heard that laughter in his nightmares.

"Oh, if I had the chance, I'd have definitely killed O'Brien and the others," he said. "There would have been no problem killing them.

"After a while, I felt no pain from the beatings because I was overflowing with hatred—pure animal hate. Yet hatred gave me something to retain my pride and dignity. If you don't like somebody you can't let them get the best of you. Hatred keeps you from suffering. And the more they hit me, the more I hated back.

"But the beatings affected me more than I wanted to admit. In a few months I developed a nervous blink. Guys would ask, 'What's wrong with you, you're always blinkin' your eyes.' I felt it, but I couldn't control it. Tough as you try to act, the tension still shows up on you." An astigmatism developed, and soon Comfort was examined and fitted for glasses. He would always have to wear them.

In his cell he read the only book allowed him, the Bible. He had read it before, but now, perhaps influenced by his circumstances, he read it seriously, and was surprised by the contents. He recalled: "It's a very violent story filled with cruelty, deception, murder, rape, and war. You read from how Cain slew Abel and go right up to the Crucifixion."

Once out of solitary confinement, Comfort regularly borrowed books from the prison library and read them avidly at night. Many of those books were classics and, considering his situation, bore ironic titles: *Crime and Punishment, Of Human Bondage, Les Misérables,* and *Civil Disobedience.* The Sherlock Holmes stories were other favorites.

Time went by, days lengthened into weeks, weeks into months. By day he worked outdoors, chopping trees in winter and growing vegetables in summer.

He had made numerous friends among the cons and had been accepted by the New York City gang. Even the curly-haired kid he'd fought on his first day became a buddy.

To Comfort's surprise he was released on parole from Coxsackie after two and a half years. The year was 1951, and he was nineteen. When the doors opened for him, he was determined never to return. He wanted never again to breathe the same air with men such as O'Brien and Lynch.

Coxsackie had scared Comfort. He knew nothing about parole, but with a thirty-year sentence hanging over him, he felt confident in his ability to fulfill the stipulations of it.

Through a friend Comfort's father secured a job for Comfort in an automotive-parts plant. The assembly-line job of poking at passing carburetors with a magnetic rod to test for defects proved to be as tedious as prison work. Comfort's growing boredom was not lost on his mother. She worried anew over his mounting restlessness. They had numerous talks. She attempted to convince him that a life of crime was not the best choice and with his intelligence he could go far in any area he chose to follow. He listened but would make his own decisions.

The strictures of parole were confining and embarrassing. At work his parole officer would periodically come by and inquire about Comfort.

When his parole officer, Lyndon Franks, learned who Comfort was dating, he called the girl's mother to inform her of Bobby's prison record.

The parole officer, in effect, hampered a normal social life by preventing him from dating some girls. But others enjoyed dating Bobby—the tough, notorious "Hatless Bandit." They found it exciting, dangerous. Besides that, he had developed into an attractive young man, with strong facial features, deep-set brown eyes, and a wiry, well-proportioned build.

Comfort had experienced his first sexual encounter while in reform school, of all places, at age thirteen. Two older girls, daughters of the housefather of his cottage, had coyly led him into the woods behind the baseball field and initiated him into the world of sex.

Sexual intercourse was a parole violation for single men. If Comfort took a girl to a motel, he invariably was forced to do so with the stealth of his burglarizing days. On one occasion, before he entered the motel room, he kiddingly asked his date to go in first and look under the bed for Franks.

Another restriction was the 11 P.M. curfew. A minute late constituted a parole violation. Sometimes Franks sat in his car outside the Comfort home and waited to establish Comfort's exact moment of arrival.

In time, Comfort broke more of the rules. He was not permitted to drive a car, but he sometimes did. He wasn't allowed to associate with known criminals or other parolees, but he did.

Unofficially, he had quit his job at the carburetor factory. Using his father's liaison there, he could be reached by telephone immediately if and when Franks called or came by.

To earn money, Bobby gambled—another activity forbidden to parolees.

His father had told him about "mechanics," men who could manipulate cards like magicians. It fascinated him. He found a book on the subject in the local library and read it, followed the diagrams,

34

and practiced diligently in front of a shaving mirror. He would sit endlessly on his bed, perfecting false shuffles and setup deals.

It wasn't long before Bobby had become an expert "card mechanic."

At first he played alone, with blackjack as his game. Later, he played poker with a partner—dealing the partner winning hands.

Besides the gambling joints that flourished in town, Comfort frequently played at church clambakes and numerous private games. He was pocketing five hundred dollars a week, five times his salary at the carburetor factory, with no comparison in the pleasure.

Coming home from a card hustle one night, Bobby Comfort entered his house at ten minutes to eleven. He had noticed Parole Officer Franks's car parked down the street. No problem. A friend, Tom Sapolin, phoned shortly after Comfort had closed the front door. He said that a fight was brewing, and he needed Bobby's help. Would he come right away?

At eleven-twenty Comfort hurried out the side door and down an alley several blocks to where he met Sapolin.

"What's going on? Where's the trouble?" asked Comfort.

Sapolin smiled. "Nothing's wrong, Bob," said Sapolin. "I just needed some company and figured this was the only way I could get you out of the house."

The next morning Comfort received a phone call from Franks ordering him to appear at the parole office immediately.

When Comfort arrived at Franks's office the heavy parole officer was smiling. "Well, big shot," he said, "we got you this time. You ran out of your house at eleven-twenty last night."

"I was just going for a cup of coffee," Comfort said.

"Bullshit. I don't care if you were helping old ladies across the street. You broke curfew, I caught you, and you're going back to the can if I have anything to say about it."

Comfort had believed that Franks was after him. He could understand the reason for Franks's personal vendetta against him, since he had known Comfort was blatantly violating parole regulations. Franks was embarrassed that he could never catch Comfort—until that night.

Comfort was remanded to the county jail to await a review by the parole board meeting in Albany. Comfort was more upset with himself for his stupidity than he was with Tom Sapolin. It had been an error in judgment.

Two weeks later Franks and another officer entered Comfort's cell and advised him of the board's decision.

"Okay, Comfort, pack up, you're heading for Coxsackie today," Franks said triumphantly.

"For how long?"

"One year. It should've been longer. I'd like to see you off the streets for good."

Comfort couldn't believe he was being sent back to prison for a year for so minor an infraction. But he sat silently, controlling his anger. If he smacked Franks, he'd have more years tacked on the sentence.

Comfort was processed out of the county jail. Handcuffed to Franks, he was led into the back seat of a sheriff's car where he would be taken to the New York Central Railroad Station in downtown Rochester. During the short trip Franks, his gun on his hip, gloated. "Some tough guy," said Franks. "This is the way all you punks end up."

Comfort remained silent, ignoring him. When they arrived at the station and entered the waiting room, Franks's partner—the driver of the car—headed for the telephone to report in to headquarters.

"Sit down," ordered Franks, pulling the handcuffed prisoner toward a vacant bench in the waiting room.

"Fuck you," said Comfort, "I'm not sitting down."

With his left hand free, Comfort shot a cracking blow to Franks's face. Instantly, he pulled Franks toward him. Franks jerked for his pistol. "Go for that gun, you asshole, and I'll take it and blow your goddamn brains out right here," Comfort said.

"Bobby, take it easy, no one means any harm," Franks said.

"Shut up," Comfort said. He shoved Franks against the wall. "Now *I'm* telling *you* what to do."

"Bob, you're asking for trouble."

"I'm in enough trouble now. A little more ain't gonna hurt me. I told you to shut your fucking mouth."

Comfort saw Franks's partner walking toward them, then

36

suddenly stop. The man's mouth dropped when he saw his partner and the prisoner. He rushed back to the phone.

In a few minutes five additional parole officers appeared at the station.

The waiting room quickly emptied of frightened train passengers who had been watching the drama unfold. The seven officers were alone with Comfort in the cavernous room.

"If you come after me," Comfort said to them, "I'm going to kill this son of a bitch."

The officers huddled. One whispered instructions, and they all charged. Comfort kicked Franks in the balls and repeatedly hit him in the face, until he himself was clubbed and kicked into submission.

One of the parole officers handcuffed Comfort's other wrist, and, with Franks again standing, the two officers dragged Comfort to the stairway leading to the trains. They pulled the beaten prisoner up the steps, accompanied by the five reserve officers who moved up behind the trio.

Comfort, feigning injury, took each step slowly, attempting to regain his breath and gather his strength. When they reached the top step, Comfort placed his right foot against the top step and, heaving, catapulted his body backward, flipping over and pulling the two men handcuffed to him crashing down the stairwell toppling onto the officers a few steps below.

Excruciating pain shot through Comfort's body. His arms felt as though they were being torn from their sockets. But his anger was too intense for him to care.

All of the men hurtled backward down the wooden stairwell.

Franks and his partner landed on Comfort at the bottom of the stairs. Comfort was kicked and pummeled and, finally, dragged to the train for the ride to Albany. It was a remarkable sight: Comfort, bruised, clothes ripped, with seven lawmen around him. Passengers stared at them as they boarded the railroad car for the ride to Albany. All seven guards accompanied him.

As the guards were about to take their seats, Comfort stopped them.

"Nobody sits," he ordered. "I'm standing all the way. I'm not gonna enjoy this ride—and no one else will either."

"Hey, look—"

"The first guy that sits down, I'm kicking him in the face. I'll drive his head through the fucking window."

He glared at the guards.

"I'm just one guy, but I'm gonna bite your jugular out, I'm gonna tear your nose right off your face with my teeth. I'll die, but you'll die, too. Not all of you, just one. Which one wants to be him?"

The guards stared at each other. After a moment Franks said, "Okay." He was convinced that Comfort meant it.

"Nobody sits," said Franks.

Shortly after the train started on the eight-hour trip, one of the guards, lighting a cigarette, said, "For Christ sakes, let's all sit down and forget the whole thing."

"No," said Comfort, "we ain't sittin' *or* smokin'."

The guard put out his cigarette.

"And no one eats, either," said Comfort. "If any of you bastards leaves to eat, I'll kill the guy that's closest to me."

The seven parole officers and Comfort stood for the entire ride.

In Albany the station was teeming with police and patrol cars. The group was met by a police captain. Comfort stood handcuffed to two parole officers. The captain walked up to the prisoner and looked him up and down. "This is what we're all here for? This one skinny kid has brought out the entire army? What shit."

The captain laughed.

Comfort kicked him in the balls.

For that attack Comfort received an additional one and a half years tacked onto the one year for breaking parole. Comfort knew what would be next. The straitjacket, the box, and a terrific beating. But to his amazement nothing happened. Comfort was placed directly into the prison population and, three weeks later, was transferred to Great Meadow Correctional Institution in Comstock, New York.

Through the prison grapevine, Comfort learned that some convicts serving time for armed robbery had received much lighter sentences than the possible thirty years he was burdened with. Some second offenders were doing less than ten years. His sentence was considered so outrageous by the convicts that they called him "Zip to Thirty."

Bobby could not fathom the reasoning that went into handing down such inconsistent prison terms. He decided that there was no logic to it, but that the judges, reflecting personal bias, malice, or incompetence, meted out an arbitrary brand of justice, and that they were nothing more than a heavy-handed extension of a hypocritical system.

After two and a half years, Comfort was once again released on parole. It was 1955. He was twenty-three and still faced nearly twenty-five years of parole, and with it the ever-present threat of being returned to prison—for the slightest misstep—with no possibility for appeal.

This time, free but not free, there were none of the anxieties or feelings of apprehension similar to those that accompanied his first return to society. Although his first prison experience had frightened him into a determination never to return, these last years had hardened him. If he had to return for any violations, he would accept it with a completely fatalistic attitude.

Once again another job was waiting for him outside, this time as a store clerk. The job existed only on paper. In actuality, he and his friend Tom Sapolin and a few others had organized an extortion ring. They scored on gambling joints, nightclubs, and bars. No one dared refuse openly, but someone did report his activity to the police, and Comfort was promptly whisked back to prison.

After two more years in a cell, he was paroled; but a year later he was found "conspiring" to commit burglary and went back behind bars.

It was the third time in the decade that he had been remanded to prison for parole violation. In 1959 he was released again.

Now Comfort again hooked up with Davey Nelson, his boyhood accomplice who had grown into a skillful burglar, and they proceeded to go on a safe-cracking spree all over Rochester.

A safe that Comfort had set his sights on was the huge one standing in the rear offices of Siebert Motors, the largest auto dealership in Rochester.

It was Sunday night, the right time, when all the used-car and service-sales money would be resting in the safe until Monday morning awaiting the usual bank deposit.

At 10 P.M. on the quiet, moonless night, the two hoods walked at a casual pace to the Siebert showroom on quiet South Avenue.

Davey Nelson pulled a crowbar from his tool bag. He wedged the bar and forced the wood-framed glass door open with one deft motion.

The two men raced across the street into the darkened entrance of a vacant store and waited. Bobby allowed that fifteen minutes would be sufficient time for the police to arrive, anticipating that Siebert Motors might conceivably be equipped with a silent alarm device.

Fifteen minutes. Nothing. Comfort decided it was safe.

After checking the deserted street for any movement, the two men crossed the street and entered the showroom.

They walked past the Lincolns and the Mercurys on the floor and proceeded into the rear office.

Davey Nelson dropped the bag, extracted his tools, and began hacking away at the hinges of the black safe.

So intent were they on their objective that they were shocked into immobility when the sounds of sirens and screeching tires broke the outer silence. The cops had arrived—late—but were there nonetheless. Comfort and Davey were trapped. They had no choice but to give up.

 **5**

The Monroe County Jail in Rochester, New York, was called by everyone in town, including the prisoners, "Skinner's Hotel." It was run by the city's most venerable politician, the bald, three-hundred-pound sheriff, Albert W. Skinner, who had been elected to the post continuously for thirty years, and whose name and appearance became synonymous with the prodigious old structure. A massive four-story, red-brick bastion, surmounted by a series of white battlements, the jailhouse resembled a medieval fortress, and in some ways it was. In 1959 it was the longest-standing public building in the city, having been built over one hundred years before.

The prison was a half mile from the county courthouse, and was the "holding tank" for the accused men, women, and youthful offenders who were to ultimately stand trial when the court calendar turned up their cases. During trial dates the manacled prisoners would be transported in one of the sheriff's green prison vans from the jail to court for appearance, and returned as the process required. Even after a guilty verdict, a prisoner might be detained for months in the county jail, pending ultimate disposition to one of the various state penal institutions that are situated along the northern tier of New York.

In fact, overcrowding in many of the state penitentiaries frequently compelled prisoners to remain at "Skinner's Hotel" for the full length of their jail terms.

Inside, the men's part of the prison resembled a monstrous chicken coop, with three tiers of dark iron-mesh cells that looked out onto an open area known as "the pit." Since the jail was situated in the downtown business district, there were no outdoor areas for prisoners to exercise, so they were confined for their recreation to the pit, which was nothing but a concrete floor with wooden benches and six long wooden tables. Released from their cells at 6:30 each morning until 7 P.M., the overnight lockup hour, they ate their meals, played cards, talked, and slept on the floor of the pit.

High above the enclosure of the pit was a huge skylight that offered the only visible daylight, screened though it was by coats of encrusted dirt and grime accumulated over the past century. Evening light came from long fluorescent tubes suspended from pipes hung from the ceiling. All cells had the usual one bare light bulb, a cot, and a toilet bowl. At night the cacophony of sounds made sleep difficult, with prisoners continuously shouting to one another, radios blaring, and toilets flushing. The only access to and from this entire area was through a heavy iron-barred door at the north end of the pit. Twenty-four hours a day, two of the sheriff's guards sat at an old desk in the passageway outside the door. This passageway and those on the three floors above ran between the thick brick walls of the prison building and the bars of the pit.

Perhaps one reason the county had been so slow to build a modern facility was that the jail served its purpose so well. Never had there been a single successful escape, though there had been several attempts. But the iron bars and the dense walls of the prison proved tougher than the resolve of any prisoners who had ever considered a breakout.

Sheriff Skinner took pride in this and in his staff, which he outfitted in what he considered handsome uniforms, exemplifying spit-and-polish efficiency. To evoke a military air he favored woolen uniforms for his men, even in the dog days of summer. Skinner had

42

a team of highly trained German shepherds he personally cared for, and he enjoyed the attention of the press, which wrote appreciative stories about his disciplined organization. And if the prisoners were somewhat inconvenienced by the filth of the prison, the rats, the noise, the miserable food, he philosophized that they deserved no better. Skinner agreed with the general belief of many leading penologists that prisoners were in jail to be punished for their crimes against society. He didn't believe in rehabilitation "nonsense." He was not a social worker, he said, he was a prison warden.

The date was November 6, 1959, and Bobby Comfort (who, as a parole violator, had been denied bail) sat and pondered his fate that morning.

Comfort appeared out of place in these surroundings. Although he had been held for more than two months pending his trial, he was carefully groomed. He wore an expensive sports jacket, slacks, and black loafers. All of the prisoners wore street clothes, since Skinner's budget did not provide for uniforms. Most of the men wore wrinkled, dirty clothing.

It was during these times that Comfort realized what he could expect when his trial came up on the calendar. The Siebert job alone could bring him ten to twenty years for breaking and entering, and, with the added twenty years remaining on his parole, he'd be an old man before he was released from behind bars.

He sat at a far corner of the pit passively watching the movement of prisoners in front of him.

At 10 A.M. Comfort took note of the gate guards passing a plumber through the separated passageway outside the pit. The passageway led beyond the pit around a corner to where a similar detention area existed for women prisoners, and yet another for youthful offenders.

The old building frequently sprang leaks, and plumbers were routinely called in.

A plumber, clad in overalls, busied himself working on a water pipe at the end of the corridor. Bobby Comfort had placed himself at the back of the pit next to the wall of iron bars. The plumber's large open toolbox revealed wrenches, elbow joints, pipe cutters, washers, a hacksaw, and hacksaw blades.

Comfort grew increasingly interested in the toolbox. Unobtrusively, he moved to a seat at the far end of the bench, within arm's length of the open box.

He glanced some sixty feet down the pit to the guards' desk. The guards were otherwise occupied with paperwork and rarely looked up.

The other inmates in the pit, numbering about a hundred, continued their noisy activities, as oblivious to the plumber as were the guards.

Shortly, a group of "trial prisoners" were returned to the pit for lunch, and were immediately surrounded by clusters of fellow inmates curious about the sentences meted out to them. The noisy return also signaled the opening of the gate by the guards, and simultaneously called the lunch hour to the plumber's attention. He checked his watch, dropped his tools in the box, pulled the lid over its bulging contents and shoved it against the wall near the pipe. Then, clutching a brown lunch bag and thermos, he moved down the corridor past the guards who waved him out the far entrance.

With the tumult continuing around him, Comfort reached down, raised the lid of the box, and quickly withdrew four small six-inch hacksaw blades. He pocketed them in his jacket and moved away.

Realizing that the plumber, on his return from lunch, might notice that the blades were missing and possibly report their disappearance to the guards, Comfort moved to a bench on the other side of the pit. He sat down, and placed the four blades into the joint where the seat met the thick leg of the bench. He wedged the blades securely to ensure that they would not drop out if the bench was jarred. That accomplished, he turned slowly away. He had only to wait out the plumber's reaction.

At 1:30 P.M. the plumber returned, nodded to the desk guards, entered the passageway, and proceeded to his repair job. He knelt, opened the box, and extracted wrenches and other tools and slammed the lid shut.

Comfort watched the man's actions and soon felt confident that, for the time being, the missing blades went completely unnoticed.

Again, action in the pit. Names were called for afternoon

44

trial appearances, and soon the pit was reduced by twenty men.

Assuming the unlikelihood of discovery of his cache, Comfort was already formulating a plan for their future use.

At 4 P.M., his work completed, the plumber repacked his tools. He adjusted a few tools in order to facilitate closing the lid. Comfort watched. Suddenly, the plumber looked searchingly about. Then, locating a messy putty can, he dropped it inside the box and snapped it shut.

The plumber walked to the outside desk, exchanged a few words of good-natured banter with the two guards, and walked out of the compound.

After dinner the bell rang, signifying 7 P.M. Lockup. Reluctantly, the inhabitants of the pit moved to their respective cells, where they were locked in for the night. Thus far, no missing blades had been reported.

The following morning Comfort related the previous day's events to his friend and accomplice Davey Nelson, awaiting trial in the "holding tank." Comfort also spoke quietly with Joe Barnes, a long-time acquaintance. Barnes was a prison trustee who performed odd jobs and menial tasks for the police guards and had relatively free access to areas outside the pit.

Comfort titillated Barnes with the suggestion that a break might be possible, explaining briefly about the blades he had hidden.

Not surprisingly, Barnes "wanted in," and agreed to examine the few possible weak spots in the building.

Obviously, it was impossible to saw through the thick iron bars that framed the outside passageway, or the windows in the kitchen. But by that afternoon Barnes confirmed that a ventilation shaft above the boiler room, around the corner from the pit, might be easy to work on, providing he was given enough time and some good blades.

Barnes explained that the shaft in the boiler room led to the roof four stories up. The shaft was small but, according to Barnes, wide enough to accommodate their bodies.

Comfort slipped him a blade the next morning, and later that day the trustee came back with a positive report.

For four days Barnes worked diligently in the boiler room. One

45

evening before lockup, he told Comfort it was done. "Now tell me how the hell you're gonna get outta the pit?"

Comfort's plan was simply conceived, and actually had its origin in an incident that had occurred the previous week.

He had caused a minor riot in the pit concerning what passed for lunch in "Skinner's Hotel." On that day the pea soup was gray, as usual, the bread hard enough to loosen a tooth, and the rice was gummy.

Comfort, watching a grain of rice being carried off by a roach, shook his head and said, "This is the only prison in the world where you've gotta catch the food before it runs away." He stood up and walked with his tray to the garbage drum. "Here's where this shit belongs," he shouted, and dumped the food into the can. He then lit a match and set fire to the can. Immediately, the two guards sitting outside the door burst in and extinguished the flame. Sheriff Skinner quickly appeared to investigate the disturbance for himself. Learning that Comfort had been responsible, he dealt with him firmly: bread and water for a week. Comfort took this as an improvement.

What had struck him about the incident was the way the guards reacted. He saw that they did not lock the gate behind them as they rushed in. He mentally filed this information.

As a result of this incident, Comfort realized he would need to create a diversion in the pit, some action that would force the guards to move inside.

Subsequently, he called on yet another "short-timer" with whom he was acquainted, and enlisted his help. Frank Nova, a large black man, guaranteed Comfort that he'd be ready when he got the signal.

As Comfort explained to Davey Nelson and Barnes, "We'll put ourselves at the corner near the guards' desk. Frank Nova will be waiting at the other end of the pit near the kitchen. I give the signal, then he starts the rumble. The guards'll open up, move in, and we run out the gate."

"What if the screws lock the gate behind 'em?" asked Barnes.

"They'll be too excited to think of it—the fight's gotta be a fast blowup," said Comfort.

46

"How long can they keep it up?"

"I told him we need fifteen minutes."

"When do we make the break?" asked Nelson.

"Tonight—just before lockup. After dinner they never take a count," said Comfort.

At six forty-five Comfort, Barnes, and Nelson stood in their prearranged positions near the guards' desk. In the far corner, diagonally across the long room, Nova looked toward Comfort for the signal. Comfort nodded.

They watched the muscular Nova walk up to an unsuspecting black man and shout, "I'm not gonna take that shit from you, you fuckin' nigger," and punched him across the table. Dinner trays flew, prisoners hollered. Other men jumped into the fight. The two guards leaped up and, as Comfort had anticipated, hurriedly unlocked the gate and rushed through the crowded room to restore order. But the second guard slammed the gate behind him! Comfort's heart dropped. The guards ran across the pit. Comfort moved to the gate and turned the handle—it was open!

Comfort and Nelson, with Barnes in the lead, ran low past the guards' desk, down the passageway, to the boiler room. They burst through the door and into a room full of steam-hissing pipes, oil burners, and generators. Barnes led the way to a series of asbestos-covered steam pipes that rose fifteen feet to the ceiling. The men had to climb the pipes to get to the opening of the vent. As they moved forward, the boiler-room door banged open again. They froze. Three black men ran into the room. Comfort immediately realized the men were prisoners.

"Can we hoof it out with you guys?" one of them asked.

"Okay, but close that fucking door," Comfort rasped.

They began to shinny up the pipes, Barnes in the lead. At the top he reached over and opened the shaft by yanking free the two iron bars he had previously sawed. The shaft was now free for access.

The shaft was big enough for a man to crawl into, and once inside it widened to about three feet square. It vaulted to the top of the building, which Barnes had estimated was thirty-five to forty feet above where he was now perched.

Bobby peered up at the shaft, but darkness had fallen and he could not see to the top of the vent—four stories above—although he could feel the draft of winter air that blew in from the opening.

Looking back down into the boiler room, he saw the remaining four figures hugging the pipes at various heights off the floor—waiting in tandem for the next man to move up.

Barnes swung up the soot-encrusted opening, first bracing his back and then bringing his feet up into a fetal position against the opposite wall of the tin shaft. Slowly, he began inching his way toward the top.

Comfort moved directly behind Barnes into the shaft. As he did so, he was showered with the aged encrustation and clinging clumps of dirt that had been loosened by Barnes's body. He suppressed a cough as his lungs filled with the dust and choking particles.

It was five minutes before the soot-covered bodies of all six prisoners were finally inside the shaft.

The ruckus in the pit would have subsided by this time, according to Bobby's calculations. Order should have been restored, but six prisoners were missing without leave. Comfort hoped there would be no cell count after the night lockup.

As the men moved up the shaft, the cold air hit their sweating, convoluted bodies. It was a tiring and torturous maneuver. Suddenly, Comfort heard a dull thud.

"Son of a bitch!" cried Barnes.

"What's the matter?" Comfort asked.

"Hit my head on the fuckin' bar," Barnes said. He had reached the top and moved through the ninety-degree elbow of the shaft, only to be confronted with another iron bar across the vent opening.

"How thick is the bar?"

"Feels thinner than the others."

"Well, get the blade out and start working—you're the only one who can do it."

Barnes began sawing.

Davey Nelson, directly below Comfort, hissed, "What the fuck's going on?"

"We're stuck," said Comfort.

"How long's it gonna take?" asked Nelson.

"How the hell do I know?" replied Comfort.

Minutes passed, and after what seemed an hour, Barnes muttered, "Got the son of a bitch!" At the same time Comfort heard the iron bar snap apart.

Barnes pushed through the curved open end of the vent and dropped onto the rooftop, six feet below. Comfort followed.

No guards! Comfort had wondered, climbing up the shaft, if anything had gone awry below that would bring Skinner's guards onto the roof to meet them. Obviously, their absence had not yet been discovered.

His entire body ached as a result of the cramped position he had endured during the hour-long climb. His knees were locked, his stomach felt knotted. It took him a few moments to bring his bent body into a completely upright position.

Shivering in the cold wind that whipped across the roof, he moved over to the edge and peered down between the battlements. The streetlamps and the headlights from the moving traffic brightly lit up busy Exchange Street more than fifty feet below him. Workers heading for the bus depot and home, intermingling with late-evening shoppers, crowded the sidewalks.

Comfort moved across the roof, checking the sides to determine the best route down. He decided quickly which was the most practical way.

"Barnes, give me the rope," said Comfort.

"Don't have it," said Barnes meekly.

"What?"

"I forgot the goddamn thing."

"Shit," said Comfort, controlling his temper and voice.

He raced to the front of the roof, leaving the group huddled near the shaft.

He returned after completing his second inspection, faced the five men, and said: "Here's the way I see it. One, we can stay here and freeze our nuts off 'til they come up and get us; two, you can go back down and give yourselves up; or three, go down the only way we can—on the front of the building by the drainpipe."

"In front of all those people down there?" asked one of the black men.

"You got a better idea?" asked Comfort.

"No."

Neither did anyone else.

Comfort hurried to the edge of the building, climbed over the decorative limestone facade, and began his descent.

He clambered down the rusted drainpipe, ripping his sleeve on a dislodged pipe strap. Finally, he landed on the roof of the lower prison building and was now approximately fifteen feet above the street.

Comfort peered out over the edge of the lower prison roof. Removing his jacket, he tied it around his waist, swung out over the roof with his fingertips gripping the roof's edge, and extended himself full length above the sidewalk.

Passersby noticed the figure above and skirted the area, anticipating that the man intended to drop onto the sidewalk. They showed no particular concern and continued on their way, oblivious to the possibility that he might be an escaping prisoner.

He released his grip, and dropped safely. His hands burned from cuts and scrapes; his knees felt like clay, but with freedom so close his adrenaline gave him the impetus to stand up and walk away. Putting his jacket on, he joined the momentarily curious crowd walking around him and moved toward the train station.

As he became part of the pedestrian traffic, he glanced over his shoulder and saw two men dropping from the roof onto the sidewalk.

Comfort coolly continued on past the courthouse and the police station, hailed a passing taxi, and took it to 171 Bedford Avenue, his cousin Jenny's home.

On arriving, he asked the driver to wait. He rang the doorbell of the two-story house. Jenny answered.

"Bobby!"

"Hold it down." He pushed past her into the foyer.

"What happened, what are you doing here?"

"Jenny, what—" It was her husband, Phil, coming in from the next room. "Bobby!"

"I'll explain, but I need a few bucks to pay for the cab."

"Sure," said Phil. He handed Comfort five dollars.

In a few moments Comfort had paid the driver and returned. Jenny nervously bolted the door behind him.

Comfort hurried to the window in the living room and, standing to one side, drew the drapes together. He turned to Jenny and Phil, who were watching in amazement, and told them what had occurred at the jail. He said he wanted to wash up and that he'd leave in a minute.

"I don't have any money—I'll need some," he said.

"How much?" asked Phil.

"Maybe fifty bucks."

"No problem," said Phil.

"Something else," said Comfort. "Five minutes after I'm gone I want you to call the cops."

"Why?" exclaimed Jenny.

"So they don't cause you any problems. They might find out I stopped here, and they'd accuse you of harboring an escaped convict."

He added: "Report that I broke in here and asked you for money. Tell them I hit Phil when he tried to make me give myself up—that I took your money and ran out. Remember, five minutes after I go."

He washed, straightened his shirt and torn pants. Grabbing a handful of hard candies from a candy dish, he placed them in his pocket and kissed Jenny on the cheek.

Cautiously, he slipped out the front door into the cold night and headed for a friend's house where he planned to hide out with Davey Nelson until the heat died down.

Minutes after Comfort had departed, Jenny, following his direction, called the jailhouse.

The desk sergeant refused to believe that there had been an escape, for the obvious reason that he, the sergeant in charge, would have been notified and alarms would have been transmitted to every police car radio in the county.

"Lady," the sergeant said, "Comfort's still in his cell," and hung up.

But feeling uneasy, the officer called Skinner's office and reported the peculiar phone call directly to the sheriff.

Sheriff Skinner thought it impossible that Comfort or anyone else could escape from his prison. However, he decided to make a routine cell check.

The next morning, November 11, the *Rochester Democrat*, with big, bold front-page headlines, announced.

14-STATE HUNT PUSHED
FOR 6 JAIL BREAKERS

The story described the escape, and went on to say:

> This was a well-planned escape. You don't do those things in two minutes, Sheriff Albert Skinner said. . . . The six are being sought in a 14-state alarm. Expanded forces of the Sheriff's Department, Rochester Police Bureau, and State Police are digging for clues. . . .
>
> The discovery (of the break), Skinner said, came at just about the same time as a telephone call from a cousin of the 27-year-old Robert Comfort. . . .

On a TV news report Sheriff Skinner, his fedora shading his eyes and the buttons on his suit jacket straining from his huge girth, told a reporter, "It's nothing. We'll have them all in a couple of days."

He was two-thirds correct. Barnes and another escapee were caught in a day. Two others gave themselves up. Only Davey Nelson and Bobby Comfort remained at large.

Skinner appeared on TV again the next day, this time with a little more authority in his voice. "We've got four of them back; the others are cold and hungry," he said. "They're hiding out like rats. They're trapped in the cold. They'll be giving themselves up soon."

Comfort and Nelson had found their way to the home of an old friend, Paul Chase. Chase and his wife had no qualms about putting up the two fugitives.

After four days in the Chase house, Bobby decided that the dust had settled sufficiently to permit them a relatively safe passage out of town. New York City was Bobby's destination. He felt that the city was big enough for him to get lost in.

He had visited New York several times in the past and knew

ex-cons from Coxsackie and Great Meadows who would help them find "jobs" quickly.

Borrowing money and a couple of parkas from Chase, the two escapees slipped into a local parking lot that night, found an old De Soto with its key dangling in the starter switch, hopped in, and, with Davey at the wheel, drove down Plymouth Avenue.

One squad car passed them going in the opposite direction, but the officers didn't look their way. Davey turned onto the thruway and headed for Manhattan.

◆ 6 ◆

November 16, 1959, Brooklyn, New York

A cold steel-blue afternoon. The two prison escapees in the tan De Soto pulled up to the curb on a quiet street lined with leafless trees and rows of two-family brick houses.

Bobby Comfort and Davey Nelson carefully wiped the entire car clean of fingerprints with rags they found in the glove compartment. Then they abandoned the escape vehicle.

Breaths steamy in the cold air, they huddled against the cold and walked two blocks to the BMT subway. They disappeared down the entrance.

They took a train to Times Square and then jumped on the shuttle to Grand Central Terminal. From there they would go to Slick Felix's house, which was on East Fortieth Street, a few blocks from the station.

When the Forty-second Street shuttle rocked and screeched to a halt, the doors rattled open and a mass of five o'clock straphangers came pouring out. Bobby and Davey pushed against the incoming horde. As they waded through the crowd, Bobby was startled to see a pretty young woman staring wide-eyed at him. "Bobby?" she asked hesitatingly.

He looked closer at her and replied uncertainly, "Millie?"

"Yes," she said.

"I can't believe it. Eight million people in New York City and I run into you!" Millie was one of his sister Rosie's best friends.

"What are you doing here?" she asked as she was jostled by a man hurrying past.

"Vacation," he said. "Say, it's good to see you."

Bobby took her in fully with his eyes. She had long dark hair and wore a tailored gray coat with white gloves and black high heels.

"You look terrific," said Bobby.

A flush crept into her cheeks. "Thanks," she said softly.

"Millie, this is Davey," said Comfort. "Davey, meet Millie, she's from Rochester—I'm sorry, I don't remember your last name?"

"Condello," she said.

"Right, Condello," he said.

As they spoke, they were forced to move in little circles to avoid being spun around by the rushing crowd in the raucous cavern.

"You know, I thought you were in jail."

"Not as of four days ago."

"They let you out?"

He looked around. "We let ourselves out," he said.

"Escaped?"

"Shh! Jesus!"

"I'm sorry."

"Okay," he said.

"When did you get here?"

"About an hour ago."

"Where are you staying?"

"I don't know yet. We've gotta make some calls. Which way are you going?"

"I've got an apartment in Brooklyn."

"Brooklyn? We just came from there."

"Well, how about coming back with me?"

He smiled, then took her by the elbow and, with Davey Nelson following, pushed onto the train to begin their return journey to Brooklyn.

Millie related how she had left home two months before to make her independent way in New York. She had been bored with the small-town atmosphere of Rochester, her parents' constant nagging, their old-country ideas, and the restrictions they placed upon her social life. She was aggressive enough, in rapid succession, to land a job as a bookkeeper at Abercrombie & Fitch and to secure a two-bedroom apartment which she shared with another Rochester girl, Cathy Rile.

It took an hour to go by subway from Grand Central Terminal to Millie's apartment on Avenue K. Considering that the girls had been in the city for only a short period, the place, surprisingly, was completely furnished and comfortable.

Millie repaired to her bedroom to change. At her suggestion the men took out a couple of beers, sat, drank, and waited. Soon Millie emerged in a tight red sweater and form-fitting tan slacks that accentuated her curves. Bobby looked at her admiringly.

Millie's olive complexion was smooth. Her lips were full and she smiled easily and confidently. It was her brown eyes, though, that told the most about her. They were candid, yet not naïve; there was a radiance in them that suggested a lively, strong spirit.

Her roommate, Cathy, a short redhead, arrived later that evening, and the four of them, over TV dinners, agreed to Millie's idea for Bobby and Davey to share the apartment temporarily.

The men would take Millie's room and the girls would stay in Cathy's. Cathy, too, knew of Bobby and thought the whole adventure would be fun. She readily agreed with Millie that the men could stay until they found something to do and a place to live.

Within a few days Comfort and Nelson had made contact with several ex-cons, including Slick Felix and Al the Horse, who were "working" the New York area. They joined forces, and by the second week of their Brooklyn stay, their unlawful ventures were netting a thousand dollars a week.

"I was on the lam like the sheriff said, but I was on the lam in the top nightspots and clubs in town," recalled Comfort. "I convinced Millie to quit her job at the department store and I took over all expenses. By now we had gotten very close."

Davey Nelson and Cathy, though, remained just friends. But Davey insisted that Cathy quit her job as well. No one could work from nine to five every day if she was partying all night and going to bed at the crack of dawn.

Millie never questioned Bobby as to his source of money, and he never volunteered the information. For Millie, at age eighteen, the entire experience with Bobby was what dreams are made of. She had fallen for the charms of an exciting man ten years her senior. He was gentle and generous to her. However, she was too practical not to recognize the drawbacks to this romance. Bobby was a thief, an escaped convict, and his exploits in New York were a continuation of his life of crime.

One evening as Bobby came up the stairs of the Brooklyn apartment building, he heard screams. It sounded like Millie. He took the stairs two at a time. He burst into the apartment, spotted a whiskey bottle on the coffee table and Millie's ripped blouse on the living-room floor. The screams were coming from the bedroom; he raced in. Millie was being held down by one of Comfort's partners—Al the Horse. He seized Al, who was taller and heavier, and slammed him against the wall, and hit him in the face and hit him in the stomach, surprised at how soft he was. Al collapsed. Bobby pulled him out of the apartment and threw him down the hall steps.

Millie was shaking, but she wasn't crying. Bobby was surprised at her control. She explained in a halting voice what had happened: Al had come by the apartment and asked if he could wait there for Bobby; Millie said yes; he was slightly drunk, gradually became abusive, and then made advances to her. When she resisted, he got mad.

This incident showed Millie another side of life in Bobby's world, and it frightened her. Yet she had to admit to herself that she felt protected by Bobby.

Comfort, for his part, felt he could not subject her to another such experience, for her sake, and his. As long as he was on the run, Millie might prove to be too much of a responsibility.

Shortly after the incident, Comfort took Millie to dinner at a small Italian restaurant. He gently informed her that it just wasn't feasible for them to continue together, and he had made arrangements to fly to Florida to be with his sister Rosie and her husband. He'd be going alone. Davey Nelson had declined to accompany him and was headed for Pittsburgh where he had friends. Millie listened, and reluctantly accepted his decision. She saw that there was no uncertainty in his eyes.

That night Millie decided that she, too, would leave New York City, to return to Rochester and spend Christmas at home with her family.

Two days later Comfort, carrying Millie's luggage, took her to Grand Central Terminal.

As they stood on the platform in front of the train, he opened her purse, tucked ten $100 bills inside, and snapped it shut. Bobby pulled her to him and kissed her.

"Will I ever see you again?" she asked.

He looked into her eyes. "I don't know."

"Do you want to?"

"You know I do."

7

December 20, 1959, Jacksonville, Florida

With a small suitcase in one hand and a garment bag slung over his shoulder, Bobby Comfort stepped off the plane in Jacksonville and was met by his sister Rosie and her husband, Joe Gustino.

He hadn't seen them since they moved from Rochester over a year before. He enjoyed them both—Joe, with his languid manner that concealed a clever, crafty mind, and Rosie, who was as effervescent as Joe was laid-back and, in her own way, equally wily.

It was obvious from their deep tans that they had taken to Florida like natives. Joe, a large man, wore an expensive pastel suit; Rosie, a lissome redhead, had on a blue off-the-shoulder dress and a string of white pearls.

In his Lincoln Continental, Joe drove back to their luxurious rented oceanfront home as Bobby and Rosie caught up on news. Comfort inquired about the family back in Rochester, and Rosie was delighted to learn about the romance between her brother and Millie, her best friend.

Comfort had always liked Rosie, always thought she had a good head. She invariably acted older than she was. Now, at age eighteen, she smoothly complemented a man nearly twenty years her senior.

Joe Gustino had been raised on a farm in the rural town of Newark, New York, forty miles outside of Rochester. As a youth during the Depression, he labored in farm fields for a dollar a day. He soon learned that big money was in the city, and found that he took to card playing in a way he did not take to plowing fields.

The term "hayseed" sometimes seemed an apt characterization of him, but his skill at cards earned him thousands of dollars a week. He was cunning, and bold in action, in direct contrast to his mild demeanor.

Anticipating Bobby's visit, Joe had secured a set of phony I.D.'s, including a New York driver's license, in the name of "Tony Borelli."

The fact that Bobby was an adept card "mechanic," like Joe, would become a profitable coincidence. And Joe, Bobby, Rosie, and friends spent several weeks together gambling around Jacksonville. During this time Rosie had heard a great deal from Bobby about how much he missed Millie. One afternoon, without Bobby's knowledge, Rosie called Millie in Rochester. It didn't take much persuasion to convince Millie to accept a plane ticket from Rosie and fly down to Florida.

For Comfort it was a joy to see Millie again, and the couple spent the next few days frolicking on the beach, shopping in the oceanfront stores, and making love.

On some evenings they visited the most exclusive hotels and restaurants. On other nights, Comfort and Joe played card games. The men were expansive and charming with their unsuspecting victims as they lured them into "a friendly game."

After a steady diet of this for a few weeks, Bobby and Millie headed for the Fontainebleau Hotel in Miami Beach, to be alone, and to listen to Lena Horne, his favorite singer, who was performing there.

Although he had set out for a relaxing week with Millie, by

the second day Comfort couldn't resist a "good score." Walking out toward the hotel pool in the early morning, he noticed a man sitting alone at his cabaña table shuffling a deck of cards. Brief overtures followed, and Comfort was invited to join him for a game of cards.

Between breakfast and lunch, the man went the way of all Comfort's victims, to the tune of eighteen thousand dollars. As the game ended, the man shook hands, tossed his towel over his shoulder, and walked toward the hotel lobby. Comfort sat and looked out at the ocean.

It always amazed him how unsuspecting some intelligent, streetwise people could be. Even casual games in the sunshine turned out to be windfall capers for Comfort.

Although card hustling was profitable for him, strangely enough, it conflicted with his moral code.

He didn't like the designation "card cheat." Friends were important to him; he liked people and hoped they liked him. He was "a stand-up guy," and friends could rely on him. It gave him a character foundation and self-respect. Cheating at cards diminished this and reduced him to a hustler.

He differentiated between robbery and card cheating. There was no hypocrisy involved in robbery. It was a thing you did— straight out. The intention was clear to the victim from the beginning, but to cheat a man who was open and friendly, and who presumably trusted you at the card table, began to gnaw at his sensibilities.

In fact, during that morning game, he found himself losing concentration. Fortunately, the man had been an easy mark, and Comfort used no deception to win his money.

Oddly, however, the brief hotel stay moved his thoughts in another direction. Seeing the gaudy splendor of the Fontainebleau at the height of the winter season, and observing the jewel-laden women in the lobby and at the nightspots, he began thinking of robbery again.

What also struck his eye was a printed notice on the door of his suite which suggested that hotel guests place their valuables in safe-deposit boxes at the cashier's desk.

"Is jewelry secure in those hotel safe-deposit boxes?" he casually inquired of the bellhops. "Should I put mine in? Do other guests?"

Comfort was assured that it was common practice, that the jewels and money were safe there. Jewelry thefts sometimes occurred in rooms, he was told, but nothing had ever been stolen from the safe-deposit boxes. "It's safer than Fort Knox," one of the bellhops had said.

"That's good to know," said Comfort. "I feel better already."

When Bobby and Millie returned to Jacksonville, Joe upbraided Bobby for having paid the thirty-six-hundred-dollar hotel bill.

It was an unwritten law that hustlers were never to pay a bill. They must appear to have paid it, and leave by the front door, gracefully. Bobby was still learning.

It crystallized a lifelong trait of Comfort's: "I become a big spender when I've got the money. I decide to just give it away. I don't think about it until I'm broke. I forget about the future as soon as I have money. It always happens. And every time, I swear it's never going to happen again."

Considering the carefree life-style he was leading, it was difficult to keep in mind that he was an escaped convict. It all seemed a long, long way from Rochester and the Monroe County Jail. Bobby couldn't imagine being caught, now that four months had passed.

A poker game was set up at the large, sprawling home of a local big-shot politico. The game had been arranged by a friend of the man's who was also acquainted with Joe and Bobby and their hustle.

The friend preferred Bobby to play the game rather than Joe. The crowd was to include some of the more sophisticated, monied people of Jacksonville, and Joe looked "too rough around the edges" for the occasion, the friend said. Bobby looked benign, innocent, and more attractive.

It was a game with high stakes and presented few challenges to Comfort. He won five thousand dollars that night, which he would split with Joe and the politico's friend.

The nights in Jacksonville were some of the most beautiful Comfort ever experienced. He relished the drive back to Joe's house, along Highway A1A, following the line of the ocean. Palm trees outlined against the starry sky, the full moon shining on the calm dark waters, and the fresh, tangy smell of ocean air were unlike anything in Rochester—or a state prison. It was on one of those moon-filled nights, returning with a pocketful of poker winnings, that he pulled into the driveway and heard rustling in the bushes. He tensed. Suddenly, he was blinded by a flashlight. He felt the lead coldness of a gun at his temple.

"Don't move, Comfort. Police."

Both car doors swung open.

"Hands off the wheel slowly and move your ass out here, Comfort, nice and easy—now move," barked a cop.

"Hey, my name's not Comfort. My name's Borelli, Tony Borelli," said Bobby. "Check my wallet."

"Bullshit, we're takin' you in." He was handcuffed.

After they went through his wallet, they checked him into the Jacksonville County jail. His fingerprints established that he was Robert Anthony Comfort, escaped convict.

The extradition papers for Comfort's return came through in a few days.

On the plane back to Rochester with two local detectives, Comfort pondered who might have provided the police with his identity. The only people in Jacksonville who knew it were Joe, Rosie, and Millie. Had one of them inadvertently said something on the phone to a friend or relative in Rochester? Was the phone tapped? He would never learn how the police found him.

Comfort was acutely aware of the hard steel handcuffs on his wrists as he sat beside the plane window and looked at the billowy sea of clouds. He lay back in his seat and tried to sleep in order to deaden his thoughts.

Bobby Comfort's return was big news in Rochester. At the airport the scene resembled an official welcoming party for a visiting dignitary. Politicians, police, and a battery of reporters and television crews were on hand. Sheriff Albert Skinner proudly repeated his prediction of four months before that the escaped convict would be captured.

In short order Comfort received a 5-to-10-year sentence for the attempted Siebert automobile showroom burglary, and a 3½-to-7-year term for prison escape, the sentences to run concurrently. In addition the judge, in his final determination, decreed that Comfort because of repeated parole violations must also serve the remaining nineteen years of his original sentence.

From the Monroe County Jail Comfort, handcuffed, was transported by station wagon to the Attica State Correctional Facility. Within two hours the conical-shaped towers, ugly high curving walls, and network of intersecting catwalks of the giant prison complex came into view. Bobby Comfort, twenty-eight years old, saw little hope of his being freed until he was almost sixty. Escape? No one had ever escaped from Attica. The wagon drew closer, and Comfort, seeing the concrete mass looming in front of him, muttered to himself, "So that's my tomb."

◆ 8 ◆

March 7, 1960, Attica, New York

The iron-bar door of Cell 26 on Tier 4 of A Block was opened by a guard, who motioned for the prisoner inside, Number 29108, Robert Anthony Comfort, to step out.

Wearing the standard drab-green uniform and paper-thin prison-issue shoes, Comfort was led through a series of low, shadowy tunnels and innumerable gates to the huge textile mill, the pride of the Attica penal institution.

The plant contained more than 150 assorted looms, threaders, bobbin machines, spongers, and other assorted mechanical devices, each seeming to vie as the most ear-shattering piece of equipment in the building. The mechanical monsters, cranking out textiles by the yard, often impaired the hearing of those unfortunate enough to have labored in the mill for even a short period of time.

Comfort was designated to work at one of the large looms as a helper to the chief operator, another convict. Above the din, the operator shouted directions, with vague hand motions and finger pointing. He briefly indicated the loom's danger areas and cautioned Comfort to be alert on the job.

Inclined as he was to abhor handling anything more mechanical than a rubber band, Comfort knew that this mill would never suit him as a long-term work assignment. The next morning the civilian plant superintendent approached Comfort at the front end of the loom and told him to sign a waiver on a page in his record book. His signature would attest to having received proper instructions, which qualified him to work on the loom. It also, not incidentally, rendered New York State free of responsibility in case of accident.

Aware of the implications if he signed, and recognizing an opportunity to avoid work on the machine, Comfort refused to comply. The foreman then signaled to the other side of the room for Sgt. Richard Maroney to come over.

When he heard the problem, the sergeant said, "It's just routine, Comfort, this book is nothing. It's just to show that you know how to operate the machine."

"I haven't been instructed in the use of the machine," said Comfort. "Besides, if the book doesn't mean anything, why do I have to sign it? I'll work on the machine, but I won't put my signature on that statement."

"You've got to sign the book."

"No, I don't."

He was taken to the warden's office. Superintendent Walter Wilkins had a stiff, erect posture and a deep voice.

"Comfort," said Wilkins, "you have until noon to do as you're told."

"Where do you think you are? In the Westerns or something? It's ten o'clock now, and I'm not signing the book at twelve o'clock high, or one o'clock or two o'clock or three o'clock."

"Yes, you will."

"I'm not signing the fuckin' book, sir."

Comfort recalls the warden saying, "In that case, smart-ass, we're throwing you in the box. You'll think straighter in there."

Within minutes Comfort found himself in the isolation cell.

66

Stripped of all clothing, he was given a metal bucket and pushed into the dank, dark room. The only light in the cell filtered through the small pane of glass in the metal door.

"You're not gettin' outta this hole 'til you sign the book," said Sergeant Maroney. He banged shut the door.

(Years later, Maroney—he would be promoted from sergeant to lieutenant—remembered the incident very much the way Comfort recalled it, though from a not unexpectedly different viewpoint. "Comfort was a troublemaker and a smoothie," Maroney said. "He was kind of a quiet operator. He wanted to be a big-time operator. Yeah, I remember he wanted to be a big shot, like a lot of 'em did.")

At night Comfort heard other convicts hollering to each other the inanities that helped them maintain human contact and their sanity.

"That light there on the tier, it's a pretty green."

"It ain't green, it's blue."

"That bulb ain't blue, you motherfucker, it's green."

"Bull-sheet. It's blue."

"You asshole. Green."

"Them hacks done got to your mind and your eyes."

"Fuck you."

"Hey, anyone else can see that light?"

"Yeah, man, it's green," someone said.

"Blue, man," said another.

On into the night the dialogue continued over the color of the light bulb. Comfort, with no choice, listened but never joined in.

"Some of the convicts down there were so tough or crazy that they'd do anything," recalled Comfort. "Guys would throw their shit bucket in the guard's face. Sure, they knew they'd be beaten up bad for it, but it made them laugh, and it broke up the day."

Every few days Comfort, stark naked, was led out of his cell to a small room where a prison guard ordered him to sign the book.

Each time he refused. Down flew a billy club on his head and shoulders. He was returned to his cell only to be subjected to further torture when the guards sprayed tear gas into his cell.

The only person he saw, besides the guards, was a prison trustee, who delivered his food daily and emptied his bucket.

Comfort believed his solitary confinement was totally unjustified and illegal, but he knew that the warden would never buckle under in the face of this challenge to his authority.

Isolated, he was permitted no visitors, and he understood that all letters were read by prison authorities. It seemed obvious that there was no way out of isolation except to sign the book. After three weeks Comfort hit upon an idea. It was a long shot, but he had to try it.

He prevailed upon the sympathetic trustee who delivered his rations to help him. The following day as he ate the dry, cold mashed potatoes, Comfort found two pencil stubs embedded in them.

Each day on torn sheets of toilet paper, Comfort scribbled a few lines preparing a petition to the court, asking relief from unlawful confinement in the strip cell. The petition was accompanied by his crude "motion for show cause," requesting the court to order the warden to justify Comfort's illegal punishment concerning his right to refuse to sign the statement that he knew how to work the loom. With a rudimentary knowledge of the law acquired during his previous prison terms, he was familiar with the legal avenues open to him.

Each day the trustee tucked the toilet paper squares into his sock and delivered them to yet another convict friend in the general population who recopied the scribbled notations onto lined notepaper.

This laborious process continued for seventy days, until Comfort had completed the "motion." Finally, the recopied material, consisting of five handwritten pages, was smuggled into his cell. Comfort hid the folded sheets under his shit bucket.

Now he needed the signature and seal of the prison's chief clerk, who served as the notary for the prison population.

A note was dropped on the chief clerk's desk, advising that the prisoner in Isolation Cell 104 required notarization of a document.

A week passed. Each night when his cell was examined by the

Guard, Comfort lay on the floor feigning sleep, covering his folded papers.

On the eighth day his cell door flew open and Sergeant Maroney burst in. "The chief clerk's out here, he says you got papers for him to sign," Maroney shouted. "Show me those fuckin' papers."

Comfort removed the five sheets of the petition from under his bucket. The sergeant grabbed the petition, read it, his face became enraged. "Damn you!" he said.

Comfort walked out into the passageway, where he met the chief clerk. Comfort had not shaved or showered for the more than two months that he had occupied the strip cell. He was acutely aware of his stench, as was the chief clerk, who stepped back before speaking to him. The clerk advised Comfort that the handwritten material would have to be typed into a formal document. The clerk's wife could type the pages for a small fee.

The following day the clerk reappeared with the typed pages in triplicate. He witnessed Comfort's scrawled signature, affixed his notary seal to the three-page "show cause," and placed each set into individual envelopes for mailing.

The documents were then forwarded to the warden of Attica, the state attorney general, and to the State Supreme Court judge presiding over the Attica jurisdiction.

The next afternoon Comfort was transferred from isolation into segregation. The rapidity of the transfer was never explained to him.

The segregation cell boasted luxury appointments compared to his former "isolation" cell, in that Comfort now had a toilet, a sink, and a bed.

Maroney visited Comfort on several occasions, asking him to drop his legal action and offering him a return to the general population, with a promise of "no mill work." Comfort adamantly refused.

He languished in that segregation cell for more than seven months while his crude petition crept through the judicial process. When the court finally processed and upheld his petition, Warden Wilkins was ordered to release Comfort immediately from solitary confinement and return him to the general population.

Comfort was sent back to a regulation cell in C Block, flushed with victory and congratulations from the other cons.

He received numerous requests for legal assistance from the convicts. He became an "in-house" legal aide. He had plenty of time to devote to this, for the warden kept his promise. Bobby Comfort never again performed any work in the prison.

After Comfort's arrest and extradition to Rochester, Millie, in Jacksonville, was left at loose ends. She was still feeling rebellious and, on a dare, responded to a newspaper want ad, and was hired as a "bunny" by the Playboy Club in New Orleans. Leaving Rosie and Joe, she flew to Louisiana.

She would be earning over $250 a week in the Playboy Club, but the strange working hours and the customers' constant advances ultimately forced her, after six months, to quit the job.

During this time, thoughts of Bobby were often with her, and she wrote him regularly. Finally, Millie decided to fly home to Rochester.

In many ways Millie mirrored Comfort's limited view of the future. When she thought of him in prison, she never considered the meaning of a long sentence. She was nineteen years old now and in love, and Bobby, though behind bars, was alive. She had faith that things would work out for them.

After several attempts to secure visitation privileges to see him in Attica (passes usually are reserved for family members only), Millie's persistence paid off.

The inspector at the Attica gate had rummaged through the bag of groceries Millie had brought; then after an hour's wait she was waved into the visitors' stalls at the reception center.

She sat down in front of the wire-mesh separator and saw Bobby pass through the convicts' entryway. Bobby looked thin, his face drawn, and his eyes lacked the animation that she had come to expect. She bit her lip to hold back tears.

He took a seat across from her. She put her fingers up to the

70

wire mesh to touch him. She jumped as she heard the guard nearby shout, "Hands off the screen, lady!"

Comfort shot the guard a swift, angry glare. Then he turned back to Millie, shaking his head. Their conversation at first was tentative, given the circumstances, but it soon warmed.

"I baked you a cake," Millie said.

"C'mon, Mill, I know you can't bake."

"Really, Bob. I thought I ought to learn, and I know how much you like chocolate cake."

"Devil's food?" he asked with a laugh.

"Straight chocolate," she replied, smiling.

The talk soon changed to their future.

"You're wasting your time coming here," he said.

"No one's forcing me," she said.

"I'm in here for a long time. Go out and live some kind of normal life. There's no hope for us and you know it."

She looked him directly in the eyes. "I think there is," she said.

A guard broke up their conversation. Visiting hours were over.

As Comfort returned down the dark tunnel to his cell, his stomach felt hollow and his head hurt. He thought of how beautiful she looked and of the small feminine things he liked about her, even the casual way she ran her hand through her soft hair. It was difficult, very difficult, seeing her.

Life in prison had once been described to Comfort as equivalent to a man swimming in shark-infested waters. It was an accurate appraisal. Convicts could be as dangerous as prison guards.

"You never know when a convict might explode," Comfort recalled. "You might say something wrong, without even meaning it. You could look at somebody and not really be looking at him, maybe just daydreaming, and the guy would say something like 'Hey, motherfucker, who you lookin' at? What's the matter with you?' If you take that, you're in trouble. Boom, you've got a fight on your hands."

Certainly, the undercurrent of danger inherent in prison life remained. But as time went on Comfort no longer had the urgent need to assert an image of toughness, to battle the guards and intimidate other prisoners. Respect still had to be gained from them, but his sharp edge had been blunted. Perhaps it was his age—he was reaching thirty—or Millie's influence, or that the prison system itself began reflecting a less brutal attitude toward men behind walls.

He had secured hi-fi equipment complete with earphones for his cell, and for the first time in his life enjoyed classical music and opera, particularly the works of Verdi and Mozart.

He read a great deal, and continually worked on improving his vocabulary. He loved words, and it was fun for him to drop sesquipedalian words into his conversations, sometimes intentionally flummoxing friends who weren't sure if he was praising them or insulting them.

He also took part in theatrical groups in prison, a popular activity in Attica. Most criminals Comfort knew fancied themselves actors—not just street-savvy con men, but stage actors or vaudeville comedians. He found it part of the mechanism of the criminal ego. When he met Willie Sutton in Attica, he found that the notorious thief prided himself on his nickname, "the Actor." Sutton maintained that his ability to use disguises was essential to him in his bank robberies and daring prison escapes.

Comfort was particularly friendly with a chubby, bald robber and cop killer named Donald Borello. Borello, too, viewed himself as an accomplished stage presence.

"I worked with him on comedy skits," Comfort said, "and Don had the place in stitches, he always did.

"One time we did a skit about the old Romans, and we had to wear short togas. Some guys and I stood around looking real serious and holding spears—well, sticks, the guards weren't going to let us have spears—while Don jumped around the stage singing and dancing in his little dress.

"He was a violent guy, he'd kill people at the drop of a hat, but he could be very funny."

Aiming to keep in good physical condition, Comfort played

halfback on the prison football team, ran ten miles a day, and punched a heavy bag. He attained the honor of prison bridge champion. But his most consuming interest by far was law.

Comfort grew friendly with Jerry ("The Jew") Rosenberg, a con with a rapid-fire Brooklyn accent. Comfort and Rosenberg had met at Great Meadows in the mid-1950s and discovered a mutual interest—the law: the reading, the analyzing, the interpretation of the legal structure in America. They had engaged in lively legal discussions. But these were short-lived, in consequence of Comfort's parole release from Great Meadows and Rosenberg's transfer to Attica. In Attica now, in 1960, their friendship resumed. Although each was serving a long sentence (Rosenberg was doing life for the murder of two New York policemen), they searched for ways to possibly beat their cases.

Scrutiny of law books and an understanding of the legal ramifications of their specific crimes and convictions might reveal to them some extenuating circumstance that could minimize their sentences.

Comfort, like Rosenberg, felt that the law was made by smart people who provided, in the maze of legal mumbo jumbo, an "out" for other smart people.

Cynical from his experiences with the judicial system, Comfort believed that the authorities and the courts used tricks, deceptions, and lies to convict—even in airtight cases.

Rosenberg's contention centered around a simple theory. "The way they got you in is the way you can get yourself out," he said. "I don't need justice. I'm just trying to learn to play their game."

Rosenberg, in fact, decided to study seriously for a law degree. Eventually, he passed the bar and became the first convict to defend a suspect in a court trial, traveling from Attica to the trial court in handcuffs.

Comfort had Millie send him law books. Tomes such as *Penal Law, Supreme Court Decisions*, and *The Code of Criminal Procedure* lay stacked on the floor in his cell, along with his favorite books, those by the renowned defense attorney Clarence Darrow.

In the prison library, which he frequented daily, he had come across one book that was to influence him and provide him with a deeper understanding of the human condition, insofar as it related to crime. The book was Clarence Darrow's autobiography. Darrow's compassionate insight into the world of courts, crime, and prisons—Comfort's world—made a profound impression on him. Comfort committed entire passages to memory. Darrow wrote:

- On prison guards: "There is a mixture of sadism in every human being that makes him enjoy another's misery."
- On prison rehabilitation: "Humiliating men, degrading them, dressing them in stripes or any other brand of prison uniform, substituting numbers for names, shaving their heads and depriving them of everything that a human being desires does not help but only destroys them."
- On judges: "To mete out justice, the judge must understand the prisoner. This he does not do, and cannot do. . . . To know life, one must have lived. The only approach to understanding is through imagination, and this gift is bestowed on few."
- On human behavior: "Everyone is more or less capable of most things that others have done, but some of the inducing causes are absent among some of us and we are spared."

Comfort spent every evening reading his books under the bare bulb in his cell.

Lying on his bunk one late winter evening, and skimming through the pages of amendments to the New York State Correction Law, he came across a paragraph that literally made him sit bolt upright.

"The term of an imprisonment of a person given an indeterminate sentence can only be held for a maximum of five years," he read.

The amendment was dated April 6, 1949—*five days before* he committed the crime for which he had received a thirty-year sentence. His sentence for robbing the grocery store at age sixteen was zero to thirty years—an indeterminate sentence!

*   *   *

74

Either old Judge O'Connor had not kept abreast of the changes in the law, or was so incensed at Comfort he refused to apply them. Whatever, Comfort, according to that amendment, had been unlawfully imprisoned for five years and three months.

In the following days Comfort composed and submitted two petitions to the courts; one, a writ of habeas corpus (contending illegal imprisonment), which he sent to the original-sentencing county court in Rochester, and the other, a writ of coram nobis (a plea to correct an injury caused by a mistake of the court), which he mailed to the Wyoming County Courthouse in the Attica jurisdiction.

Five months after he petitioned the court, Comfort received a response to his challenge of the original judicial decision. The County Court upheld his position.

The *Rochester Democrat and Chronicle* reported the story on Sunday, November 6, 1960:

19-YEAR TERM VOIDED
BY JUDGE'S RULING

Robert A. Comfort, 28, convicted burglar and jail-breaker, wasn't on parole and consequently can't be required to serve nineteen years as a parole violator before beginning a five-to-ten-year Attica Prison term imposed last April 20, County Judge George D. Ogden has ruled.

When Comfort first arrived at Attica . . . he was told by prison authorities, he alleged, in a petition he sent to the Court, that he must serve some nineteen years as a parole violator first. . . .

Without aid of an attorney, Comfort sued . . . and Judge Ogden upheld his petition, saying that the commitment was erroneous because of an oversight. . . .

Comfort didn't savor the victory for long. Although he had fought and won release from the yoke of nineteen years of parole, he still faced a 5-to-10-year sentence on the Siebert burglary charge and a concurrent 3½-to-7-year stint for escape.

He was not encouraged when he was called before the Parole Board in February 1963. It was just a routine appearance, and he did not hope for a release.

Seated at the end of a long table, Comfort listened as one of the parole officials said at one point, "Well, Comfort, this escape among other things doesn't look good for your case."

"I've got to be honest with you," said Comfort. "If I was doing thirty years right now—thirty years in which I was illegally imprisoned—I'd be looking to escape again."

"I can understand that," came the reply.

"The court said I was illegally imprisoned, and before, when I kept telling you, you didn't believe me," Comfort said heatedly.

"Let's not get excited," said another member.

"You sure as hell would be excited if you served five years more than you should have," Comfort countered.

"There is something very positive in your record," said another board member. "Your psychiatric report says you are a well-adjusted personality and you have a very high IQ. Under the right circumstances you could be a credit to society."

A week after the review Comfort received an official letter from the Parole Board. Two words jumped out at him: "Parole granted."

◈ 9 ◈

June 15, 1963

A gray overcast morning. On the gravel parking lot outside of the Attica prison walls, Millie Condello sat behind the wheel of a blue four-door Chevrolet. She smoked a cigarette and waited for Bobby.

There was no question that she belonged to this man. She had hardly dated during the three years he was away. Her friends upbraided her for her foolish loyalty, and her parents pleaded with her to forget him.

She was brooding over a bitter argument that had erupted over her using the family car to pick Bobby up at Attica, when she looked up and saw the heavy iron door open and Bobby emerge.

He spotted her, but his noncommittal prison expression never changed. He came to the car and got in. She leaned toward him, but he sat stiffly, looking straight ahead, and said, "Drive out, Mill, I don't want to put on a show for the screws."

After a few minutes of driving over bumpy country roads, she turned onto the smoother Route 98.

Suddenly, his mood changed. He slipped his arm around her soft shoulders, and with a smile said, "Let's head for the bushes."

She frowned. "After three years, is that all you've got to say?"

"I'm sorry, Mill, you have a right to expect something more romantic, more sentimental. Okay—I missed you and I'm crazy about you."

She glanced at him skeptically.

"That's better," she said.

"Now, can we head for the bushes?"

They broke into laughter. Shortly, the car turned off the road.

A few weeks later Millie moved into an apartment in Rochester with Bobby, despite the intense protests of her family.

Comfort had never met her parents. When Millie asked her mother if she would like to meet Bobby, she encountered, "What for? I can read all about him in the newspapers."

This attitude seemed to draw the headstrong Millie even closer to Bobby.

They had been living together for about a year when, one morning at breakfast, he said, "Well, do you want to get married or what?"

It was the first time the subject had ever been raised. Millie coolly finished buttering her toast, and then looked up. "Is that your idea of a proposal?" she asked.

"Something along those lines," he said. "I was thinking that we might as well get married. We'll invite a lot of people and we'll make a nice score."

"Some men ask a woman to marry them because they love them," she said.

"Well, I do, don't I? Otherwise I wouldn't be part of this conversation, right?"

*   *   *

Millie became Mrs. Robert Comfort. True to Bobby's prediction, there was an outpouring of cash and gifts from the Condello and Comfort families and friends.

The festivities over, the newlyweds settled into a normal domestic routine, at least what Comfort considered normal.

He became involved in a number of illegal scams, which included diamond switching, traveler's checks and money-order forgeries, and passing bad checks. He did these things outside of his hometown to minimize the risks, traveling as far west as Chicago and as far south as Georgia.

Life for the Comforts was good and money plentiful. The couple regularly enjoyed parties and nightclubs. Bobby bought Millie expensive clothing, jewelry, and perfumes. She relished life with Bobby again, and on a permanent basis.

While in prison Comfort had filed a civil action suit against the State of New York for the judiciary's error of unlawful confinement.

Although his legal rights were suspended for the period of his prison sentence, he wanted to begin the process, anticipating the time when he would be released and free to pursue the case.

In the ensuing months he corresponded with a Rochester attorney, Norman Palmiere, a family friend, who felt Comfort had legitimate grievances against the state.

In late March 1965, nearly two years after his release from Attica, Comfort received word from Norman Palmiere that the long-pending civil suit had finally been placed on the court calendar.

On April 22, 1965, Comfort, accompanied by Palmiere, traveled to Buffalo and the court of claims.

The bailiff called the first case on the docket, "Claim #27461, Comfort versus The State of New York, the Honorable John R. Cooke presiding."

It was to be a one-day documentary trial, with Special Assistant Attorney General Hamilton Ward, Jr., representing the state.

At one point in the proceedings, State's Attorney Ward asked Comfort, "What do you recall of the commitment order with reference to the time of your sentence?"

COMFORT: "It was an indefinite sentence. Under Article

13-A—that is, pursuant to Article 13-A of the New York State Correction Law, Section 343, it was interpreted as five years."

The judge smiled, obviously amused to hear such legal phraseology from an ex-convict.

WARD: "When did this amendment take place?"

COMFORT: "It was amended to—"

"Objection," called Palmiere, rising from his table before the bench. "I ought to be the one answering those questions. I'm the attorney, not Comfort."

JUDGE COOKE: "Well, I'm wondering if he knows . . ."

PALMIERE: "If Mr. Ward is asking the questions to test Mr. Comfort's knowledge of the law, I don't think the witness is qualified. Legally, that is."

Judge Cooke fixed Palmiere with a stare. "Perhaps not legally, but apparently he has answered questions quite well."

The judge added, "We understand of course that Mr. Comfort is not an attorney, and if he makes a mistake, we will take his position into consideration. It seems the only way to get the facts of the matter."

Besides the legal side of the issue, Comfort also answered questions pertaining to his employment and earning capacity in the various jobs he held while on parole. The court would then determine the monies Comfort might have earned providing he had been gainfully employed during those five years and three months in question.

The trial concluded that afternoon.

On June 30, 1965, Judge Cooke handed down his decision. Comfort learned of it in a letter from the court to Norman Palmiere.

Judge Cooke's opinion read in part:

It is . . . evident that if not confined, [the claimant] could have been gainfully employed.

Claimant, in his claim, sets forth two separate items of damage: (1) loss of time from work and (2) shame, humiliation, loss of freedom and mental anguish. As to the first item of damage, claimant should be entitled to a recovery, but as to the second, from the history of the criminal record, parole violations and continual disregard for the law, this Court finds no cause of action.

The Court finds, therefore, that the claimant is entitled to an award of $15,000.

"I wasn't overjoyed at getting the fifteen grand, but it did come in handy," Comfort would recall, "but it could never make up for the stretch I got as a kid. Thirty years for robbery for a first offender who was sixteen years old? That's not justice. Thinking about it, I'd get so damn mad. That was blood money and it could never make up for the five years—the seventeen hundred days—that I spent in a nine-by-six cage.

"It sure affected me in a lot of ways—some ways I'm not even aware of. And I don't want to torture myself by being angry now. But I will admit that it was the toughest money I ever got in my life."

◆ 10 ◆

From the moment he legally became Millie's husband, Bobby was accepted into the Condello family. And because he exhibited interest in her cooking, he became a favorite of Mrs. Condello's.

But, flattered as she was by his praise of her lasagna and manicotti, she remained realistic about her daughter's future.

Rose Condello felt it her duty to convey the old-country customs about the traditional role of a wife in an Italian family:

"You make your bed, you sleep in it. You marry, you stay, no matter." And she warned Millie that the police would forever be in her life.

It was true that when a major crime was committed in the Rochester area, the police invariably rang the Comfort doorbell, regardless of the hour.

Since Comfort was still under parole supervision, he suffered this harassment. But nothing incriminating was ever uncovered by the police in their searches of his home, although his activities were less than pure.

It was during this period that the marriage ties were tested. The intrusions of the police and Millie's heightened anxieties did not help to keep the marriage running smoothly. Millie resented the frequent police searches and, in rare shows of temper, occasionally became belligerent. She was overreacting, for only she knew of Bobby's illegal activities; and feeling guilty and apprehensive, she struck out blindly when she felt her marriage threatened by Bobby's possible arrest.

The restrictive covenants regarding parole during the 1960s prohibited a parolee from "associating with known criminals."

The old adage of "guilt by association" and the illogic of it inflamed Bobby Comfort. It was a restraint he refused to abide by.

When Norm Huck, an extortionist and a lifelong friend, was released from Attica, Comfort had no compunction about hanging out with him. One night, shortly after Huck's release, Comfort was awakened at around 3 A.M. by a phone call. Cynthia, Huck's live-in girl friend, was on the other end. "Norm's dead," she sobbed. "They found him on the side of the road, shot three times." There was something in her voice that Comfort found suspicious.

"That's nice," said Comfort, and hung up the phone.

Millie was awake. She put the night table light on.

"What was that all about?" she asked.

"Huck's been killed."

"Oh no! What happened?"

He repeated what he had just heard.

"What's that got to do with you, Bob?"

He was sure from the sound of Cynthia's voice that the cops had put the girl up to the call and were listening on the phone. His curt response to her was his recognition of the cops' presence.

"The cops'll be here next," he said. "They're going to try to set me up for parole violation on this one—that's for sure. They'd love to pin this on me. It's a big one, murder."

In less than ten minutes the doorbell rang. It was the police.

Comfort was taken to headquarters for questioning. The police wanted to trace Huck's activities that evening. Comfort was their prime source, since they learned that at 10:30 P.M. he had been seen in the company of Norm Huck at a local pool hall.

Bobby offered the police no information about Huck's associations, although he would learn through the grapevine that there had been "a contract" out on him. Huck's murder would never be solved.

Unconvinced of Comfort's answers, the police took him into custody and held him over in the Monroe County jail. The charge: "Parole violation—associating with known criminals."

He was again taken to Attica, where the State Parole Board was in session. In green prison garb and assuming a most pleasant manner, Comfort exhorted the parole panel with an unusual monologue. He began by explaining that there had been no involvement on his part in any criminal activity, that his relationship with the deceased, Norman Huck, had been as an old friend, and that their chance meeting at the pool hall had been strictly social.

"You tell me that I'm not supposed to associate with ex-cons," he went on. "Okay. Well, why don't one of you go ahead and invite me to your house? I'll be happy to come and hang around with your son or daughter. But you obviously don't want to introduce me to your family. So who do I associate with? Who do I know that's not an ex-con, or Mafia, or gang lord or something? Who do you think I've met in my life? Rochester's not a big city. Everyone *knows* I'm an ex-con. I can understand your not inviting me to your home. A person's past is all you have to judge him by. I believe in that. You judge horses by past performance if you know how to handicap. So I can't blame you for being wary of me. But the question is, who are criminals—are they ex-cons?

"If I happened to be in a bar with Martin Luther King or Socrates or Jesus Christ—I'd be back in jail for parole violation, right? Martin Luther King's a criminal, and Jesus Christ was one of the worst. He and Socrates. They both got the death penalty. King only got a jail sentence.

"They're ex-cons, but one won the Nobel Peace Prize, one was a great philosopher, and the other is considered by half the world to be God. Well? I don't know who to associate with if I can't socialize with the only people I know."

Friends like Huck, Tom Sapolin, and Davey Nelson were obviously not the equivalent of Christ, Socrates, and Martin Luther

King, but the board acknowledged that Comfort had made a salient point. However, he was not sufficiently persuasive. In November 1967 he began a sixteen-month prison term.

It was different now for Millie. She had been married to Bobby for more than two years, and there was a routine to their lives. This time Millie had lost her husband. She hurt in a way she never had experienced before. When she needed him emotionally, he wasn't there. When her father died, she faced the tragedy without Bobby. Millie was pregnant when Bobby went back to Attica, and when it turned out to be a tubal pregnancy, ending in a miscarriage, his absence was painful to bear. Those were the times she resented him, and she viewed his imprisonment as a selfish act.

And because of Bobby's free-spending ways, she had been left with little money, another fact that gnawed at her. Millie went to work in the family's Italian restaurant. Periodically, she received a visit from Comfort's parole officer, Joe Dean.

"Millie," he said, "you and Bob are in love, but if he doesn't straighten out, he's going to spend most of his life in jail. You'll wind up a grass widow."

His words did not fall on deaf ears. It was a thought that until now she had avoided.

When Millie visited Bobby in Attica, he sensed a distinct change in her. She told him, "I don't know, Bobby. I can take it now, but I don't see myself taking it forever. Some things have got to change."

Millie's visits were unpleasant for Comfort. "There was no real enjoyment in the visits because I was helpless," he said. "It was a depressing period." He finally realized then how much she meant to him and how much he really loved her.

For the first time he began to question whether she would wait for him. She was a "sticker," Comfort believed, but not a martyr.

◈ 11 ◈

December 1968, Attica, New York

> Mrs. Antenor Pation in black velvet and enor-
> mous pearls. . . . Raven-haired Diana Vreeland . . .
> was fabulous with billowing sleeves and a golden
> diamond-encrusted eagle hanging from her neck. . . .
> The Diamond Ball, always one of your most glitter-
> ing affairs. . . .

Comfort subscribed to numerous newspapers in prison and
read them all avidly. But it was the society news, particularly in the
"Suzy" column of the *New York Daily News*, that captivated him
above all else.

At first he read Suzy simply for amusement, enjoying the
gossip that surrounded rich people. He liked reading about their
material acquisitions: their opulent homes, their great paintings,
their precious jewelry.

He read about Prince Richard of Gloucester, the Italian ambassador, and the Moroccan consul general; of Jacqueline Kennedy Onassis and Marjorie Merriwether Post; of the Biddle Dukes and the Rockefellers. The gossip columnist detailed the season's social events, the diamond and charity balls, and other society activities that took place in the ballrooms of the great hotels in New York. In almost every column, the designer clothing and jewelry were always described in detail.

Comfort recalled his Fontainebleau experience and the glittering women whose gems were secured in the hotel's depository overnight.

At thirty-five Comfort believed he was at an age when he ought to be socking away enough money to live in the style he wished—without working.

The only way to get that kind of money was to go for a big score. He could always pick up ten thousand dollars in a card game, or cash phony money orders; but when he read Suzy's columns, and her accounts of the wealthy, he was hooked. They've got it, he thought. I want it.

Comfort envisioned the jewels that must be contained in safe-deposit boxes in the big city hotels where the rich stayed and played. There could be a bigger score in one of those hotels than in several of the biggest banks.

From casual chats with prisoners from New York, Comfort learned about good "heist" men and about one in particular referred to as "Sammy the Arab." One con, Bill Komis, told Comfort that he knew Sammy well and had been with him on some jobs. He described Sammy as slick, careful, neat, with good scores, and, as far as anyone knew, had never spent a single day behind bars. Comfort was skeptical about Komis's glowing endorsement of Sammy the Arab, in light of Komis's reputation as a heavy drinker and small-time crook. Comfort couldn't fathom why an A-1 heist man would associate with a Bill Komis.

One afternoon, in a corner of the prison yard, Komis and Comfort, both expecting to be released shortly, talked about their futures.

"What plans have you got when you're sprung?" Komis asked.

"I'm heading for New York," Comfort said. "My sister lives

in Yonkers, and I'll stay with her for a while before I make any plans."

"I'll give you a call—I'm not too far from there. I live in the Bronx."

"That'll be fine, the name is Gustino."

"Yeah. Okay. I'd like you to meet Sammy the Arab," added Komis, attempting to ingratiate himself with Comfort. "I got a feeling you'll hit it off. Sammy's always lookin' for a good man. Maybe we can all do something together."

"Maybe," said Comfort.

Bobby Comfort awakened early on the morning of April 19, 1969. It was the last day of his sentence. He had slept poorly the night before, in anticipation of his release. He slipped into his gray cotton prison uniform and shaved in the cold-water sink. He took the framed photograph of Millie and placed it in his bag with a few other belongings. The picture had been the single decorative piece in his windowless cell. He rolled up his bedding, which he would drop off at the supply room, and then sat down on the lumpy mattress that had been his resting place for the past sixteen months. From behind the bars he looked across the passageway, through the long, steel-grated window, and saw the dawn breaking slowly across C Yard.

He now had a goal: to make that one tremendous score. He would approach it gradually, leaving no room for error.

It would be his challenge, his gamble, in an area he felt he had done his best work—planning and executing robberies. If he was caught, if he lost this shot, everything could be lost—his freedom, his wife, life as he wanted it. But he felt he had to try.

There was no need to discuss this with Millie, he thought. He knew it was best that he keep his own counsel. Not that Millie messed up. She was very clever, very tight-lipped. But it was best—what she did not know would be that much less for her to worry about.

His cell door was opened electronically. He walked toward the guard waiting beside a sliding steel door at the head of the passageway.

Comfort and the jailer walked through the long, dark, low-ceilinged walkway. Jailers sitting on high stools turned the locks to allow the pair to pass. Every twenty yards they stopped to allow the next steel door to open.

They passed the stark mess hall, with its nailed-down stools and its small enclosed balcony, where guards equipped with tear-gas guns overlooked the prisoners at every meal.

They passed the sheet-metal shop, trudged up the winding steel staircase, through the hospital corridor, and into the package room.

Comfort then went through the ritual he knew so well: he dropped off his bedding, was fingerprinted, photographed, shed his prison garb, changed into a smartly tailored suit, shirt, and the paisley tie that Millie had brought a few weeks earlier, and received an I.D. and the forty dollars of New York State money to help him start his new life.

He was told that his wife had arrived and was waiting outside the front gate.

He straightened his tie and stepped out into the warm spring air of the prison yard. He was not yet free. Around him loomed those stark, massive, sand-colored walls of the fortress called Attica. Above him rose one of the fourteen six-sided turrets, each of which was topped by a peculiar architectural cupola. A rope was being used to lower the guard's shit bucket. Comfort stepped up his pace, to get beyond the odor.

The official prison exit through the last turret consisted of three massive sliding iron doors. A guard sitting beside a glass-enclosed box pressed an electronic buzzer. The heavy doors slowly moved; each of them took precisely ten seconds to open. With Millie waiting, they seemed to take an eternity. Finally, he was free.

Millie was standing beside the car in the gravel lot. She looked like a vision to him, in a white silk blouse, tight-fitting black slacks, and high heels.

As soon as they got in the car and shut the doors, they turned to each other—and this time he disregarded the guards watching him. He embraced Millie, holding her tightly until she gestured for air. He indulged himself in the constantly dreamed-of luxury of the taste of her soft lips against his, and the sensual touch of her silky blouse and her softness pressing against his body. He allowed himself this, but only briefly.

"Let's get out of here, Mill," he said. "I want to get as far as I can from those walls and those hacks."

Millie drove. After her many visits she knew the route well, only this time she vowed it would be the last time she would ever take it. It was like a recurring bad dream. She drove through the farmlands on Route 98, and then through the small town of Attica, and then onto the thruway. However, instead of moving north, they headed south to Yonkers, New York, where the Gustinos had moved from Florida.

Comfort had told Millie that New York was their new destination. It was where the big-money cardplayers were; and if he would ever make a bundle again, it would be in New York.

"I don't need millions, you know," she said.

"If we're going to have kids, we're going to need money, right?"

"Do you know what I want, Bobby? I want to live a normal life like other people," she said.

"You know what I want?" he asked after a moment.

She turned and smiled. He enjoyed his ability to make her blush.

"Do I have to guess?" she said.

"Well, it has been sixteen months, Mill," he said.

"Do you think you're the *only* one?" she said sharply.

He realized he had offended her.

"I know you don't go fooling around," he said. "Don't you think I know that after all these years? Who else would stick by me like you have? You either have to be a saint, a fool, or in love with me, and it doesn't take a genius to figure which it is." He paused. "I love you, Millie."

They drove in silence with Bobby's left hand resting on her shoulder. She spotted a motel and turned the car into the driveway.

They didn't reach Yonkers until the following day.

90

◆ 12 ◆

On a morning shortly after the Comforts arrived at the Gustinos' home in Yonkers, Bobby walked into the kitchen where Joe, Rosie, and Millie sat having their morning coffee. In yellow hard hat, denim shirt and pants, and heavy-soled work shoes, Bobby stood before them, lunch pail in hand and with a very long face.

He reluctantly had acceded to Millie's wish to give legitimate work a try. Joe had outfitted him for the construction job that he'd obtained through a friend.

"You look great, Bob," said Joe, smiling.

"Different, anyway," Rosie added, laughing.

"Well, this new image will take some getting used to," said Millie.

"A lot of getting used to," said Comfort.

Arriving at the construction site in Yonkers, Bobby found that the foreman had been expecting him. He was assigned to mix mortar in a large gravel-mix cement truck. The noise was ear-

91

splitting. He looked around and saw the construction gang digging and sweating in the sun, and the hod carriers bending under their heavy loads. He breathed in the dust that had been stirred up in the deep, excavated pits. Bobby turned to the foreman and said politely, "Excuse me, be right back."

He walked onto the street and hailed a passing cab.

As he came through the door of the Gustino home, the three people he had left at the breakfast table were still talking over coffee.

"I knew you weren't going to do it for long," said Joe, "but I thought you'd last at least until lunchtime."

Comfort had been in Yonkers for a few weeks when he received a call from Bill Komis. The ex-con from Attica wanted to know if he was still interested in "work."

"Always interested in work," said Comfort.

"You remember Sammy, the guy I told you about? He wants to know if you're up for a meet tomorrow."

Comfort said yes.

The following night in Manhattan Comfort walked up Broadway to Seventy-fifth Street and stopped in front of an old black canopy with a sign reading Plaka Steak House. It was a misnomer: the Plaka was more of a tavern than a restaurant. Inside, the lights were low and the bar on Bobby's left had a display of overhanging glasses. To Comfort's right were three booths upholstered in shiny black plastic. In the middle booth, below the mural of a Grecian port scene, sat Komis and another man. Komis motioned Comfort over.

Bobby slid into the booth and shook hands with Komis, who then introduced him to Sammy Nalo. Sammy the Arab, as he was often called, was impressively dressed in a well-cut dark suit. He looked to be in his mid-thirties. His black hair was combed flat and slick on his head—Comfort was certain Sammy wore a rug.

Sammy raised his left hand and motioned to the bartender.

92

Bobby noticed the large pink star sapphire on Sammy's fourth finger.

"George," said Sam to the bartender, "refill us and give our friend here . . ." He paused.

"Scotch and a little water," Comfort said.

"Bill tells me you're looking for work," said Sammy, turning to Comfort.

"That's right. I understand we're in the same line."

Sammy nodded.

"What do you have in mind?" asked Sammy.

"Looking for someone to work with. I just got to New York."

"I know, you've been away," said Sammy.

"That's right."

"Let me tell you up front, it's been my habit not to work with guys who've done time," Sammy said.

Comfort looked directly at him. Sammy returned Comfort's direct gaze.

"It's a good habit," said Comfort.

"Oh?" said Sammy, surprised by the reply.

"Sure, I can't blame you. If you don't want to connect, I can understand. No hard feelings." Comfort stood up.

Sammy held up his hand. His fingernails were manicured.

"I don't mean to give offense," he said. "C'mon, sit down."

"I'm not taking offense," said Comfort, taking his seat.

"Nothing personal," added Sammy, "it's just that anyone who's been in the joint is a loser—I mean, had to lose at a job—and I'm a success."

Komis hadn't said a word, his eyes shifting from Comfort to Sammy and back. Komis wondered why Sammy was going through this strange routine, since he had appeared so anxious for this meet.

"But," Sammy continued, "you definitely come highly recommended. A lotta people say good things about you . . ."

Comfort was not about to remain on the defensive.

"Heard the same about you," he said.

Sammy smiled. "Okay," he said. "Okay. I think we'll be workin' together."

Bobby was not happy with the tone of Sammy's voice. It

sounded arrogant, condescending, as if he had been weighing *him* in the balance, while Comfort usually was the one who did the weighing. This was a role reversal for Comfort.

"I think maybe we'll see," Comfort said, showing some annoyance.

Sammy nodded. He stood up to leave. "I know you've only been out a few weeks—and you're gettin' settled. Here's five hundred dollars. I'm sure you can use it."

"I'm good, thanks anyway," said Comfort. At the moment he had less than fifty dollars to his name. The roles between the men had reversed again. He had no desire to create an obligation in their first encounter.

When Sammy rose, Comfort noticed that he hadn't finished his drink. A good sign, Comfort observed. He never wanted to work with men who liked the bottle. As Sammy walked out, Bobby's eyes followed him to the door. He was surprisingly short, even with the lift-heel shoes he was wearing. Comfort had also noticed that Sammy had a little paunch; by contrast, Comfort, who had been running ten miles a day and lifting weights in prison, was lean and hard.

"What do you think?" asked Komis.

"I'll have to sleep on it," said Comfort. "I don't know."

Comfort did like Sammy's poise and forthrightness. He was cocky, but Comfort could deal with that. When Comfort left the bar, he had a feeling that Sammy was the man he wanted. It was Sammy's move now; either he would want to go in with Comfort, or not. Sammy would have to make the call. Two days later he did.

Comfort agreed to meet Sammy in a bar at Lexington and Thirty-ninth Street the following night.

"Komis told me you had big plans, Bob," said Sammy after they sat down at the bar. "But he didn't know specifics. That's good. You keep things to yourself."

Comfort stirred his drink and looked at him. "It's not a good idea to go into details until you're ready to work. I wasn't going to spell it out to Komis because he's not the kind of guy I confide in."

"Agreed," said Sammy. "He's a good worker, but he gets too nervous."

"You mean he hits the bottle," corrected Comfort.

"That's what I mean," said Sammy. He continued: "What's your plan?"

"I need someone good with his hands, who's handy with tools, and I understand you can open safes; if you can open safes, you can open safe-deposit boxes," Comfort said.

"What's so hard about that? I've never done 'em, but aren't they just a crowbar-and-hammer whack?"

"That's all."

"You got two hands, don't you?"

"But I'm just not good with tools. Besides, it's too much like work—and I'm scared to death of work."

Sammy leaned back and laughed. After a moment he said, "But don't you think robbin' takes work?" he asked.

"Sure, but you do have to get money some way. And if we do the type of thing I have in mind, we'll ultimately hit the score I know is possible. Then we never have to do another thing except lie around on our yachts."

"Keep talking," said Sammy.

"What I have in mind are hotels," Comfort said.

Sammy stared at him. "Why hotels?"

"The right ones are loaded with what I'm after."

"There's plenty of money in banks, too."

"Not really, just lots of cameras and plenty of paper—some marked, others not negotiable," Comfort said.

Sammy's face registered no surprise, but his voice rose. "You want to explain that?"

"People come to a hotel for a visit and put their valuables in safe-deposit boxes," said Comfort. "There are also people who live in hotels permanently who keep their jewelry in the hotel safe-deposit boxes. These people are rich—I mean super-rich: I'm talking about dukes and duchesses, oil and steel magnates, people of that cut."

95

"If you want ice, what's wrong with jewelry stores? I've done 'em. They're pretty good."

"Stores are too risky to do. They're designed to expect a robbery, so they install alarms in case guys like you and me think about robbin' them."

Sammy nodded. "That's true. Have you ever done a hotel?"

"No. Which is why I'm here talking with you now. I want to find the right guy."

"I've been in hotels, but cash was all I had in mind. There's a bunch of people around, like security, and sometimes there's only one entrance for a getaway. It's risky. But I gotta admit, I've never thought about the safe-deposit boxes."

"Decent scores can come out of a box even in small hotels," said Comfort, "and we'll have to start that way in order to get enough money to finance the big jobs later. I mean, we'd need time and money to do it right, to investigate the right places; and we'll have to pay the best people to get the right help. And the planning has to be perfect."

"I don't know," said Sammy. "There's a lot to think about. Why are you so sure it'll work?"

"Because I saw Humphrey Bogart do it," Bobby Comfort said, smiling.

"Humphrey Bogart! Are you a comedian, or did stir do that to you?"

"It sounds funny, but the idea came from *High Sierra*, a Bogart movie I saw as a kid. They showed a hotel in the mountains, and the character was named Mad Dog something, and he robbed the safe-deposit boxes."

Sammy's look had changed from amused to engrossed. "I think I mighta seen that movie."

"I don't know if you remember, but there was a million dollars in jewels in those safe-deposit boxes."

"But it was only a movie. What makes you think stuff like that is really in the boxes?"

"There's a hotel nearby. I can explain it better there."

Sammy was eager now. The men walked to a Lexington Avenue hotel Comfort had passed earlier.

They entered the lobby. Comfort went through a low-voiced, lengthy discourse explaining the simple construction of the safe-deposit boxes, the lack of security people, and the best hour to strike.

It all appeared logical and easy to Sammy. He agreed to try this very hotel as a test run.

They would go in wearing dark suits, Comfort said, in order to avoid any suspicion.

"And I'll put on a wig and false eyebrows," said Sammy. "What're you putting on your face?"

"Nothing," said Comfort, "because I go to the desk first."

"But they can identify you."

"No they can't. Remember, I'm a stranger in town. They've got no mug shots on me."

Comfort believed that as long as he entered the hotel without disguise, he was just another guy coming across the lobby to check in. "But if I wore a fake nose or fake eyebrows," he said, "the clerk might take a closer look at me. This way, the clerk hardly looks at me. When I get to the desk, I say, 'Turn around and don't look at me.' All that takes two seconds. There couldn't be much identification in that time."

The following Sunday at exactly 2 A.M., the two men walked through the unguarded door, and, in less than an hour, walked out into the dark, rainy night with the contents of ten boxes, the hotel's cash receipts, and the drugstore and coffee-shop money that had been readied for early-Monday-morning bank deposits.

The take was mostly cash, with a few diamond watches and three rings. It totaled twenty-two thousand dollars.

What they left behind was the night clerk and the elevator man tied to the radiator pipes in the back room.

It was agreed in the opening phases of their association that Sammy would select the target hotels while Comfort learned more about the city.

On a Monday Sammy would inspect a hotel marked for the following Sunday's action. Daily, he visited, observed, and gathered pertinent details. He repeated the procedure at night.

Comfort found it difficult to believe how cautious Sammy was, and wondered why.

"Sammy, why do you have to check and recheck?" asked Comfort. "The hotels aren't that big. There's a basement, we know where the restaurant is, where the shops are, where the boxes are, and we know who's around at what hours."

"We can't be too careful," said Sammy.

"But you always want me to look around, too. Why?"

"You might see something I missed," Sammy replied.

To begin Sammy selected transient hotels. They were now realizing between fifteen thousand and fifty thousand dollars per hotel on their takes. And in the first year they had taken more than twenty-five such hotels.

Some of the hotels chosen were larger, and required an experienced heist man who would accompany them for a stipulated percentage.

The swank Navarro on Central Park South was one. In the dark early morning of September 14, 1969, the three men, dressed in tuxedos, came through the front door and took over the hotel. Bobby controlled the front desk, Sammy was to crack the safety boxes, and Tommy, a third partner, was the lookout at the entrance. Unexpectedly, a chartered bus containing fifteen members of a Mexican *mariachi* band pulled up to the curb. Having just finished an engagement, the musicians, still outfitted in their gaily colored costumes and black sombreros, began to unload their instruments.

Tommy called to Bobby, "What the hell do we do now?"

"Let 'em in," Comfort called back. "Make sure they're all in the lobby, then lock the door."

Tommy ceremoniously opened the glass door as the group trooped in, lugging their instruments and luggage through the door to the middle of the lobby. Comfort stood at the front desk impersonating the room clerk.

Out of view at the far end of the front desk, on the floor near his feet, sat the seven hotel-employee hostages, handcuffed, with mouths and eyes taped.

Tommy clicked the door shut as the last musician entered.

The group's leader, tassels from his sombrero dangling in front of his eyes, approached Comfort and said in uncertain English that his group had reservations for the night.

"Okay," Comfort said, "would you and your caballeros move over against the wall, please?"

"I no unnerstan'," the band leader said.

Comfort pulled a gun from his waistband. "This is a stickup— move over there." He motioned with the gun in the direction of the wall.

The leader's face blanched. He turned and began to explain rapidly to his wide-eyed group.

"Don't speak in Spanish," Comfort said sharply. "I don't understand."

"English they *no comprenden*," was the leader's reply.

"They *comprende* this, don't they?" Comfort said, extending his .38.

"*Sí, sí, señor.*"

The hotel employees were occupying the only contained area of the hotel lobby, and no other space existed that would accommodate the fifteen additional hostages.

Comfort looked down at the open drawer of the front desk and noticed two keys tagged for the lavatories.

He snatched the key marked Men and walked toward the leader, at the same time motioning to Sammy and Tommy to herd the men in the direction of the brown door he pointed to at the end of the lobby.

Pressing the leader to move forward with a gentle nudge of his gun, Comfort led the way, and the group shuffled after their leader. Comfort stopped, unlocked the door, snapped the toggle switch and peered into the tiled lavatory. He saw two urinals, two stalls, and three sinks. He estimated that in this emergency, the room was large enough to hold ten people, uncomfortably.

The three bandits resembled rustlers as they herded the fifteen men into the room. There was one small overhead window for ventilation, not large enough to allow escape.

After the guitar players, floppy sombreros and all, were squeezed into the room, there wasn't enough space for another castanet.

Comfort locked the door, then turned and surveyed the lobby. The bags and miscellaneous musical cases were strewn across the lobby floor, resembling a military obstacle course.

Quiet once again. Sammy returned to the safe-deposit boxes, Tommy returned to the door, and Comfort smoked a cigarette in relief.

Soon after Sammy commenced hammering at the safety-box hinges, a muffled voice was heard, emanating from the men's room. The voice was singing a Mexican song. Other voices joined in until, a minute later, there was a clamor loud enough to resound through the entire lobby and beyond.

Realizing that the singing would surely arouse the hotel guests upstairs, and unquestionably lead to calls to the desk or to the police, Comfort had no choice. He rushed back to Sammy. "Let's get the hell out of here," he said, "the place is coming apart." He helped Sammy close the suitcase containing the loot from the truncated heist, and the robbers fled the Navarro. As the front door closed behind them, they could still hear the refrain coming from the men's room.

The abbreviated night's work netted the trio a hundred thousand dollars.

The fruits of his criminal labors provided Bobby and Millie with a very comfortable life. They had a sporty new Thunderbird, a luxury apartment on fashionable East Seventy-fourth Street in Manhattan, and their wardrobes matched their swanky address.

They were on frequent shopping sprees for suits, dresses, nd home furnishings. The more Comfort spent, the more he wanted. They enjoyed the best the town had to offer in restaurants and entertainment—the Four Seasons, the Copa, "21," the Starlight Room at the Waldorf, as well as the favorite haunt of his new partner, the Port Said at Twenty-eighth Street and Eighth Avenue.

Comfort was a little surprised that only a few brief newspaper stories appeared describing the succession of daring burglaries. He assumed that hotel managements would rather suffer their losses without publicity, or, perhaps, the robberies were not

100

yet big enough to command much newspaper space. One small item in the *New York Daily News*, however, reported that numerous complaints about a recent rash of hotel thefts had been registered with the New York Hotel Association. The mayor's office sent directives to the police commissioner. The city's tourist office demanded an end to this growing menace.

Albert Seedman, then commander of Manhattan South detectives, recalled that he had a "hotel squad" that "responded to all hotel crimes. Hotels were their beat." Sometimes they would just sit in hotel lobbies, as if they were hotel guests, and observe the goings-on. They also sought emerging patterns, and sent inquiries to police departments in other cities. "Maybe these guys matched somebody else somewhere else," said Seedman.

The police were limited, though, in what they could do to stop the hotel jewel thieves. They would go through their "prevention phase" of "extra vigilance," as Detective Lieutenant Edward O'Connor, who would become commander of the Manhattan Robbery Squad, would recall. "Patrol officers would stop in at unspecified, sporadic times to hotels to make sure nothing strange was going on. Of course, they had to use common sense. They could be talking to the hotel clerk, but it might actually be one of the criminals."

Hotels were urged to install alarm systems, or to improve their alarm systems. But all were aware that if the hotel clerks were surprised at gunpoint by the robbers, there was precious little they could do. They would have no chance to activate the alarm system. Lieutenant O'Connor added that "there was no way of telling when the gang would strike again." So the police would go through their routines of trying to track down leads, of checking photographs and fingerprints, and of seeking sources of information from records or the grapevine. "It was a continuing effort, and we had to keep it alive until some development gave us substance. We learned more of their methods of operation, of their physical descriptions—we were seeking some tidbit of information, some break that would crack their wall."

But so far, the police had frustratingly little.

◆ 13 ◆

The closer Bobby and Sammy worked professionally, the closer they grew personally.

Comfort learned that Sammy Nalo was born in 1931 in Detroit, to immigrant parents from Iraq. His family came from a farming area, known as Chaldea, at the southernmost portion of the valley of the Tigris and Euphrates rivers.

Sammy never liked to be called "the Arab." He was Chaldean, he emphasized. He was proud of his heritage, and grew up believing that he had been born under a star. He also adopted the historical Chaldean philosophy that man is a natural sinner, that he was born to pursue material gain.

He loved to gamble and, as a youth, would have men place bets for him since he was too young to be allowed in bookie parlors. He began stealing as a boy to pay off gambling debts. Like Comfort, he burglarized stores and homes. He was caught several times, but his longest jail sentence was only for eleven months, at age eighteen. Sammy moved to Manhattan in the early 1960s, where he began a skein of armed robberies and had only minor brushes with the law. His ineptness at gambling quickly dissipated the easy money from the robberies. His procession of women, especially topless go-go dancers and belly dancers, was another drain on his take.

Sammy maintained several apartments in the city, and Comfort soon learned to differentiate among them. Sammy's hideout spots were usually shabby affairs, contrasting with his much finer living quarters on West Forty-fifth Street, directly in the center of the theater district.

During this time Sammy had one girl he particularly liked, a topless dancer named Diana DePeña. She was a thin, attractive blonde who had undergone silicone shots to fill out her breasts. Diana claimed she spoke seven languages and came from a wealthy Venezuelan oil family. The important thing for the five-foot-four Sammy, Comfort knew, was that he could attract tall, beautiful women.

Occasionally, Bobby and Sammy would meet Joe Gustino for a day at the track. Joe knew a lot of owners, jockeys, touts, and always had some kind of tip. Some worked; most didn't.

One afternoon Joe told the other two men that he had a "sure thing" in the second race. "Look," he said, "this is a fix. This ain't just the smart money. This is a *dead* fix."

.The three put up five thousand dollars and won ninety thousand.

Comfort had never seen Sammy as animated as when he collected his thirty-thousand-dollar winning share. His dark, deep-set eyes flashed with excitement, and his voice quavered.

Sammy began betting five and ten thousand dollars on succeeding races. He didn't refer to the form sheet; he bet with no apparent rhyme or reason. He couldn't get to the window fast enough to throw down the money.

He lost one race after another. Comfort stared at him. "What's got into you?" he asked. "You're dropping a bundle. You don't know what you're doing."

Sammy shot back, "For Christ sakes don't bother me when I'm busy! Fuck off!"

Comfort flared. "Who the hell are you talking to? I oughta beat the living daylights out of you, you baldheaded midget!"

Sammy's eyes widened in shock.

Comfort wheeled around to Joe. "C'mon, I'm leaving," he said. "Let that little asshole walk home."

He pushed his way through the crowds.

Sammy ran after Comfort.

"Bob—"

"Get away from me, or I'm going to kick your balls right through your head!"

Bobby and Joe left the track without Sammy.

Comfort's anger persisted, and, in the following days, he refused to answer any of Sammy's urgent phone calls.

"I wouldn't talk to him," Comfort said. "Then I get a four-page letter from him about our friendship and partnership. He said we had gone through so much together, that we were such a good team, that we shouldn't break up like this. He said, 'I don't know why you got so mad. I should have gotten mad. Okay, so I was a little abrupt, but you did call me a baldheaded midget and other names.' He added, 'You know when I'm at the track I get excited.'"

Comfort eventually agreed to a reconciliation. In less than a week the two partners were back together.

Sammy was obviously a man of extremes. He could be cool and composed, but also could exhibit a violent temper. When an acquaintance belittled Sammy's short stature, he immediately cracked off an antenna from a nearby car and chased after the bigger man, trying to stab out his eyes. Other times he was considerate and generous. On one occasion he surprised Millie with a cocktail ring he had had made for her. Once, when Comfort was arrested in New Jersey on a speeding charge and got into a brawl with the arresting State Police officer, Sammy hurried to the station house and put up the bail money.

Sammy wasn't a man who read books, but he avidly read the *Wall Street Journal* to check his investments. He also kept abreast of the business world in general—and his business world in particular: he began reading "Suzy."

In the late summer of 1969, Millie learned that she was pregnant. Near the end of her term, she and Bobby moved back to Rochester. Millie preferred to be near her mother and her own

104

doctor. That was fine for Bobby. He could drop down to New York—fifty-five minutes by plane or five hours by car—to do what he had to do, and return. And Rochester was safer for him than New York: the more robberies he committed in Manhattan, the less he wished to be seen there.

The Comforts moved into a large garden apartment in an exclusive town house on the outskirts of Rochester.

Up to now, Comfort and Sammy had made several hundred thousand dollars. But much of it had been spent. Sammy, the chronic gambler, was always in debt, and Comfort, for his part, gambled little but *gave* his money away. With a baby on the way, Millie, for the first time, began urging him to save. But he had a habit of being loose with a buck that was hard to change.

It was Bobby's lifelong pattern to show affection for people by lavishing money or presents on them, family and friends alike.

Millie began to question some of these "friends" who benefited from Bobby's generosity. She was certain that many were parasites and would disappear if Bobby's wallet shrank.

He didn't see it that way. He couched the gifts in the form of loans, but everyone knew that repayment was neither expected nor forthcoming.

"You've got a marker from every deadbeat you ever met," Millie told him. "I don't understand you. Do you think you can buy friendship?"

He felt she didn't understand that friendship meant helping a guy when he was down.

On February 24, 1970, Nicole was born, precisely nine months after the day her father had been released from the Attica Correctional Facility. When the infant arrived home from the hospital, her room was overflowing with hundreds of dollars worth of stuffed animals. And she was surely the only infant in the neighborhood wearing forty-dollar knit dresses and fifteen-dollar embroidered booties.

Millie, happy with the baby, grew increasingly unhappy with the style and the speed with which their money melted away.

"There's always more where this came from," Bobby told her. "We're not going to run out."

"You sound like you've got a license to steal. That this can go on forever. Don't you see, we've got to save for the future, for Nicole. I don't want to nag, but, Bobby, I think every woman wants security."

Although Millie handled some of the money that came in, she never asked, nor did Bobby explain, its origin. She knew that it was less than legitimate. She was led to believe it came from gambling and card games.

Over breakfast one morning, she said, "We've got twenty thousand in cash in the house. Why don't we invest it in a business, some kind of store? Or put it in a bank. You can get some kind of job."

"Who'd hire me? An ex-con, nearly thirty-eight. What can I do? And what kind of business do I know? About the only thing I could do is tend bar, and you won't let me do that."

"Why not?" said Millie, her eyes narrowing.

"Because you're jealous."

"I don't like you drinking—that's what you'd do if you were behind a bar."

"That's not the reason. You're worried about broads sitting in those bars like you saw in Jacksonville."

"No I'm not." She didn't sound convincing.

"You're jealous. I remember how you punched one who walked up to me at a party and asked me to dance."

"You're saying I don't trust you," she said, "but you go to New York anytime you want and I don't go with you."

"Because you know you can trust me," said Bobby.

The next time Bobby went to New York, he told Millie that Mel Dunne, an old friend, had called to ask if he'd be interested in a big card game in Yonkers. "Unbelievable—doctors, bankers— Mel said even a shipping millionaire would be there," he told her. Millie never complained about his card playing; it was the safest vocation he had.

When Comfort returned home two days later, he walked in smiling broadly. He hugged Millie in the living room and handed her several rolls of bills bound with thick rubber bands.

106

She placed the money in the pocket of the apron she was wearing.

"Must have been some card game, Bob," she said.

"I told you it would be."

"The big-shot shipping millionaire must have been there."

"Yeah, he was."

"How's Mel?" she asked.

"Good. Great. He said hello."

"I know."

"You do?"

"He called last night."

Bobby blinked.

"You lying bastard," Millie shouted. "I know where you've been. Playing cards my ass! You've been out sticking up people. Otherwise you would've told me the truth."

"Millie—"

"I don't want this money," she screamed. She snatched the rolls in her apron pocket and threw them at Bobby.

He blew up. He picked up one of the rolls of bills. "You don't want it?" he said. "Then I don't either," and he threw it out the open window. "You probably don't want anything else in this house! Money I brought in bought everything here. When the hell did you ever complain about where it came from before?"

He grabbed the draperies and ripped them down. He picked up the coffee table, threw it against the wall, shattering the wood. He knocked over a stuffed chair, then jumped on the back to break it. As he did, he swung his arm and the lamp crashed down.

Millie sat down on the sofa, crossed her legs, and lit a cigarette. He pulled a picture off the wall and broke it in half. He smashed the lamp tables and flung a set of encyclopedias across the room. The room was in a shambles. Except for the sofa, the only untouched piece of furniture in the room was the TV console with a soap opera in progress. Comfort kicked in the screen. Sparks flew in all directions. He yelped, yanked his leg out of the television set, staggered back a few steps clutching his shin, and fell onto the couch.

Millie calmly exhaled a stream of cigarette smoke.

107

"You don't seem to care that I'm in pain," he said, rubbing his leg.

"You don't seem to care about lying to me, you don't care about smashing up my house—" Her voice cracked slightly, her eyes moistened.

"Okay," he said gently, straightening up, "I lied to you about New York. I'm sorry, Millie. But I'm doing the best I can for us. You know I'm not going to do anything to hurt you. Christ, you're all I've got, you and the baby."

"More bullshit," she said quietly. "You think you can con your way out of anything, don't you?"

"I'm not trying to this time. What I told you is the truth."

He reached over, took her cigarette, and crushed it out in the ashtray on the floor. She looked at him without saying a word. Then he put his arm around her shoulders tenderly and bent to kiss her. She did not draw away.

◈ 14 ◈

There were hundreds of hotels in New York, but only a dozen or so first-class, part-transient-part-residential hotels that could net Comfort the big scores he envisioned. These hotels were all located in an area bordered by Thirty-fourth Street on the South, Seventy-sixth Street on the north, Park Avenue on the east, and Seventh Avenue on the west. Comfort traversed streets and neighborhoods from Murray Hill to the elegant art galleries of upper Madison Avenue, looking and learning about hotels.

He and Sammy eliminated the bustling, mammoth, multi-entrance hotels with late-night activities, like the Hilton on Sixth Avenue, the Americana, the New York Sheraton on Seventh Avenue, and the Waldorf-Astoria on Park Avenue. Besides the manpower required to cover the various entrances, Comfort found the hotel clientele undesirable for his purposes. The majority of the guests were either button-down corporate types in the city for organizational meetings and conventions, or tourists, sometimes with several children in tow, taking advantage of "five-day special" rates.

In Comfort's view the safe-deposit boxes in those hotels were strictly low-yield, maximum-risk.

His excursions—sometimes with his partner—took him to Park Avenue south of Grand Central Terminal. He learned from newspapers and the underworld that, aside from the Jackie Gleason penthouse suite at the Doral at Thirty-eighth and Park, the guests there, and at the nearby Tuscany and Sheraton-Russell, were predominantly department store, dress, underwear, and costume-jewelry buyers. Although these hotels were ideal because of their single entrances, small staffs, and minimal security, Comfort was certain that the take would be small: no gems, and loads of credit cards. He immediately discounted these hotels.

Farther uptown on Park Avenue, at Grand Central, he observed the Commodore, the Biltmore, and the Roosevelt. These were smaller than the Hilton, but they seemed "commercial."

Proceeding north on Park Avenue, he began to get different perceptions. Except for the Waldorf (though he was interested in the Waldorf Towers—living quarters apart from the hotel itself), Comfort's attention was captured by the sophisticated tone of the Barclay, the Drake, and the Regency. They looked rich to him—and ripe.

North again on Fifth Avenue, he was attracted to the Gotham, the St. Regis, the Plaza, the Sherry Netherland, and the crown at Sixty-first Street—the Pierre.

Farther uptown on Madison Avenue stood the exclusive Carlyle, where, Comfort knew, President Kennedy had stayed when in New York. He marked that one for "possible."

After weeks of careful consideration, Comfort and Sammy decided to take the Sherry Netherland, a relatively small but patrician hotel with wealthy permanent residents. On a wintry Sunday morning four men in business suits, posing as guests, took the staff hostage, broke up the safe-deposit boxes, and in less than an hour made off with over one million dollars in gems and cash.

In the months to come Comfort and Nalo—sometimes with others—robbed the St. Regis, the Drake, and the Carlyle.

Since they were getting 80 percent of the wholesale value of the gems, and the split went only three or four ways, it amounted to over half a million dollars a job. Others could retire on several scores like that—which were some of the biggest in New York history—but not Comfort.

He decided that the Regency, on Park and Sixty-first Street, might be the best hotel to take next. Industrialists like Henry Ford II and Robert Sarnoff, chairman of RCA, and various other celebrities were often guests.

Sammy, too, thought highly of the Regency, so the partners agreed that Comfort would check in to "get the feel of the place." This marked a change in the *modus operandi* the men had been using. Comfort rented a suite. The Regency was a fairly busy hotel; and Comfort would lounge around the small red-carpeted lobby for short periods. He enjoyed sitting on the well-padded Louis Quatorze sofa set against the brown walnut-paneled wall. He watched the lobby activity at random hours, becoming familiar with the permanent staff, including the unobtrusive men with a silver button pinned to their lapels: the hotel security guards. There were only a few guards during the busiest hours. At three and four in the morning, when he casually walked out of the hotel, Comfort noted that only one guard appeared to be on duty.

Comfort paid particular attention to the area around the front desk. With appreciation he noted the seven-foot gold-leafed ebony clock—he always liked quality antiques. But he was more interested in what he could see of the area behind the partition of the front desk: the bank of safe-deposit boxes.

He learned the layout and the operation of the hotel. He checked out all the alcoves, the stairwells, the kitchen, and the telephone room in the basement.

Within three days he felt he knew all that was needed to take the Regency.

Comfort never drew diagrams—that was only for movies, he said. "We aren't architects, so why draw where a column in a building is? Or where a post is?" he explained. "You don't do that—you go in and you observe and you remember where things are—because you're interested enough to remember. If it's a bank—it's just one room. What's to remember? If there are cameras, you squirt them with paint. Hotels don't usually have alarm systems the way banks do—unless maybe at the cashier's window. If you've got a gun, show it, and tell people you mean business. They'll listen.

"I've never seen young guys guarding banks or hotels. No commandos. There's no real protection because robbery is never expected. People are lulled into a false security by luxurious surroundings.

"In some ways robbery of a hotel is easier than the stickup of the corner grocery store. The grocery store is where the guy's own money is, and this guy will fight. He's worked hard and he's mad and you can't blame him. It's very personal. You know, one-on-one.

"In a hotel heist the people we're robbing aren't there in the lobby. So I don't see the suffering. They get the news the next day. The clerks are told, 'Give the robbers the money.' Usually they do."

Comfort met with Sammy and detailed his findings at the Regency. They determined that the size of the lobby and the lack of late-evening traffic required the services of only one additional partner.

Sammy chose an old friend, "Milty from Miami," to round out the trio. Sammy and Milty had combined on jobs a few years back, and Sammy vouched for his competence.

Comfort didn't meet Milty until two days before the scheduled robbery. When they met, Comfort had reservations about him immediately. He seemed loud and boastful.

His gaudy checked sports jacket and white shoes showed the flashy stamp of Miami Beach.

Accompanying Milty to buy a tuxedo, Comfort grew annoyed when Milty caused a hassle by demanding a yellow Scottish cummerbund for his tux.

"This isn't for a fashion magazine," said Comfort. "Why don't we just take what they've got."

"I got very particular tastes," explained Milty, finally settling for a red cummerbund.

On the following afternoon the three men met in Bobby's suite in the Regency. They planned to take the hotel from the inside, because Comfort felt it would be easier and less risky than coming through a locked front door at four in the morning.

The men sat in the room for nearly eight hours. Bobby believed it best that they stay together before the robbery—"so no one would show up late, and everyone would understand his assignment."

They played cards, watched television, ordered room service. But as the hours wore on, it became obvious that Milty was growing increasingly uncomfortable. He began to sweat, and his hand shook so badly that he spilled his coffee.

"You okay?" asked Sammy.

"Yeah," said Milty. He did not sound convincing.

Comfort looked at Sammy. "Think it'd be better if we do this another time?" he questioned.

"What do you think, Milt?" asked Sammy.

"I don't like this sitting-around crap," said Milty. "I'd feel better if we'd come in from the outside."

"Got any objection?" Sammy asked Comfort.

"All right, we do it from the outside," replied Comfort.

They checked out of the hotel, repaired to Sammy's apartment and waited there.

At 3:45 A.M. on August 16, 1970, the tuxedo-clad trio, having parked their car on Madison Avenue, each armed, carrying suitcases and tote bags, walked to the Regency Hotel entrance around the corner of Sixty-first Street on Park Avenue.

Of the three men only Sammy wore a disguise—a rubber nose and glasses, his bald pate covered with a curly dark wig under a snap-brim black hat.

The men knocked at the locked door. Through the glass clustered with small fleur-de-lis designs, a security guard stared out. Comfort said, "Reservations." The guard unlocked the door, and the three men pushed in, guns showing. They quickly took as captives the guard, two bellhops, the elevator operator, the desk clerk, two porters, and three guests. All were led out of sight and into a room next to the front desk. The hostages were handcuffed and their mouths and eyes taped. They were ordered to sit on the floor.

Milty watched the hostages while Comfort stationed himself

at the door, which gave him a full view of the front desk. He could also control the switchboard from there. Sammy took the two suitcases and the tools and went back to the safe-deposit sections behind the desk to begin hammering.

About ten minutes into the robbery, two men in work clothes knocked at the locked front door. Comfort, acting as the security guard, asked their business. They said they were elevator repair men responding to an earlier call from the hotel.

The two elevator repair men moved in with their tool bags. Comfort locked the door behind them. "Gentlemen," he said. They turned to him. He opened his jacket and let them see the gun in his waistband. He never wanted to terrify anyone in this situation, out of fear they might become hysterical or even violent. If he stayed calm, they usually stayed relatively calm, too. "It's a hold-up—just move over there," he said, motioning to the room where the captives were.

"Jesus fucking Christ," said the taller repairman. "Every time I go someplace, something happens to me!"

"Just walk over there, please," said Comfort.

"My luck, I gotta come to fix an elevator and I get involved in this shit. If I don't come home on time, my wife'll think I'm out fooling around."

"Hey," Comfort interrupted, "would you *mind*? Get over there!"

"All right, all right," said the tall mechanic.

The elevator mechanics sat down. Comfort applied the handcuffs to them. In doing so he removed their watches. After the handcuffs were fastened, he replaced their watches.

"Hey," the shorter mechanic said, "you ain't robbin' us?"

"No, I'm not."

"Well, Jesus Christ," he said. "Yeah, have a good time. It's all right with me."

Sammy resumed hammering. Milty taped the men's mouths.

A few minutes later the phone rang. Comfort walked over and picked it up. "Front desk," he said.

It was a hotel guest asking for a wake-up call at 7:30 A.M. for Room 1121. He had to make a plane for Chicago and said he was so worried about it he couldn't sleep.

114

Comfort took his room number.

"Will I get called for sure?" the voice asked.

"Yes, sir," said Comfort. "I'll be on the desk personally. There'll be no problem. You'll be the first one I call at seven-thirty." Click.

He didn't like lying to the man, but he had no choice. They would be gone by seven-thirty. He wanted to leave a note at the front desk for the wake-up call but decided against it for fear his handwriting would provide an unnecessary clue. He walked over to the hostage area, located the desk clerk, and said in an even voice, "We'll be out of here soon. Just remember a wake-up call for Room 1121 at seven-thirty if you get a chance."

He returned to the front. He heard the pounding of the hammer on the hinges, the clattering to the floor of a broken deposit-box cover, and the silence that followed, which signaled each opened box with its contents was being emptied into the suitcases.

Comfort looked up at the gold wall clock. It was 5:30 A.M.

The time reminded him of his home on Jefferson Avenue in Rochester, and that shortly his daughter would be stirring in her crib. She would be six months old in exactly one week. He had to remember to bring a stuffed animal home for Nicole's sixth-month birthday.

He paused in his thoughts and glanced again at the clock—a quarter to six. If he didn't want to celebrate the six-month anniversary in the Tombs, they'd better pack and get the hell out of the hotel.

When Comfort went to the safe-deposit area, he saw Sammy muttering to himself. The boxes had been difficult to unhinge. He couldn't get adequate leverage in the spaces between the desk and the boxes. Only seventeen boxes had been ripped open. Sammy had expected to open at least twenty-five, maybe more. He already had several hundred thousand dollars in cash, and enough jewels to keep at the boxes with enthusiasm. Beads of sweat were running down his face from the frustrating effort in the crowded space.

"We've gotta go," said Comfort.

"There's a whole section I haven't gotten to," Sammy complained. "It's a crime to leave it, isn't it?"

"Aren't you ever satisfied? We've got over a million," said Comfort, glancing at the contents of the open suitcases.

"But there's a million more in this section, believe me."

"We don't have time. In about forty-five minutes this lobby starts to come alive."

"I know," said Sammy, "but we would take this whole damn section with us."

"What are you talking about? How you gonna take it out?"

"Drag it out."

"Down the street?"

"To the car."

It was a thought. Comfort, too, was reluctant to give up the loot that might be in those unopened boxes. The hotel's safety boxes were of a prefabricated variety, constructed in sections that consisted of ten boxes across and four boxes deep. There were four sections in the wall unit, installed one atop the other to the height of almost seven feet. Because of the weight of the sections, they were stacked without any additional anchoring; and the complete assembly was finished off with a wood molding on the top and the sides.

Both Comfort and Sammy knew that the individual sections were movable once the molding was removed.

"I've got an idea," Comfort said. He instructed Milty to watch the door, and raced out onto Park Avenue. He turned right at the corner and moved rapidly down Sixty-first Street.

During his short stay at the hotel, in his nocturnal wanderings in the area adjacent to the Regency, Comfort had noticed a typical New York scene. Early each morning a window cleaner serviced store fronts of the specialty shops along Sixty-first Street, before the start of the working day.

At the time, Comfort marveled at the man's industriousness and ingenuity. His two water pails and carton of rags were set upon a narrow metal-framed dolly, which he pulled from storefront to storefront. Comfort remembered the dolly.

As he moved up the empty street in the early-morning light, he turned the corner at Sixty-first, and saw the window washer.

He walked up behind the man in the checkered cap. "I need

116

you," said Comfort evenly. The man turned and saw Bobby's gun.

"Hey, mister . . ." the man said.

"Just come along with me," said Comfort, "and bring the dolly."

The man obeyed immediately. Comfort and the window washer rolled the dolly into the hotel. They brought the dolly around to the rear of the desk, directly under the boxes. With the help of the window washer the three men struggled to inch the unit out from its mooring in the wall.

Finally, with the section half-exposed, Comfort instructed the men to place the unit facedown onto the dolly. In that manner, when they reached the street, there would be no immediate recognition of the boxes and less attention given to them.

Precious minutes ticked by. The heavy box came out slowly and, finally, with one man at each corner of the dislodged steel unit, they lowered it onto the dolly, lengthwise and upside down.

They pushed the dolly out from behind the desk and moved to the door, where Comfort stopped.

He turned to the window washer, pressed a hundred-dollar bill into his shirt pocket, apologized for the inconvenience, handcuffed his wrists, taped his mouth, and set him down in the captives' area. Milty grabbed the jewel-laden bags, placed them atop the unit, and the three men walked out the door.

As they guided the frail dolly around the corner, moving up Sixty-first Street, the heavy section began to wobble precariously. Sammy moved in front and pulled, Milty took up the rear and pushed, and Bobby, in the middle, attempted to keep the section and the heavy bags balanced.

Moving down the street, they were confronted with the sidewalk cracks, and the scraping of the front end of the box drew sparks as the metal struck the cement.

Comfort looked nervously up and down the street. "This is the craziest, stupidest goddamn thing I've ever done," he said.

"We're almost there," said Sammy. "Another couple of minutes."

The three finally reached the corner of Madison Avenue and

Sixty-first Street. They had less than fifty feet to go to make their getaway car, a 1963 red Rambler station wagon.

The sight of the car quickened their efforts. Finally, sweating and cursing, they reached the car.

Comfort kept looking south down Madison for sight of a patrol car. He knew that no foot patrol worked Madison Avenue.

Sammy moved to the rear of the wagon, pulled up the top flap, and lowered the tailgate. Milty put the two suitcases on the back seats. Then the three men heaved the steel unit onto the tailgate and pushed it into the back of the wagon. The unit proved to be too long for the rear section. They had to let it hang out on the tailgate. Comfort anxiously motioned the men into the wagon. He slammed the top flap down.

Sammy moved around to the driver's seat; Milty climbed into the front seat, exhausted. Comfort wedged in beside him. Sammy started the motor, put it into gear, and then drove the car to the Queensboro Bridge, heading toward a friend's home on Long Island. They had advanced down the street for a block when they heard a sudden ear-shattering crash from the rear of the wagon.

They turned instantly. They immediately realized that the springs under the rear wheel had collapsed under the strain of the heavy safe deposit boxes; the car scraped along the street.

"What are we gonna do?" asked Milty.

"Just obey the speed limit," said Sammy.

"That's the least of our problems," said Comfort. "What we have to worry about is getting arrested for slowing up traffic."

As the car crossed the Queensboro Bridge, the rear bumper, hanging low, banged against the steel grid. The men continued looking anxiously behind them as the bumping of the wagon echoed loudly in the dawn.

The next morning, accounts of the Regency heist were all over the newspapers. In their completely anonymous way, Comfort and Sammy had become instant celebrities. This was the first of their robberies to make headlines, and they enjoyed it. The robbery grossed more than a million dollars. But they learned that they had missed a chance for a great deal more. While the robbery was taking place in the lobby, Elizabeth Taylor and Richard Burton were in a suite thirty stories above.

In the *New York Daily News*, Comfort read:

> None of Liz's fabulous collection of gems, valued at over two million, had been deposited in the hotel's safety deposit boxes that night. They had arrived late and decided to keep her fabulous gems in the suite.
>
> One of the first things that East 67th Street detectives did was phone the Burtons' suite to inquire if there had been any trouble there. . . .
>
> Liz and Burton slept through the whole drama. A spokesman said: "They didn't know what happened and are here for a rest. They aren't even eating out." . . .

Comfort and Sammy were disappointed but not depressed at having missed the Burtons' gems. The heist had been successful. Reporters praised them for their "professionalism," stating that no one was hurt or unduly harassed.

"They were so courteous," one of the hostages was quoted as saying, "that when I walked through the door with my friend, I said to him, 'Isn't the security here wonderful?' Then one of them pointed his gun at us, and told us to join the other hostages."

◆ 15 ◆

The world of wholesale and retail gems in the United States is contained, for the most part, in one stretch of concrete on Forty-seventh Street between Fifth and Sixth avenues in Manhattan. With the exception of several delicatessens and take-out shops, the street consists almost exclusively of jewelry dealers. Up and down the street, neon signs extend from the buildings telling the bustling crowds: We Buy and Sell Diamonds; Jewelry Bought and Sold; Gems Here.

In the store windows are dazzling displays of precious stones to satisfy the tastes of anyone from an Arab potentate to a newly engaged couple.

Along this block-long enclave, extending from basement cubicles to street-level booths that remind one of the giant public markets around the world, to offices in buildings rising up thirty floors, may be found the brokers, the middlemen, the buyers and sellers who create over four billion dollars in sales each year. Fifteen thousand people work in this glittering section of Forty-seventh Street.

Each weekday morning at 9 A.M., the transactions for diamonds and other precious gems begin. The raucous noise at any given hour of the day is generated by milling crowds: some trading on the sidewalk, others at the curb, while uniformed security guards converse over raspy walkie-talkies—unlike the hushed elegance of Harry Winston or Tiffany's on Fifth Avenue, ten blocks north and a world apart.

Although the clandestine nature of the diamond trade is legendary, the negotiating techniques are widely known. Personal honor is esteemed and respected. Gems worth hundreds of thousands of dollars are traded by verbal agreement, and deals are consummated with nothing more than a handshake. Not a single signed piece of paper need be exchanged.

On an afternoon weeks after the Regency robbery disappeared from the front pages, Bobby Comfort and Sammy Nalo edged their way east down Forty-seventh Street through the tide of people. Sammy, like many others on the street, was carrying an attaché case, empty except for a handful of diamonds wrapped neatly in tissue paper.

The partners had taken only a sampling of the Regency jewels to be fenced. If the buyer liked their merchandise, and paid the right price, he would be invited to a "meet" to negotiate for the remainder of the loot.

The dealer they were heading to see had been recommended by a mutual friend. They had not dealt with him before.

When the men reached their destination on the south side about midway down the block, they turned left into an alley which led to an interior courtyard, and then to a doorway.

Entering a dimly lit vestibule, they took a narrow flight of stairs up to a heavy metal door. The door bore no name and a seeing-eye in combination with a two-way speaker. Comfort rang the bell. Shortly a click was heard.

"Who is it?" came a voice over the speaker.

"We have an appointment," said Comfort.

"Name?"

"Herbert," said Sammy. That was the name he had given on the phone.

"One minute."

Shortly, the door opened and they were ushered in.

There were two rooms. The large front room had a series of glass-topped display cabinets containing velvet-lined trays of diamond rings, necklaces, and bracelets. Against the wall was a huge Mosler safe, open, revealing stacks of wooden drawers containing other jewelry.

In the rear room Sammy and Comfort could see a man with a loupe to his eye, bending over a table examining a stone held in tweezers. Behind the man was a smaller safe. Above him was a window with thick steel bars, the only window in the office.

"You have the merchandise you called about, please?" asked the dealer.

Sammy placed the attaché case on the counter and opened the clasps. He extracted a tissue-paper packet, and undid it, revealing five brilliant diamonds.

The dealer took the packet to the man in the rear workroom.

Comfort and Sammy sat on two folding chairs and waited.

"Gentlemen," said the dealer on his return, "we can offer you eighty thousand dollars."

"We may not know the market like you do, but our appraiser told us not to settle for less than one hundred thousand dollars. So that's our price," said Comfort.

"Just a minute." The dealer retreated to the back room and this time closed the door. When he again appeared, he carried a handful of bills.

"It's a deal," he said. "One hundred thousand dollars."

Bobby took the money, counted it, placed the bills inside the attaché case and locked it.

"We've got some other stuff we didn't bring down," Sammy said. "Interested?"

"Definitely."

"Okay, we'll be in touch and set up a meeting with you next week," said Sammy.

They shook hands. The dealer unlocked the heavy door and the two well-dressed customers departed.

The entire transaction had taken no more than fifteen minutes.

◆ 16 ◆

October 1970, Rochester

Bobby Comfort passed several lazy months at home after the Regency robbery. The newspaper stories about the heist had long disappeared. No clues came to light, and not one stickpin ever surfaced that could be connected to the theft. The hostages were still telling whoever would listen about the harrowing experience they had endured under the gun of the thief in a tuxedo that fateful night at the Regency.

For the most part, once the robbery disappeared off the front pages, it dropped from the top of the list of unsolved crimes at the New York Police Department. A harassed, overworked, and undermanned police force welcomed the opportunity to bury the memory.

One evening Comfort, in his easy chair at home, was sipping a can of Bud and watching the David Frost television interview show. Millie was in the bedroom diapering a squalling Nicole.

When Sophia Loren was introduced as a guest on the TV show, Bobby sat up and gave her his undivided attention. As beautiful as the sloe-eyed, buxom Sophia Loren was, he was immediately attracted to the huge diamond ring that glittered on her finger. He leaned forward in his chair. Look at *that*, he said to himself. It's got to be worth at least a quarter of a million dollars!

Sophia Loren was asked if she agreed with some critics that her performance in her new movie *Sunflower* was her best since *Two Women*.

"Very much indeed so," said Miss Loren with a distinctive Italian accent. "It is a picture I care very much about. It is a story based on the everlasting pillars of human feelings. . . ."

Comfort leaned closer toward the set and decided that the ring must be a king-sized marquise cut.

He got up and went into the kitchen and called Sammy in New York.

Sammy picked up the phone.

"Hello, Richie," said Comfort. He knew that Sammy Nalo always liked him to use one of his aliases.

"Oh, hello, Tony," said Sammy.

"I got a little business in mind," said Comfort.

"Call me back at 691-2128 in exactly ten minutes," said Sammy.

"Ten minutes," replied Comfort, and then hung up.

Bobby left the apartment and drove to a pay phone.

"She's wearing a rock you'd love," Comfort told Sammy, as he reported on the TV show featuring the movie star. "It's as big as your fist. And she's got to have other stuff, too. She's supposed to have an apartment in the city. You think we can get her address?"

"I'll check it out," said Sammy.

Two days later Sammy called back. He had learned from a show-business contact that, when in New York, Sophia Loren lived in a twenty-second-floor penthouse apartment in the luxurious Hampshire House, a combination condominium and hotel on Central Park South. She had a secretary, a maid, and a nursemaid for her twenty-two-month-old son, Chipi. Her husband, Carlo Ponti, was in Italy. Ponti's son, Alex, in his early twenties, had been seen

124

around town, but Sammy's sources were not certain whether he was staying in the apartment, though they had determined that she would be in New York for a few weeks. Two armed bodyguards were with Loren constantly.

"I think she's got a few million in jewelry up there—come on down, and we'll look it over," said Sammy.

The report was crisp and to the point. "I think it's worth a check," said Comfort. "See you soon."

For the first time in their partnership, they enlisted a woman to help them with surveillance. A man standing around the lobby watching Sophia Loren might seem too obvious. A woman, on the other hand, could go relatively unobserved.

Gloria Competello, a tall blond friend of Sammy's, was hired as the lookout. At the Hampshire House she took a suite which by chance was directly below that of Sophia Loren. For a week Gloria stayed close to the hotel, eating in the hotel restaurant, sitting in the black-and-white marble-and-mirrored lobby. She tracked the times and reported daily on Loren's schedule.

Although Comfort respected the actress, for she had successfully risen from a poor family in Naples—the same town his grandfather's family came from—the coincidence did not divert his intentions.

Comfort's research told him that some ten years before, Sophia Loren had been robbed in London. Her response then was that it was not "just," that the theft made her feel as if something integral in her life had been torn out of her. In a news interview she said her jewels represented some of the rewards in her "struggle with life."

She had married the rich Carlo Ponti, who had lavished jewels on her. "She would have plenty of money left—I didn't have to worry about her starving if I robbed her," rationalized Comfort. "She still had great earning power. Sophia Loren wasn't going to go hungry."

At nine-thirty Saturday night, October 11, 1970, Sophia Loren and her secretary stepped out of her limousine and entered the Hampshire House. Gloria Competello, sitting on a sofa in the lobby, watched her step into the elevator. Gloria immediately called Sammy's apartment on Forty-fifth Street. He and Comfort were waiting for the call, as were two other men—their partners.

"She just came home," said Gloria Competello.

"Check to see she doesn't go back out," said Sammy.

Gloria called back at 2:30 A.M. "She hasn't left. It looks like she's in for the night."

It was no secret to Comfort that the squad cars from the Central Park Precinct did heavy patrol in this exclusive, wealthy section of the city. He also knew that changeover of the police shift was at 8 A.M., so he selected 7:30 A.M. for the hour of the job, realizing that the cruisers would be heading for the station house and not poking around hotels. He had told the men that they had about one hour to work the job.

At exactly 7:30 A.M. on that cool fall Sunday morning, a green Ford and a blue Chevy pulled up to the canopied entrance of the Hampshire House.

Motors were shut off, and the four men stepped out onto the sidewalk.

Comfort swiftly checked up and down the almost deserted thoroughfare. Overnight cars filled the park side of Central Park South. There were a few cruising cabs—but no patrol cars in sight.

Comfort and "Pete" entered the lobby through the revolving door, Sammy and "Stan" following directly behind. There were no security guards. They quickly took over the hotel. Porters and maids were shunted out of sight, and Comfort manned the desk and phone. Pete was the lookout.

Sammy said to the manager: "We're going up to Sophia Loren's place—we know the number—and you're comin' with us. You're gonna get the door open. You're gonna tell her there's a gas leak, so she opens the door."

The manager, a lean, proper man in his fifties, looked at the short man in his obvious wig and fake rubber nose. "You can't go up there," he said. "Mrs. Ponti's got two guards. Armed guards. They'll kill us when we get up there."

"Well, you're gonna be the first one in the door, so you'd

better talk good if you don't want to be shot," said Sammy. "We're goin' up and we don't care who's there."

From Competello's reports, Sammy and Comfort knew about the guards. Gloria could not say whether they had left the hotel. But if the guards were taken by surprise, there would be no problem.

The bell captain, the manager, Sammy, and Stan went up to the twenty-second floor.

The manager performed as instructed, and when the maid cracked the door, the men bulled their way in. The maid screamed. Stan hit her on the temple with the butt of his gun. She fell, whimpering. They quickly checked for Loren's guards. There were none.

"Where's the master bedroom?" Sammy asked. The manager pointed and Sammy went in.

Sophia Loren, shocked out of sleep, was sitting straight up in bed, pulling on her robe, when Sammy walked into her bedroom.

Her huge eyes were full of fear. Sammy immediately tried to reassure her. He told her that they had come for the jewels, and cautioned her that she wouldn't be hurt if she cooperated.

She pointed to a nearby table where several pieces of jewelry lay in an open box. He picked them up, glanced at them, and put them down.

"Where's the big stuff?" he asked hurriedly. "We've come for the big stuff."

"Most of my jewelry is home in Italy," she said.

"What about the ring you wore on the Frost show?"

"It wasn't mine," she said. "It was borrowed from Van Cleef and Arpels. I returned it."

"Where's the kid?"

Sammy saw panic instantly transform her beautiful face, and she broke into tears. Sammy realized that she took it to mean her baby boy, when actually he was referring to Carlo Ponti's son. But before he could say anything, the movie star cried, "All my jewels are in my closet, go there, but leave my baby, please—take everything you want in the closet."

The luxuriously scent-laden closet reminded Sammy of the perfume counters at Saks Fifth Avenue. Upon entering, he was struck by the colorful array of dresses, furs, and evening gowns. Perhaps fifty pairs of shoes and boots, and a stack of boxes of stockings. The well-lighted closet enabled him to locate the jewel box immediately. However, he hunted to see if perhaps there was more than one box.

He located a second and then a third jewel box. He snatched the boxes, emptied them into a bag, and placed the boxes on a table in the living room.

During the commotion and the roundup that followed, Stan decided not to disturb the baby's room. There was no need to worry about a crying baby. However, in their haste, they overlooked another room in the penthouse, the one connecting the room where the Italian nursemaid stood listening to the noise through a crack in her door.

She quietly closed and locked the door, then tiptoed to the night table and picked up the phone.

In her best English she explained to the operator to hurry and call the police immediately, that a robbery was taking place in Mrs. Ponti's apartment.

"Yes, please don't panic, the police will be right there," the man said. "Where are you?"

"I'm in the baby's room."

"Stay there, don't move, they'll be right there."

Bobby Comfort returned the phone to its cradle.

About five minutes later the switchboard lit up with another call from Sophia Loren's apartment.

This time it was Sammy.

"How's it going down there?" Sammy asked.

"Good, except you overlooked the nursemaid in the kid's room."

"How do you know?"

"Because she just called to tell me to call the cops," Comfort said.

"What did you say?"

"I said they'd be right up. Get into the kid's room and make sure you get that nursemaid."

"We'll get her," Sammy said. "As soon as we cuff and tape 'em, we'll be right down."

"Don't take the elevator all the way. Get off a few floors above the lobby. Lots of people and their dogs are coming and going, so be careful. Just walk down to the lobby." He pulled the plug.

Finally, the nearby lobby door to the stairwell opened slowly and Sammy peered out. The four thieves, with their loot, walked out of the hotel and disappeared in the two cars.

Within ten minutes they were through the Lincoln Tunnel and into New Jersey.

As soon as it had been learned that the Loren apartment was robbed, the police responded immediately.

Right behind the squad cars that pulled up to the Hampshire House came the unmarked car of two special agents from the FBI office in New York. Their presence, just as it was after the Regency Hotel robbery, was due to the likelihood that the stolen gems would be carried across state lines, thereby making the theft a federal offense.

Reporters, too, quickly converged on the Loren apartment.

"No," Loren told the newspapermen, "I don't care about the jewelry—I don't have to wear any jewelry as long as I can have my child's arms around my neck."

Her spirits seemed high, and it appeared she cared only that little Chipi was safe.

"Have you considered wearing imitation gems?" she was asked.

"It's a good idea. I never thought of it—but I never wore anything false in my life," she said, smiling.

Sophia Loren accompanied the police detectives to the Bureau of Criminal Identification, where she examined mug shots of known jewel thieves.

She was at the police station until seven-thirty that evening. Exhausted, she told the policemen, "There are so many pictures, so many—I can't pick anyone out from them."

Comfort and Sammy had become so adept at determining the quality of jewelry that within an hour after having robbed Sophia

Loren they dumped several relatively worthless pieces into a garbage can: an old-fashioned rhinestone necklace, an iron-copper cross, some inexpensive earrings and stickpins.

The following afternoon the two partners sat in a bar in Cliffside, New Jersey.

"Sam, I was curious," said Comfort. "You didn't mention anything about Loren in bed—she's got to be gorgeous."

"Hey," Sammy said, "you know me better than that. Business comes first. But I'll admit I took a good look at her. How could I help it? Even waking up in the morning she looks better than anything else walking around the streets at any hour."

The next day, in the *New York Daily News*, the following editorial appeared:

SORRY, MISS LOREN, BUT—

We sympathize with screen star Sophia Loren in her Sunday loss of $600,000 worth of jewelry to robbers who invaded her Hampshire House apartment, and we hope the rats may be caught and convicted and all the loot recovered.

Nonetheless, we do not know why wealthy persons so often leave heaps of jewelry lying around the house or apartment—uninsured sometimes, as in the case of Miss Loren for the second time in ten years.

If one must have gems close by to gloat over and luxuriate in, why not stock up on plenty of fakes and put the genuine articles in a strong box?

Kindly pardon us if our pity for Miss Loren in this instance adds up to considerably less than 100%.

The contempt for the rich and powerful that had surfaced between the lines of the editorial was obviously shared by many of the *News*'s readers, Bobby Comfort among them.

When he read of Sophia Loren's claim that she had lost $600,000 in diamonds, emeralds, pearls, and rubies, he wondered what she was thinking of. They had received an offer of more than

$900,000 for her gems. On the retail market, they would be worth more than $2 million.

Why had she underestimated her loss? Had she simply made an error, or did she want to avoid calling attention to the value?

Well, whatever was in Sophia Loren's head was none of Comfort's business—not anymore. Feeling understandably flushed, with over a quarter of a million dollars, Comfort decided to throw a "lawn party" for his friends.

The "lawn" that he rented was attached to a large motel in Asbury Park, an oceanside resort town in New Jersey.

Comfort invited a few dozen friends and relatives to join the festivities for a week, renting forty rooms at $250 per room. Every night dinners were served in the restaurant across the road from the motel. It was an orgy of champagne and steaks and baked Alaskas. It cost Comfort $1,500 a night to feed the crowd.

One week slid into a second. Then a third. When some people left, other friends took their places. Millie grew deeply concerned. The money was again flowing through Comfort's fingers.

One night in their room after dinner, she said, "Why do you insist on paying for everything?"

"They're my friends, Mill, and we're having a good time."

"And when someone like Dom tries to pay for his own—just one night—you won't let him. Bobby, we'll be left with nothing."

Comfort went into the closet and counted out eighty thousand dollars. He handed it to her. "Why don't you take a plane to Rochester and put it in the bank? I'm serious. Take it."

"Why don't *we* take it and go back?"

"I'm having a good time. I'll leave when I've had enough."

Millie stayed. It was a decision she would regret.

She said of it much later, "It was Bobby's money. Even though we were married, it was Bobby who got the money. Not me. Maybe deep down I thought he'd resent me for taking it. And maybe I was enjoying the partying, even though I knew it was not the right thing for us to be doing with the money. But Bobby was the boss of the family, in the same way my father was the boss of my family. I was raised on that tradition."

So Millie stayed on with Bobby until the party wound to its close, one month after it had begun.

◆ 17 ◆

February 1971, New York City

On a snowy February afternoon Comfort, back from Asbury Park and in the city once again, had ducked with Sammy into a delicatessen on Eighth Avenue for lunch. They sat at a table close to the counter where salamis hung overhead. Nearby, steam billowed from the corned-beef hot-bins, partially obscuring the white-coated countermen.

As Comfort sank his teeth into a pastrami sandwich, he heard, "Hiya doin', Bobby?"

He looked up, dabbing mustard from the side of his mouth. A tall man with snow covering his hat was standing in front of him. A shorter man, bareheaded, stood alongside him.

"Am I supposed to know you?" asked Comfort.

"Federal agents," said the tall man. He pulled out his wallet and flashed his shield.

"What do you want?" asked Comfort.

"We're gonna get you two," he said.

"Why you wanna bother us?" asked Sammy. He took a sip of his soda.

"We know you guys did the Sophia Loren job and all those other hotel robberies. It's just a matter of time before we nail you."

The agents turned and tracked their way back to the door and out into the whirling snow.

Comfort grew cold as he watched them leave. Then he turned to Sammy. "I didn't think they knew I was alive down here," he said.

Sammy was stunned. "*Now* what are we gonna do?"

Comfort drank his beer. "We've got to keep relaxed," he said. "They've got nothing—otherwise they wouldn't be walking in and talking to us. They'd have us booked by now. We just have to stay nice and cool."

"Yeah, but how did they find out?" asked Sammy.

"Someone told them."

"Who do you think?"

"I don't know. You got any ideas?"

"No," said Sammy. "Let's get the hell out of here. My appetite's gone."

From then on, the partners were acutely aware of being followed, watched, or overheard.

One of the two FBI men on the tail of the partners was Joe Holliday, a member of the New York bureau's major jewel-theft division.

The FBI, like the police departments across the country, lean heavily on a network of paid informants. Rarely is a case broken without the help of an informant.

Through this method, special agent Holliday had learned that someone named "Sammy the Arab," and "Bobby from Rochester" had been involved in the Sophia Loren robbery.

Because of the delicatessen confrontation with the FBI, Comfort and Sammy knew they would have to remain inactive for a period of time.

It was Bobby's decision, not Sammy's. Sammy would periodically call and suggest a job, but Comfort was apprehensive. Not until he felt "the heat" had subsided sufficiently would he be ready to resume his work.

It was during this particular enforced lull in their hotel robberies that the name of Janet Annenberg Neff surfaced and became the object of Sammy's attention.

He read a magazine story describing her extravagantly furnished $4 million triplex apartment at One Sutton Place South.

One paragraph in particular captivated him: "Mrs. Neff's jewelry collection is reported to be one of the finest in the world." Accompanying photos added to his interest.

Sammy called Bobby and gave him a glowing account of the article. Comfort flew to the city a few days later.

On his arrival the men drove across town to visit One Sutton Place South, the most exclusive residential enclave of New York's "Silk Stocking" East Side.

They spent a week formulating their plan of attack, and once learning that Mrs. Neff was at home, the partners, using the building's freight elevator, gained access to the thirteenth-floor service entrance. Comfort held six household employees captive, while Sammy approached the shocked society hostess, who was lunching alone, and persuaded her at gunpoint to give him her jewelry collection.

Mrs. Neff acceded to his demands, and her jewels were carefully dropped into one of her Gucci overnight bags.

Trying to maintain her poise, Mrs. Neff made an appeal for the return of her ornamental crucifix pendant of black onyx and diamonds. She explained that it had very little value, but she treasured it for sentimental reasons. Comfort assured her, if circumstances permitted, the ornament would be returned.

The fencing yielded a relatively meager two hundred thousand dollars because most of the important-looking pieces were paste copies. The crucifix was valued at fifteen thousand dollars.

Although Comfort found it odd that this woman, born in the Jewish faith, should cherish this symbol of Christ, he nevertheless wiped the piece clean, with gloves on, wrapped it in a box, and called a friend to leave it with the doorman of the building.

134

Two days after the crime, on June 17, the *New York Daily News* reported: "Two items appeared identical—a gem-studded crucifix, which Mrs. Neff begged [the robbers] not to take, and a copy. They took both, but later discarded the copy and returned the original by special delivery."

◆ 18 ◆

November 13, 1971, Rochester

Five months had passed since the robbery at One Sutton Place, and in that time Bobby Comfort, at home in Rochester, took stock of his life in a way he never had before.

He knew the robberies just couldn't go on forever. He had never in his thirty-nine years had such thoughts before. Perhaps Millie's words were making a dent in his psyche, or possibly it was just a case of a man growing older.

He believed that the law of averages was no longer on his side. Still, he had that dream of *one big score*—the "retirement" job. He was determined to accomplish it before much longer.

He thought of the many hotels he had taken in the last two and a half years.

In the beginning there were small hotels, and the takes were relatively small. Later several of the bigger ones, the Sherry Netherland, the Carlyle, and the St. Regis, each could have been the score that would end his life of crime. None, however, resulted in the return he had expected. The Regency might have been the lifetime endowment, but they couldn't get to enough boxes—they were too hard for Sammy to open alone. They should have had another man on that job to help. Even the safe-deposit boxes they carted away didn't yield what he had hoped.

The Sophia Loren robbery at the Hampshire House had been a substantial take, except that even she didn't have enough "big stuff."

The next job they did would have to be *the* best hotel in Manhattan. And there was no doubt in his mind which one it would be. He had read about it in the society columns, walked through the hotel several times, and grown enthusiastic about its potential. But he was also aware of the difficulties. Could he convince his partner to go along with the job, especially when he learned of the unusual obstacles? He'd see. He would call Sammy and arrange a meeting in New York right away. Oddly, during the entire period of their partnership, Comfort had never told Sammy his dream hotel—the Pierre.

◆ 19 ◆

November 14, 1971, 1 P.M., New York City

The hansom cab rambled through Central Park, around to Fifth Avenue, and down to Sixty-first Street, where it stopped. Comfort and Sammy alighted from the coach on the park side of Fifth Avenue.

Comfort motioned toward the thick stone wall that encircles Central Park. "We can get a better look at the hotel."

From that vantage point they viewed the stately Pierre Hotel, rising forty-two stories into the sky. The cream-colored brick structure ascended in four ever-narrowing setbacks to a long, slanted, green roof that shimmered in the sunlight.

"Do you know what made me like this place so much?" asked Bobby. "It was the vault. One day I'm walking around the lobby and I see it. Then someone opens the door and I can look in. Anyone can. You see rows and rows of safe-deposit boxes. A whole roomful of them! It's the only hotel I've ever seen that has a vault. There must be a damn good reason why it has one."

Sammy was about to reply when a man in a bowler and a pinstriped suit walked past. He waited for the man to get beyond earshot.

"But a vault is harder to break into than safe-deposit boxes."

"Sam, do you have a fever? We get a guy to *open* the vault. That's why we carry guns. We don't break in with dynamite."

"Maybe the guy with the combination's off duty."

"There's got to be someone there who can open it. I mean, what if you're a guest and you come in at four in the morning and want to secure your valuables? They've got to have twenty-four-hour service."

"What I heard about the Pierre," said Sammy, "is that it's got the biggest security force of any hotel in the world—more guards per square foot than any other hotel in America."

"It really doesn't matter how many they've got. If we have good men, and move fast, we can surprise and overtake 'em. We've done it before."

"But, Bob, I remember reading when they hired the guy to head the security there. They're payin' him something like thirty grand. The guy's got to be doing something to earn it."

"Let's walk in, I'll show you the way I think we can do it."

At the Fifth Avenue entrance to the Pierre, they were greeted by the doorman in a blue, gold-buttoned jacket, standing beside a marble column. From out of the revolving door, a lissome brunette in fur coat and elegant leather boots glided past Nalo and Comfort. Just behind her a brown dachshund on a leash was trotting to keep up.

The men entered the lobby and looked down the long hall, which was nearly the length of a football field. They walked up three marble steps, and continued quietly down the hall on the plush red carpet. To the right a man was seated on a maroon silk damask sofa reading *Le Figaro*.

Large French mirrors and blue damask drapes adorned the windows. Comfort and Sammy passed a marble rotunda on the left dominated by a sunburst chandelier. Inside the rotunda were entrances to numerous rooms, a café, a supper club, and the Cotillion Room.

They passed the elevator bank, with the doors and car interiors covered in beige silk. Across from the elevators was a small, cluttered room, the office for the hotel security guards.

Beyond the security headquarters, on the left, was a gift-and-flower shop. On the right, at the end of the hall, was a cigarette-and-magazine shop.

The two men approached the T, where the hallway meets the main lobby, and there they stopped, admiring the understated elegance of the off-white-painted main lobby with its gold Persian carpets and its high, handworked ceiling and wood-carved moldings. In the middle of the lobby, below a dazzling chandelier, rested a huge fresh-flower arrangement on a polished walnut table.

From where they stood they could see the Sixty-first Street glass-door entrance. Directly in front of them was the registration desk, where a man with a gleaming bald head and gold-rimmed glasses conversed in French with a guest.

Beyond the registration desk they saw the cashier's window, and behind that, plainly visible, was the door of the vault, looking as heavy and formidable as the side of an armored tank.

"Do you see it?" said Comfort, casually, in a low voice.

"I see it," said Sammy under his breath.

"Do you know what's inside that vault?" asked Comfort.

"Do *you*?" asked Sammy.

Comfort said, "Figure it out. There's supposed to be seven hundred rooms and suites here. Now these are definitely some of the richest people in the world. A couple hundred are permanent residents. Wouldn't you guess that each has at least a million in jewels? Let's say a half million only. Okay? Plus visiting guests. I mean we're talking about forty million, fifty million—who knows how much. It'll be the biggest thing we'll ever do."

"And the toughest," said Sammy.

"And the toughest," agreed Comfort. "But I think it's worth it."

Sammy lit a cigarette. He looked across at the registration desk, where the bald clerk was rearranging some papers. Sammy drew on his cigarette and exhaled.

The men moved over to two upholstered chairs and sat down.

"There's one perfect time in the whole year to do it."

"When's that?" asked Sammy.

"New Year's Day night," said Comfort.

"You want to explain that?"

"The way I figure it, there'll be more jewels in the vault on that night than at any other time. Everybody wears their best stones for New Year's Eve parties, right? If you don't wear them on New Year's, when do you wear 'em? Visitors from out of town would be sure to bring their finest stuff. The people living in the hotel will be wearing their best stones.

"Now both the visitors and the residents would have to keep their jewels locked in the hotel's safe-deposit boxes until Monday, even if they usually keep them in bank vaults. The banks don't open until after New Year's Day. Everyone knows that New Year's Eve is about the noisiest and most active night of the year, right? Well, people don't realize that the following night, the night of New Year's Day, is about the quietest night of the year. Most people are trying to recuperate from drinking and partying the night before. This hotel lobby should be very quiet, calmer than usual, with fewer people."

Comfort wasn't certain what kind of impact his words were having on Sammy, for Sammy's eyes appeared to be glazing over.

"Sammy, are you falling asleep on me?"

"No," Sammy said. "I was just thinking, we're going to have our own little costume party *after* everyone else has had theirs."

◆ 20 ◆

December 12, 1971, New York City

In a corner of the large bright reading room of the New York Public Library at Forty-second Street and Fifth Avenue, two men sat side by side in front of two microfilm machines. Bobby Comfort was going through old copies of the *New York Times*; Sammy Nalo was working on the *New York Daily News*.

Comfort had suggested they check the library to learn something about the Pierre. He told Sammy, "You never know, maybe there was a previous robbery and maybe they put in a sophisticated alarm system. Hotels rarely spend unnecessarily on things that guests can't see. Maybe there's something about the vault in some newspaper clip. And maybe there's something about the layout or the guests or the security guards that was reported in some magazine. It's worth a try."

"How do you know so much about libraries?" asked Sammy.

"I spent a lot of time in them."

"In the can?"

142

"In and out. I got familiar with Hemingway, Tolstoy, Dickens—"

"No kidding," said Sammy. "How much time did they do?"

The crank of the handles and the whir of the microfilm machines took the two men back through the history of the famous hotel.

When construction of the Pierre was announced in 1929, it raised objections among many New Yorkers since it meant that several New York landmarks would have to be demolished.

The hotel was the project of a group of wealthy men whose aim was "to create the atmosphere of a private club or residence instead of that characteristic of the average hotel." It would be notable for "its simplicity and refinement."

On October 14, 1930, the *Times* reported the opening of the Hotel Pierre. A dinner was held in the Grand Ballroom, and included among the guests were some of the most prominent men of New York and Paris (the president and managing director of the hotel, Charles Pierre, was a Parisian). One speaker—the adviser to the kitchen—was Auguste Escoffier, eighty-five years old, renowned as the "father of French chefs." He told the gathering that "the feverish pace of today" did not allow sufficient time for meals, but he hoped that dining at the Pierre might reverse that dyspeptic trend.

Other items caught Comfort's eye as he studied the microfilm screen. On the same day that the Pierre opened, there was a story about the shooting of Diamond Jim Brady. It said that Americans like to romanticize hoodlums like Brady, and fawn over his "ill-gotten" diamonds and other appurtenances of wealth. Comfort smiled.

They learned the Pierre now boasted of resident guests such as Robert J. Kleberg, Jr., of the King Ranch in Texas, and Mrs. DeWitt Wallace, cochairman of *Reader's Digest.*

Frequent Pierre guests included Aristotle Onassis, the Prince of Wales, the king and queen of Greece, Crown Prince Philip, Kirk Douglas, and Katharine Hepburn.

In a "Suzy" column in 1965, Sammy ran across the name of Gabriele Lagerwall, a Pierre resident. He checked her name in the periodical index, and found that she was the German-born wife of the Swiss multimillionaire Adahan Lagerwall, one of the world's richest men. She appeared in a story in the October 25, 1963, issue of *Time*. The story, titled "Society," told of the Metropolitan Opera's annual opening night of the season with women resplendent in their chinchillas, minks, and jewels:

> But the eye-catcher of the evening, an auburn-haired stunner with skin like lambent alabaster and a figure like Juno, was Gabriele Lagerwall wearing a blue dyed Balenciaga mink and almost exactly $2,500,000 worth of diamonds—including a thirty-odd carat diamond in each ear and a 34.8 carat blue diamond ring (putting it just below the famed Hope diamond, which is 44.5 carats, and the 35.5-carat Wittebacher, which is on sale for $650,000. Contact J. Komkommer in Antwerp).
> . . . Childless, she spends 5 or 6 months a year in the U.S. (she has a 7½ room apartment in Manhattan's Hotel Pierre). . . .

Sammy nudged Comfort and pointed to the article. Comfort read it, then returned to his machine.

He now read that in November 1968 Richard Nixon as president-elect had taken two floors at the Pierre as temporary headquarters for himself and his staff. The hotel was Nixon's favorite in New York, and he occupied the penthouse suite on the thirty-ninth floor.

When the president-elect was there, the hotel virtually crawled with Secret Service agents. Comfort read to see if any permanent electronic devices had been installed for security. Security was so rigid, according to the papers, that elevator operators, maids, and some service employees had to show identification to pass the ever-present security agents. Comfort reached over and tapped Sammy and showed him the story.

"We gotta make sure there's no president staying at the hotel when we take it," said Sammy quietly.

"Yeah," Comfort said, "let's hope he's at the White House for New Year's."

144

As Sammy turned the microfilm machine, looking for news of Nixon related to the Pierre, a headline on page 4 of the *New York Daily News* of November 20, 1968, made him take notice: "Johnson Drops in for Dinner." The story related how President Lyndon Johnson had decided on the spur of the moment to fly into New York and attend a dinner of the National Urban League at the Hilton Hotel.

"Look at this," Sammy said.

Comfort read: "The trip was kept under such tight wraps that Johnson's movements were not announced publicly by the White House until he was airborne. He landed at La Guardia at 9:30 P.M.... The security-conscious New York Police Department was not even alerted...."

"So what?" asked Comfort.

"Nixon's weird like that, too. He likes to drop into places. What if he gets a bug up his ass to fly to New York for New Year's? You know where he's gonna stay? Right there at the Pierre!"

"Maybe he'll leave some of the jewels he gets from kings and sheikhs. Maybe he'll put them in the vault like everyone else."

"What are you *talking* about?" said Sammy. "The joint'll be swarming with Secret Service!"

"Sammy, this is a library—keep your voice down," said Comfort.

"Get serious," said Sammy quietly. "This guy does a lotta crazy things. Why do you think they call him 'Tricky Dick'?"

"But he'll want to spend New Year's either in the White House or at his home in Florida or in California. Or maybe he'll go up into the mountains. Anyway, forget it, he won't be at the hotel."

The pair spent several hours going through the files. Other than for an occasional room being burglarized, there wasn't a single mention of a major robbery at the Pierre in the history of its existence.

Now they had to decide on the number of partners they would need for the job.

Sammy needed one man to help break open the boxes. Comfort would control the hostages and operate the front desk. Men were needed to watch the two entrances. Like many hotels the entrances to the Pierre were locked between the hours of two and six in the morning. Only the Sixty-first Street entrance was available for access during that time. A security guard would be there. A fifth man should be positioned to watch the Fifth Avenue entrance and be available for an emergency.

The partners sat side by side in a booth at the Plaka and decided on a list of possible recruits. This group they selected *had* to work out, for New Year's Day was not too far off.

Comfort suggested Doc from Cleveland. He was a friend of Sammy's and had been brought along on the St. Regis job. Although young, in his mid-twenties, he had virtually retired from "the business" and was a dance-school instructor in Cleveland.

"He's smart," said Comfort, "and I think he has guts. He might be interested."

"We can find out. I'll give him a call."

Sammy sipped his drink. "Another guy I like is City. The guy we took on the Carlyle."

"The stocky guy who likes to drive. He wanted to be a race-car driver, didn't he?"

"Yeah, except he could never fit into any of those small race cars."

"I thought he was in stir."

"I heard he's out now. Even though I normally don't like doing things with guys who've recently been in the slam."

"I know, Sam, we've gone through that before."

"Okay, we'll give him a call, too."

"I'd want to call one other guy," said Comfort.

The waiter came by. "Will there be anything else?" he asked.

"We're okay for now," said Sammy.

When the waiter left, Sammy asked, "Who?"

"Country, the guy you met at a card game. A friend of mine from Rochester."

"Bob, he's a hick."

"He looks dumb, but he isn't. And he's got balls. He's been a partner of mine in cards."

"The guy's an amateur."

146

"He's done jobs upstate I know about. We can rely on him."

From a public telephone booth on the corner of Twenty-ninth Street and Eighth Avenue, Sammy called Doc.

Sammy dug into his suit pocket and pulled out the slugs he used to make telephone calls. He bought them at hardware stores for one dollar a bag—and could make fifty dollars worth of phone calls from them. Though big spenders, neither of the partners had any wish to make the phone company richer. "I'd rather give the price of a call to someone who could use it, like a bum on the street," Comfort had said.

Each slug resembled a faucet washer with the hole covered by the adhesive portion of a Band-Aid. When the slug was inserted into the coin slot, it gurgled down with ease.

Comfort stood outside waiting for Sammy to finish.

"What took so long?" asked Comfort as Sammy emerged.

"Doc thought he might be tied up," said Sammy.

"And?"

"I told him. 'This'll be the biggest score you'll ever get.' He wanted to know who else was in it. I said you. He liked that. He's coming."

Comfort then called Country, using Sammy's slugs. Country's wife answered. She said he was outside fixing the car, would Bobby hold on? In a few minutes he heard that familiar drawl on the phone.

"What kin we do you out of, Bob?" said Country.

"I got some work for you. It'll give you enough food in your pigpen to last a lifetime," said Comfort. He sketched some general details.

"Bobby, you talk so sweet, you could make a mule do a jig," said Country. "I'll be down tomorrow."

Comfort hung up.

The next man they approached was City, whom they visited in his two-room apartment on the West Side of Manhattan. City was forty, chunky, with a swarthy complexion and salt-and-pepper hair. City said he wasn't looking for work right now. He had just been released from prison and said he wanted to enjoy the "fresh air" before going back to work.

"After this job," said Comfort, "you can move to the French

Riviera and enjoy real fresh air." City patiently listened to the overall concept and agreed to join them—contingent upon the final details.

Comfort's decision not to divulge the location until a day or two before the robbery might not rest very well with the prospective partners. They might understandably consider it too risky and unreasonable. However, he felt justified in concealing the target until shortly before the planned time of the robbery.

Comfort's reasoning centered on his own axiom, "What you don't know won't hurt me." Keeping the target hotel a secret from the other men would eliminate any accidental slip that could travel the grapevine to a police informer.

Comfort also had persuaded Sammy that they bankroll their three partners to two weeks on the town—until they made the score.

He rented a suite of rooms at the Bretton Hall Hotel, at Eighty-sixth and Broadway.

"I wanted to take them around town, wine them, dine them, and get them feeling loose," Comfort later recalled.

On a mid-December afternoon the two partners, in Sammy's gray Coupe de Ville, drove out to LaGuardia to pick up Doc.

They met him at the baggage area. In a sleek sealskin coat and expensive black leather boots, Doc cut a handsome figure. He was tall, lean, with dark blond hair and a trim mustache. Comfort thought he resembled the model in the Marlboro cigarette ads.

"What's goin' down?" Doc asked in the car.

"We don't want to keep you hanging," Comfort said, "but we can't say anything for a week or so. You'll have plenty of cash in the meantime."

"As long as you guys got me on your welfare roll," Doc replied, "then I can take the suspense."

On the following afternoon Country drove down from Rochester. As arranged, Comfort met him at the Bretton Hall Hotel when he joined Doc in the suite.

"It wasn't much of a suite—actually, it was in an old West Side hotel," recalled Comfort. "The suite cost a hundred and sixty a week, and it had a small kitchen with a refrigerator. But I was sure Doc and Country wouldn't care. There was maid service, and it was comfortable enough.

"The advantage of the Bretton Hall was that no one took notice of anybody. The lobby was usually filled with bettors and touts with their heads buried in racing forms. It was a safe place."

Country blended perfectly into the "horse parlor" hotel. He wore a red-and-green-checked sports jacket that was more remarkable for its horse-blanket look than for its improper fit. Like almost everything else about Country, however, there was purpose to his style. The long sleeves helped camouflage card moves, and the outsize jacket made it easier for him to switch decks. The look of the jacket gave him the disarming quality he sought.

"Country always gave the impression of a hayseed," Comfort remembered. "He'd talk about cows and pigs, and about things the average person never heard of. He was quiet, didn't drink or smoke—and had never spent a day in prison."

Country apparently admired Comfort's numerous exploits and welcomed the opportunity to join him.

"I knew he had a lot of guts," said Comfort. "I believed he wasn't going to hurt anyone. This was important to me. I may be a criminal, but I have my rules. I don't want to hurt anyone, although it could happen, since we carried guns. But I avoided working with guys who looked for violence. That's why I wanted Country."

For the Pierre job Comfort's working name was Tony. Sammy was now calling himself Richie. Although they knew the real identities of Country, City, and Doc, the aliases were used to protect against any slip of the tongue. Such precautions were common practice for the partners. Only one of the three men who had joined them knew Comfort's true identity, but none knew Sammy's. Of the three new men only Country was told where Comfort or Sammy could be reached, and that was through a message at the Plaka or the Port Said. But it was never necessary to contact the two bosses, for they made it their business to keep in constant touch with their three hired hands.

◈ 21 ◈

Even on this overcast winter afternoon, the scene outside the Hotel Pierre entrance on Sixty-first Street reflected the gay mood of the Christmas season. Limousines, taxis, and private cars maneuvered for position, picking up and discharging guests. Luggage and brightly wrapped packages were being carried in and out. Horns blared. A doorman's whistle shrilled. In the midst of this bustle, a robin's-egg-blue Ford pulled up and stopped behind a double-parked Cadillac. The front passenger door opened and Bobby Comfort, in dark coat and gold tie, got out, came around to the other side, and withdrew two suitcases from the back seat. He placed the luggage on the curb and looked about for assistance. The lone available doorman now was directing hotel traffic, blowing his whistle to hail cabs with little result, shifting luggage, answering questions—to Comfort, he resembled a frazzled officer in the front line of battle.

Comfort, not wishing to draw undue attention to himself, carried his luggage into the cream-colored lobby of the hotel.

Inside, he turned and watched the Ford depart. It was driven by Carmen, a man Comfort and Sammy used to obtain "work" cars, paying cash for automobiles that were used for a crime and then discarded or sold.

At the front desk Comfort was greeted by the clerk with a smile and an air of European grace.

"Reservation for Dr. Wilson," said Comfort in an authoritative manner, "James Wilson."

Comfort handed him his American Express card for identification. The card was bona fide, but stolen from a Dr. James Wilson and sold to Comfort by an underworld contact. Although he showed the card for identification, Comfort would pay his bill—all charges—with cash, thus avoiding confirmation check through the American Express computer. The guest was duly registered.

"Have a pleasant stay, Doctor," said the clerk. A bellhop appeared. He ushered Comfort to the elevator. On the way, Bobby stopped to admire the holiday-season wreaths and poinsettia plants decorating the hotel lobby and hallway.

Inside his twenty-second-floor suite, Comfort tipped the bellman and then waited for his departure. When the door closed, Comfort reached into his inside pocket for his glasses. He would alternate wearing them around the hotel. If the time ever came when identification would have to be made, he might have an edge in confusing some people. With his glasses on, the room grew decidedly clearer. Bobby Comfort had been in many fine hotels before, but he was still impressed by the grace and splendor of the appointments. Now he laid his coat on one of the upholstered armchairs, walked to the large window, and pressed the electric switch that parted the full-length brown silk draperies, revealing, in the fading light, a splendid view of Central Park.

The bare-limbed trees, dense and black, extended through the park as far as he could see. The broad expanses of open area appeared in patches of brown and green. To Comfort's right was the odd conglomeration of single-story buildings of the Central Park Zoo. He thought one day he'd take Nicole there—she'd like it. To his left the Pulitzer Fountain came into view. It was there that he and Sammy had met a short month before. He took in the majestic, castlelike Plaza Hotel and, a little farther down, a smaller building, the shopping landmark, Bergdorf Goodman.

The streets were filled with holiday shoppers. From his height the steady streams of people moving in and out of shops reminded him of an ant colony. He finally turned away and went into the bedroom, where he spotted a hotel brochure on the night table between the twin beds. From it he learned that the "concierge" could assist with all foreign exchange matters, obtain theater tickets, and secure reservations for the guest if he were traveling to the Continent after a stay at the Pierre.

A card placed beside the pamphlet caught his eye. It read: "Our cashier will provide you with a SAFE DEPOSIT BOX for your valuables—The Pierre Management." Comfort elected to keep his watch on his wrist and his ring on his finger. That's the safest way, he thought. After all, hadn't there recently been a spate of hotel robberies in New York?

Later, he casually strolled around the hotel. In the Yellowbird Room, where it was said ice cubes never seemed to melt in the water goblets, he eschewed a plebeian ham-and-cheese sandwich for Eggs Benedict Pierre.

More important, Bobby Comfort was up and about to case the hotel at all hours, with special attention to the early morning.

"I just wanted to get to know what the people on each shift were doing," he recalled. "I'd be downstairs every morning at around four. Sometimes I'd come down at four-fifteen in the morning, sometimes four-forty. But whenever I came down, I saw something amazing. The vault door was *always* open. The first time I came out of the elevator and just walked slowly past the concierge's desk to the cashier's window, and beyond to the vault, and boom! The vault . . . it's wide open! There was a man in there sitting at a desk working what looked to me like a calculator of some kind. I couldn't believe it. It was like an invitation—like they wanted us to come in and relieve them of their treasures.

"At the Sixty-first Street entrance there was a guard, an older man, sitting on a chair beside the revolving door. 'Good morning, sir,' he said. 'Good morning,' I said. He unlocked the door and I went out. Every day I went down Sixty-first Street and turned right

Bobby Comfort, "The Hatless Bandit," (standing, right) at home with his mother, brothers, and sisters

Bobby Comfort and Millie Condello on their wedding day

With his parents, Mary and Joseph Comfort

With Rosie and Joe Gustino

October 12, 1970. Sophia Loren leaves her Hampshire House apartment en route to the police station following the early-morning robbery. (WIDE WORLD PHOTOS)

Four weeks after the Loren robbery, Bobby poses with his mother and Nicole.

Family portrait

Comfort and Dom Paulino

The Pierre (John Sotomayor/NYT Pictures)

January 2, 1972. The rifled safe-deposit boxes in the Pierre's vault
(NEW YORK DAILY NEWS PHOTO)

John P. Keeney, Pierre security chief, answers newsmen's questions
(UPI/Bettman Newsphotos)

Louis Rabon, bellman, was taken hostage in the main lobby.

Socialite Gabriele Lagerwall sustained the greatest jewelry losses of all the victims (LARRY C. MORRIS/NYT PICTURES)

Albert Seedman, New York City's chief of detectives (WIDE WORLD PHOTOS)

NYPD Lieutenant Edward O'Connor (*New York Post*)

Detective George Bermudez

(a)

January 8, 1972. (a) The suspects are booked. (WIDE WORLD PHO-TOS) (b) Bobby Comfort (NEW YORK DAILY NEWS PHOTO) (c) Dom Paulino (NEW YORK DAILY NEWS PHOTO) (d) Sammy Nalo (NEW YORK DAILY NEWS PHOTO)

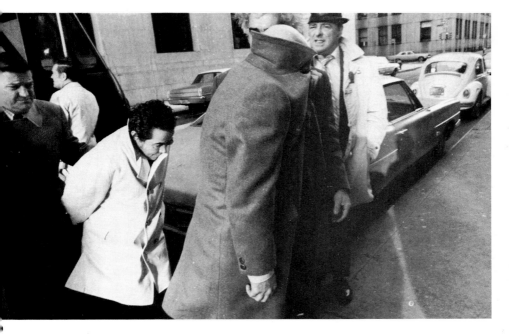

A policeman stands guard over recovered jewelry and the handcuffs used to immobilize the hotel staff and guests during the holdup. (WIDE WORLD PHOTOS)

Assistant District Attorney Richard Lowe *(New York Post)*

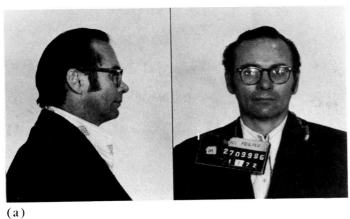

(a)

(b)

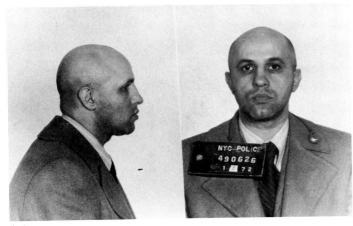

(c)

(a) Bobby Comfort and (b and c) Sammy Nalo (in and out of disguise) were each sentenced to seven years.

(a) Dom Paulino and (b) Benjamin Fradkin received one-year probations for criminal possession of stolen property. (c) Bert Stern received a zero-to-three-year sentence.

Judge Andrew Tyler (CARL T. GOSSETT/NYT PICTURES)

October 31, 1980. Five years after Comfort's release from Attica State Correctional Facility

In retirement

at Madison Avenue. Sammy was there to pick me up. He wanted to know what I'd discovered. I told him, 'The vault door is open, wide open.'

"He looked at me like I was crazy: 'What do you mean?'

"I said, 'The vault's open.'

" 'It can't be.'

" 'Well, you go and look.'

" 'That doesn't make sense to me, having the vault open.'

"But he took my word for it. 'Do you think it's just this morning that it's open, or an everyday thing at this time?' he asked.

" 'We'll have to wait and see,' I said."

If the vault door was open when they planned to come in, they could be fairly certain there were no hidden alarms to be tripped, eliminating one element of concern.

"Every single morning that I went through the lobby," remembered Comfort, "the vault door was open. One time I went into the men's room in the lobby to wait and see how long the vault door stayed open. I stayed there for about fifteen minutes. When I returned to the lobby, the vault was *still* open. This was four-fifteen. So the vault door could have been open at a quarter to four, or at three-thirty—I didn't know yet.

"I do know that it was closed by seven when I went back to have breakfast in the Yellowbird Room.

"So the following day I dressed and was down in the lobby five minutes earlier than the day before. By the sixth morning I actually saw the man opening the vault door. The time was three-forty A.M. The procedure he went through wasn't complicated. It took him exactly twenty-five seconds to disengage the alarms that were built into the system."

Comfort noted that on that "graveyard" or 11 P.M.-to-7 A.M. shift, there were seven security guards in the entire hotel. "You can spot 'em easy," he recalled. "A hotel security guard moves around looking at the people, while a guest just goes about his business. The guards have a job to do, and if they're not doing it, they like to look like they're doing it. So they'll check the desk, the cashier, and then they'll go have a look in the dining room and come back and stand in the lobby. They're circulating around making sure nothing is wrong. But just like a waiter, the security guards stand out. They usually wear cheap gray suits and black shoes. Their clothing is a dead giveaway.

"I also noticed that some guards would disappear for a few hours. I'd see them walking through the hallways on my floor, and I figured that they walked through all of the forty-two floors of the hotel."

A week into his stay at the Pierre, Comfort had reason to change an essential element of his plan.

His original idea was to take the hotel from the inside. The gang, all five of them, would sit in Comfort's suite, awaiting the hour of the proposed takeover. Prior to the 4 A.M. target, Comfort planned to call down to the desk to complain of a drunken nuisance whom he wanted removed from his suite. He would suggest that two security guards were required to handle him.

Unaware that they were being duped, Comfort presumed, the security men would appear at the door, enter, be handcuffed and taped, forced into the bedroom, and handcuffed to the bedroom radiator.

One of the guards, however, would be forced to call down to the security office to seek the assistance of two more men. They too, would suffer the same process and, based on Bobby's calculations, the security staff remaining to be contended with in the entire hotel would then number three.

Once the four guards were captured, the five thieves would take the elevator to the lobby, fan out, and take over the remaining personnel, including the three elevator operators, two bellhops, one maintenance man usually working the vacuum cleaner in the lobby, any strays that might appear, and any guests or other employees.

Comfort soon realized, however, that that plan wouldn't work.

From inside his room he could hear the bed creak next door. When the people called room service, he heard the order clearly. When one of them sneezed, he heard it.

"The walls are like tissue paper," Comfort told Sammy one night. "If we had four or five guys in the room talking, the entire hotel would know everything we were doing."

154

"At a hundred fifty a day," Sammy said, "the least they could give you is privacy. We'll have to take it from the outside."

"It'll be more dangerous. Might give someone more time to get to a phone or an alarm."

"Do we have a choice?"

"I guess not."

The following night the pair sat in Sammy's car at the end of the block on Sixty-first Street in view of the hotel entrance, watching the limousines pulling up and discharging elegantly dressed passengers, some returning from a night out, others arriving from late flights. The partners watched as the chauffeurs signaled the doorman for assistance.

Comfort now knew exactly what his entry plan would be.

On several mornings Sammy met Bobby at the hotel and drove to an apartment on West Fiftieth Street, near Eleventh Avenue, which was the planned hideout after the robbery. The apartment was a little more than a mile southwest of the Pierre. Several routes were possible, but which would be the best—the quickest? Driving away from the hotel, they would have to adhere to the speed limit; they could hardly chance getting pinched for a speeding violation.

Leaving the hotel on Sixty-first Street, they drove west to Fifth Avenue and then turned south. From there they had several options as to which of the one-way westbound cross streets to use—Fifty-ninth, Fifty-seventh, Fifty-fifth, Fifty-third, or Fifty-first? Crosstown traffic lights were not synchronized to allow a car traveling at a given speed to make every green light. In fact, traveling thirty miles an hour crosstown, virtually every light they approached would turn red.

Sammy seemed obsessed with trying to discover a pattern to the lights. The faster they got off the streets, he insisted, the better. He got no argument from Comfort. But after what seemed the hundredth trip to check the lights, Comfort asked, "How many times are you going to drive this route before it occurs to you that we're never going to catch the lights right?"

155

"We'll figure it out," said Sammy.

Comfort was getting impatient. "Don't you think this is kind of foolish, checking the lights like this—you don't even know what time we're coming out of the Pierre."

Sammy shot Comfort a deprecating glance. "This has got to be perfect," said Sammy. "We have to be prepared for coming out at any time."

"But isn't it obvious, after four or five times, how the lights are? They're not going to be different after a hundred times."

"That's why you ended up in the joint," said Sammy. "You don't check enough."

"If it makes you feel good, okay, keep going," said Comfort. "I've got nothing better to do."

Comfort sat back and looked out of the window as the tall city buildings glowed pink in the dawn.

Sammy decided that Fifty-ninth Street was out, because it only went as far as Eighth Avenue, and then they'd have to turn north to another westbound street to hit Eleventh Avenue. Sammy told Comfort that either Fifty-fifth, Fifty-third, or Fifty-first would be less visible than the larger, four-lane Fifty-seventh Street.

Comfort asked, "But what if there's a garbage truck clogging up one of those smaller streets? We're sitting and waiting for fifteen minutes before we can pass it."

"That's a thought," Sammy agreed.

"Fifty-seventh Street has an extra lane, so we'd never get hung up like that."

"Bobby, for an ex-con, you're not so dumb after all."

"Thanks, Sam," said Comfort. "I'm touched."

At two separate pharmacies the partners purchased several rolls of two-inch-wide adhesive tape. From novelty stores around Forty-second Street and Eighth Avenue, a dozen pairs of handcuffs were bought, at different times, on different days. Another ten sets were picked up in Newark by a friend. (The partners knew the police would try to trace the handcuffs that would be found on the wrists of the captives.) Handcuffs cost six dollars apiece, and were

156

easy to obtain from any novelty or game store—exactly the kind the police use.

Comfort and Sammy had obtained two "work" cars, a yellow Ford and a shiny black Cadillac Fleetwood limousine. New Jersey license plates were secured through the same source.

A friend warmed up the cars every day, parked them in an outdoor parking lot on Twelfth Avenue, and paid for them daily to avoid undue attention.

After a week at the Bretton Hall Hotel, Doc began to grow itchy.

"How long are we going to hang around here?" he asked Comfort.

"Not much longer, a week at the most."

"Let me go back. Just call when you need me. I can make more than the hundred a day I'm getting here."

If Doc left, Comfort couldn't be sure he'd return.

"I know how you feel," said Comfort, "but I guaranteeing you a half a million dollars out of this job. We need you here. I can't tell you why it's important that you stay, but it is."

That seemed to placate Doc, but Comfort was still concerned about his restlessness.

Comfort saw Doc and Country every day. As a precaution he would hop in a cab outside the Pierre, get off about a mile away, walk a block, then get another cab and take it to the Bretton Hall.

Comfort took Doc to bars around town, introduced him to friends, including some of Sammy's girlfriends, and sat around and played cards with him and Country. The days went by surprisingly fast.

Meanwhile, Comfort maintained close contact with Millie, calling her daily, sometimes two or three times a day. She had extracted a promise from him to be home for Christmas. He kept it.

Comfort flew up to Rochester the afternoon of December 24, laden with gifts; toys from F.A.O. Schwarz for Nicole and his nieces and nephews; expensive perfumes and other gifts for his mother and his mother-in-law, and a diamond-studded necklace for Millie.

Bobby never needed a significant occasion to give his wife

jewelry. He knew it made her happy when he placed a diamond bracelet on her wrist, a ring on her finger, or pinned a cameo on her dress. But he was careful never to give Millie a piece that had been part of a jewel theft. He bought all of Millie's jewels wholesale. He paid his Forty-seventh Street friends the insider's price, and the transaction consisted of two parts—cash and an appropriate paid invoice.

He reasoned that if he ever got caught for a robbery, his arrest would trigger a search of his home. Paid bills, which were kept handy, would prevent any attempt by the police to confiscate Millie's jewelry, and ultimately to charge her with possession of stolen property.

Millie met Bobby at the airport. The look in her eyes told Bobby he was going to like his stay very much. Her black hair glistened, her eyes were bright. Nicole, in the rear of the four-door, was bouncing happily up and down in her car seat.

For the next three days Bobby partied with his family. Everybody was together, his family and Millie's.

Millie knew that Bobby would be returning to New York shortly and said nothing that would create any tension. She preferred to have her man free of concern. Intuitively, she knew he had to be "working" again, but she simply did not discuss it. Although she noticed his preoccupation at times, she never questioned him.

On December 27 Millie drove Bobby to the airport, where they parked in front of the terminal building entrance. She turned to Bobby and held him tightly.

"Be careful," she said.

"Everything's going to be all right. Don't worry. I'll be home in a few days."

On the afternoon of December 30, Bobby Comfort and Sammy Nalo held a meeting with Doc, City, and Country at the Bretton Hall Hotel to tell them that the job they would do was the

Pierre, and they outlined the specific plan. "Nobody declined with a flat no, but they didn't say yes either," recalled Comfort.

"Doc and Country wanted to take a look at the Pierre for themselves. Neither had ever been there. City said he knew the hotel, and after he heard how we planned to take it, he said okay. It was that simple. I could hardly believe it."

Comfort drove Doc and Country to the Pierre and then arranged to meet at the Plaka when they finished.

"They went in separately about twelve-thirty in the afternoon and came out about two," Comfort remembered. "They probably stopped and had a drink. Country didn't know all that much about what to look for, but Doc did. And when they met us, they both said, 'It can't be done.'

"I said, 'I'm telling you it can be done. You haven't done anything with me yet that couldn't be done.'

"I knew Country would never go against me—that whatever I wanted, he'd join me. He had faith in me. Doc was different. He had a mind of his own."

"There's a lot of people in the hotel lobby," Doc said.

"We're coming at four in the morning, not at two in the afternoon," Comfort said. "And we're gonna have five guys. That's enough to handle whoever's there. They don't expect us, do they? We'll get them fast, but if something happens and we can't get them all, we'll leave. That's all."

"I don't know . . ."

"I know you can do it. I was impressed with you on the last job we did. Everything you did was right."

"You thought so?"

"Why do you think I wanted you for this one?"

Comfort was sincere. He believed that if Doc went through with it, he would do it professionally.

Comfort also knew he needed five men—four would be insufficient to cover the space and the people.

Besides, it was too late to get anyone else he could count on.

"Doc," said Comfort, "we need you."

"What happens if we've got to make a run for it—is there a driver waiting?"

159

"No, we all go in. If there's an alarm, it's going to take the cops four, five minutes to get there—probably more. We're long gone by then. We just jump in the car. It'll be parked at the front."

"I'm thinking I'm with you, Bob," Doc said. "But we have to go back. You have to show me that it's not going to be too tough."

A short while later Doc and Comfort returned to the Pierre.

"This door will be locked at the Sixty-first Street entrance," Comfort said quietly. "When the guard opens the door, we're all going in together. You, City, and Country go straight through, and Sammy and I are right behind you. Country will grab the guard.

"As we're hurrying through here, we're grabbing up everybody along the way."

Comfort walked straight to the elevators and then turned right down the long corridor to the Fifth Avenue entrance.

"What about the vault—the vault's not going to be open—they just won't leave the vault open—no place would," said Doc.

"It'll be open. I've spent weeks checking it out."

They sat down on the red damask settee facing the Oval Room.

"How long will it take?" asked Doc.

"Maybe two hours. We've got to be gone in two and a half hours, by six-thirty, before the seven o'clock shift starts coming in."

"That's a long time. The longer we're here, the more things can happen."

"But we're in control of the hotel. Complete control."

"Give me one of your cigarettes, Bob."

As they sat silently, a woman walked past. Both of the seated men subtly zeroed in on the woman's earrings.

"Those have to be ten thou an earlobe," said Doc.

"And they'll be in her safe-deposit box tonight—and every night," said Comfort.

"We should get them now," said Doc.

Comfort grinned. "Let's wait," he said. "Then we can get a few suitcases full, just like those."

"Let me think about it."

Comfort wouldn't say another word until Doc brought it up again. A little catering-to, a little subtle pressure was one thing, but he was not going to twist Doc's arm. Doc had to *want* to do the job for him to be completely reliable.

They drove to the Plaka restaurant and had a few drinks with Sammy.

Comfort recalled: "It took an effort for me not to keep building up the job and the money. I was ready to go, I was all keyed up. We had spent a lot of money. I'd been living at the most expensive hotel in the country, and Sammy and I were paying for these guys at a rate of five hundred a day to go partying for two weeks.

"We were drinking and laughing about something—it was a couple of hours since we had left the Pierre—when Doc turned to me, and said, 'To hell with it. I'm in.'

"Sammy and I both stopped laughing. We looked at Doc. He had been drinking, but his speech wasn't slurred; he was sober. Although we hadn't been talking about the job, it was all we'd been thinking about. So when he said 'To hell with it,'—oh man, I felt like kissing the guy, but I just said, 'Good. How about another drink?' "

In the weeks leading up to the scheduled Pierre robbery, Sammy read the papers to determine the whereabouts of President Nixon and occasionally mentioned the president's movements to Comfort. He didn't tell the others, because he didn't want to cause any "unnecessary anxiety." The episode with Doc warned the two partners to keep the atmosphere free of further uneasiness, even about something as remote as Nixon's hypothetical visit to New York around New Year's.

One afternoon Sammy said to Comfort, "You see what they're saying about Nixon in the papers today?"

"No, I'm leaving the administrative branch of the government in your hands."

"Bobby, the guy's a nutball, he could do anything."

"What did the papers say about him?" Comfort asked.

"He's supposed to be spending a quiet New Year's Eve with his wife at the White House, and then on the night of January first he's going to be interviewed live from Washington on NBC."

"So we don't have to worry about him anymore."

"Not unless he comes to New York after the interview," said Sammy.

Comfort checked out of the Pierre and moved in with Sammy at Sammy's Forty-fifth Street apartment.

For New Year's Eve Comfort offered to take Doc, City, and Country out for dinner, drinks, and a show at the Port Said. Doc said he'd be happy to come. City thanked him for the offer but said he had made prior arrangements. Country demurred, too. "I always like to watch Guy Lombardo," he said. "I'll get a six-pack of Coke and watch New Year's Eve come in on the tube."

Earlier Comfort had taken each of the men to different stores to buy tuxedoes. Sammy had gone with City to purchase a chauffeur's cap. Everything was ready.

◆ 22 ◆

In a dimly lighted corner of the Port Said, a crowded Middle Eastern nightclub located on the West Side of Manhattan, Bobby Comfort stepped into the dark telephone booth, slid onto the stool, and shut the wood-framed glass door. The fan and an overhead light switched on automatically.

Using a phony credit-card number, he placed a call to Millie.

The phone in his home three hundred miles upstate rang several times. Finally, Millie answered.

"For a minute I thought you weren't home," said Comfort in his raspy, emphatic voice.

"I'm home," she replied. There was an unmistakable bite in her voice. "Where are you?" she asked. "I hear music."

"I'm at the Port Said," he replied. "How's the baby?"

She brushed off his obvious attempt to change the subject.

"You're going to do more of that stupid business, aren't you?" She was practiced enough after ten years with her husband to camouflage her words on the phone.

"It's a card game," he said.

"If it's cards, how come you're at the Port Said?"

"Dropped by for a few minutes, that's all," he replied.

To Millie the Port Said meant Sammy the Arab, and Sammy had nothing to do with playing in card games.

Suddenly, the crowded cabaret exploded with shouts. Colored streamers burst into the air. Balloons floated up. Through the glass door Comfort saw revelers hug and kiss, and he heard the muffled sounds of the gypsy band strike up "Auld Lang Syne."

"Happy New Year, Millie," he said. "This is the last time we'll be apart on New Year's. I promise."

There was a pause, and a crackle of long-distance wires.

"I'll believe it when it happens." She added, "But be careful, and remember the baby needs a father—and I need a husband."

After they said their good-byes, Comfort returned to his table, now occupied by Doc and two friends—Walter Leavitt and his wife.

Leavitt ran a big wholesale fur operation in midtown, and had excellent connections in the diamond center that were helpful to Comfort and Sammy when the occasion required.

Comfort sipped his Scotch and water and looked around the club. It was heavy with smoke. The band loudly played its amplified music. As usual, the night's entertainment included a comedian, a singer, and several belly dancers. Between acts some of the men in the audience—in the tradition of the Middle East—stepped onto the stage to attempt a Greek folk dance. One of these men, Comfort noticed, now climbed onto the small bare stage. Adhering to tradition, he began his heavy-legged dance, then nonchalantly tossed a handful of dollar bills over his shoulder—to be picked up later by the band.

Comfort was struck by the man's money fluttering to the floor. The scene only served to remind him of his own repeated foolish gestures in the past—the giving away of hundreds of thousands of dollars.

It would be different after tomorrow. Millie was right. Living from day to day was over.

Comfort exhaled a Kent and then watched the smoke curl toward a revolving red ceiling light.

"Hey, everybody drunk yet?" It was Sammy, with Diana. He bent over and kissed Leavitt's wife.

"Happy New Year, Sam," said Walter. "Sit down, make yourself at home."

"Hi, Doc," said Sam.

"Whattya say, Bob."

"Hiya doin', Sam, Diana."

"Where you been?" Walter asked Sammy.

Sammy pulled up a chair beside Comfort. "At the Monkey Bar. The place is jumpin'. Looks like the night is still young here too."

They ordered drinks. After a short while Doc excused himself. "Have to check out that Irish dancer with the red hair—I've had my eye on her," he said to Comfort and Sammy, and walked to the bar. Sam watched him go. "How's he holding up?" Sammy asked quietly.

"Normal—he's up there chasing a girl, isn't he?" said Comfort.

They both looked toward the bar. Doc was in lively conversation with the dancer.

"What's new on Fashion Row, Walter?" asked Sammy. "Haven't seen you since the last fur I bought."

The conversation was interrupted by an electrical hum from the house microphone. Pete, the owner, was on stage. The men dancers had departed, and he was now introducing "the most thrilling new Oriental dancer ever to appear in New York. Her name, appropriately, is Arabic for 'Joy.' Ladies and gentlemen, the beautiful Bahijah!"

She was prettier and younger than most of the girls who danced at the Port Said. A long blue silk veil covered much of her body. Her straight brown hair fell to her shoulders, one of which was not covered by the veil, and seemed smooth as porcelain.

Beneath the filmy theatrical gauze veil, the dancer wore a beaded costume bra and slitted skirt with a wide, spangled belt. There was no slow warm-up. She came in shimmying swiftly to a fast beat.

Then the mood of the music slowed. With graceful, snaking movements, she unsheathed her veil.

Customers forgot their drinks, and conversations halted as

165

they watched the dancer. The music and the dancer's sensual presence filled the room.

Now, in an exotic writhing motion, Bahijah allowed the long, outer veil to slide slowly down the length of her body and fall to the floor.

She danced down from the stage and, moving to the beat of the music, glided from table to table. With quickened, undulating rhythms, she brought her arms up and clicked the brass cymbals attached to her long thin fingers.

An ancient ritual demanded that she titillate the men, running a coquettish finger under one man's chin, and then bending and dipping her ample breasts in front of another.

As she danced through the audience, she would slow her gyrations enough for men to place the customary bills into her thick jeweled belt, or into the depths of her sequined bra, whichever was closer to the more than eager patrons.

Bahijah danced toward Comfort's table, rolling and fluttering her stomach with great muscular control. Her sweating body looked glazed under the glow of the dim lights. Someone at the table in front of Comfort slapped a ten-dollar bill onto her wet skin, and it stuck. As she swiftly clicked her finger cymbals above her head, Walter stuffed a bill into her belt. Sammy said coolly, "Here, honey," and tucked a bill into her bra. She moved over toward Comfort, who turned to look into a shimmying bosom. He slipped a twenty-dollar bill into her hand.

Onstage again Bahijah turned her back to the audience and, in time to the vibrations of the drum solo, she furiously gyrated her hips until her skirt became a blur.

Cries of delight broke out from the enraptured audience.

Then she whirled wildly, inspired by the drummer's deafening crescendo. Suddenly, it was over. The audience cheered and applauded enthusiastically, Comfort among them.

It had been a spectacular performance.

The night passed pleasantly and quickly, and when Comfort looked at his watch, he saw it was almost three o'clock. He'd better get back to Sammy's apartment and get some sleep.

With a nod, he motioned to the waiter for the check.

Walter Leavitt made an effort to take the check. Sammy made a similar overture. "Next time," said Comfort, reaching into his pocket. He privately vowed it was the last time. He pulled out a roll of bills, paid the check, and headed for the door.

Doc was drinking with the Irish girl as Comfort waved goodbye. The night was crisp and cold. Comfort wore no coat, and he shivered a little as he gave his parking stub to the carhop.

With a screech, Comfort's 1970 black Thunderbird drew up. He climbed into the car, pulled out onto Twenty-ninth Street, and headed east.

Although the Pierre was in the opposite direction from Sammy's apartment, Comfort thought he just might cruise past the hotel. Just to make certain it was still there.

◆ 23 ◆

Bobby Comfort rose at nine o'clock. But Sammy Nalo, who had come in later than Comfort the night before, was already up and dressed, sitting on the couch reading the papers. Comfort always wondered when Sammy slept—if he did—yet he always appeared fresh and looked alert. Comfort told him that he was going to spend the day with Doc and Country at the Bretton Hall Hotel. They arranged for all five to meet at two-thirty in the morning at the hideaway apartment Sammy kept on Fiftieth Street.

"I'm not going to take the .38's with me to Bretton Hall," Comfort told Sammy. "I'd just as soon we handed them out at Fiftieth Street. I don't want Doc doing any more imagining than is necessary."

Country was at a table practicing dealing cards when Comfort arrived at the Bretton Hall Hotel. Doc was still asleep in the bedroom. Comfort took this as a good sign. From then on, he stayed close to Doc and Country.

The three men sat in the hotel room and played gin. "Country and I showed Doc how we could beat him," recalled Comfort. "He was a young kid. We did show him a few tricks, but the time dragged.

"We went out to a little Chinese restaurant a block from the hotel. None of us ate much. But I noticed that Doc was not worrying out loud anymore. He didn't try and talk his way out of it. I figured he was gaining confidence.

"I've been with other guys before a job and they'd say, 'Yeah, this is gonna be a snap,' or 'Nothin' to it.' I knew that it was always false bravado. They would crap out one hour before. They couldn't go through with it."

Country asked Comfort whether the hotel security guards carried guns. "The guards wear suits," Comfort said. "I've never seen guns on them, but that doesn't mean they don't have them. What's important is, we have guns."

At around 1 A.M., Doc, Country, and Comfort began putting on their tuxedos. Comfort needed help with his cummerbund and stays.

The three men, their changes of clothes in garment bags, left the hotel. All three wore black raincoats purchased for the occasion. Country and Doc wore black snap-brim hats.

In the yellow Ford Comfort, Country, and Doc drove to the apartment at 534 West 50th Street, located in a ramshackle area known as Hell's Kitchen. The tenement building was one of a blockful of five-story walkups, with overflowing, uncovered garbage cans lining the entrance, and a fire escape zigzagging its way up the front. A narrow entrance led to the so-called "railroad flats"—apartments that lined the long corridors with exits at the front and rear of the floors. Comfort, Doc, and Country made their way up the dark stairs, stepping gingerly over a sleeping wino. On the second floor they walked down a narrow, dark hallway reeking of the stale odor of urine until they came to the rear. From the red light bulb hanging near the door, they could make out "2C" lettered in black crayon.

Comfort knocked.

Sammy answered the door in his tuxedo, sharp as could be, down to the gleaming shine of his black patent leather shoes. City was there also, wearing a black chauffeur's cap. Four large suitcases were standing against the wall.

"The place was a dump, a pigpen. As soon as you opened a window, the place got filthy," recalled Comfort. "No one lived here. It was just used for our jobs. I wouldn't stay there under any conditions. Cockroaches, bugs, probably rats, though I never saw any. There were two bedrooms, a small kitchen, and a living room. And the furniture? Stuff that even the Salvation Army wouldn't accept. Two worn-out couches, four wobbly chairs. Two funny lamps, one long one, one on an end table. A broken coffee table, and a large kitchen table, which was the only thing that looked halfway decent.

"There were blankets hanging on the walls—to cover some holes. And there were two beds in the bedrooms, but I don't think anybody had ever slept in them. The place had a good refrigerator, filled with beer and Coke. There was no food. Nobody would eat there.

"But people did live in the other apartments in the building. And there were several on the floor. You'd see them when you went to the bathroom. There was one toilet for the whole floor.

"It was unusual for Sammy to have this dump, he was such a spotless guy. He was like that guy in "The Odd Couple." If he had to take a shit, that would mean he would have to take a shower. I used to call him The White Glove.

"But this neighborhood was perfect for our purposes. Nobody around there cared what was going on, and nobody would say anything if they knew. They didn't want cops snooping around.

"Of course, we had carried in suitcases and were dressed sharp when we came. That's not fitting for the neighborhood, but it was three in the morning. But look, there's a risk to everything. You just try to keep your risks to a minimum."

Sammy wore a complete disguise—a fake nose, glasses, and a long-haired wig. City had dyed his hair black. Country was equipped with a false beard and fake eyebrows. Doc wore no disguise: there was little chance he could be traced back to the Midwest. Comfort, just before entering the hotel, would don a blue knit ski mask. In all previous hotel robberies, he was the first man

170

through the door and never wore a disguise. He was first in because it was up to him to decide whether to proceed with the job or scratch it in a split second. However, with the Pierre it was most logical that the first man to enter would be the chauffeur, followed by his two passengers, then Comfort and Sammy.

"For the next hour or so, we stood around the apartment—I mean stood," recalled Comfort. "None of us actually sat down, it was too goddamn dirty. We walked around; we leaned against the kitchen table. Five guys all dressed up, with no place to go until three-thirty A.M.

"We were all edgy. No one was in a laughing mood. It was hot in the apartment, so I opened the window. Sammy was talking a little louder than usual, as he normally did before a robbery. The other guys were pretty quiet, which I liked. Country drank his Coke. Doc lit up a joint. Sammy asked him if it wouldn't dull him—'No,' Doc said. 'It'll relax me, and I'm having just one.' He switched to real cigarettes after that. City had a couple of beers. So did I.

"My biggest concern was, would all these guys keep their heads in case something went wrong? And if they would remember to do the few simple things I had talked about over and over. I looked at them and thought that my future was in their hands, and theirs in mine. Our freedom and our fortune was tied up with each other closer than blood brothers. One big mistake meant deep trouble.

"What would it take for one of these guys, if he was caught, to turn stoolie? I trusted Sammy and I trusted Country. Doc and City I knew, but not as well; but for the next five years—or until the statute of limitations ran out on our job—I knew I'd be thinking about where they were, what they were doing—who they were talking to . . ." Comfort checked his watch. "It's almost three-thirty," he said. "We'd better get started."

"Yeah, right," Sammy muttered, glad to be on the move.

Sammy went into the closet and parceled out a gun and white gloves to each of the men. He also gave each one two sets of handcuffs, then put the ten remaining sets into the black satchel that contained the heavy tools—hammers, chisels, pliers, crowbars, and adhesive tape. Country was given two empty suitcases, and Doc and City one each.

The three hired partners would use the limousine, following Comfort and Sammy in the Ford.

Comfort reminded Country again, "If I happened to miss somebody in the hotel and you see him, get him."

Then Comfort faced the group and said, "Look, there's nothing to be ashamed of if you're too nervous or tense or feel you don't want to go along. Tell me now. If you don't feel right, pass. There'll be a lot more jobs we can do together." He paused. "Because once we go through that door—there's no turning back."

He looked around the room. He glanced at City. "I'm okay," City said.

Comfort turned to Country. Country smiled, revealing the funny gaps between his teeth. "Ready."

Doc leaned against the wall, arms folded, head down.

"Doc?" said Comfort.

Doc looked up. He looked at the other men. "I like the sound of that half million," he answered. He was not smiling.

Comfort glanced at Sammy, who appeared almost grotesque in his disguise. "That wraps it up," said Sammy. "Let's move."

The men walked out of the apartment and along the dark hall and down the stairs. Doc, Country, and City went out the front door. Sammy and Comfort remained in the vestibule until their three heads had disappeared out of view. Then the two partners stepped out into the cold night.

◆ 24 ◆

As Bobby Comfort descended the stone steps of the building on West Fiftieth Street, he was troubled by a feeling that something was not quite right. Then he realized it was the street—it looked darker than usual. As if it had been painted black. The cars, the houses, everything. He stood for a moment on the sidewalk, wondering. Then it struck him. The light on the overhead streetlamp was burned out.

"Anything wrong?" asked Sammy beside him.

"Nothing," said Comfort.

The wind blowing hard off the nearby Hudson River cut through him, and he shivered. He fastened the top button of his raincoat; then he and Sammy walked briskly down the black street.

Their yellow Ford work car was parked on Eleventh Avenue just north of Fiftieth Street.

Sammy revved up the motor and turned on the heater. He cursed when the heater died.

They sat waiting for their partners, hands in their coat pockets, the windows growing steamy from their breath.

Comfort was always on edge before a job. He knew Sammy was nervous too. He could tell by the rise in Sammy's voice and in the restlessness of his eyes. But once we're inside, he said to himself, once we have the place under control, the butterflies disappear, it gets very calm.

He pulled out a cigarette and lit it.

Maybe this kind of thinking was a sign of getting old. He had never felt quite this nervous before a robbery. Maybe it was the magnitude of the job, the possibility of making the score he dreamed of. Maybe he had built the job up too much in his mind. Maybe his efforts to relax Doc had had the boomerang effect of unnerving himself. He could understand how guys could lose heart in a job. He felt for his ski mask in his coat pocket. He would be wearing a mask for the first time. He had decided on this after the last robbery; he had read the newspaper account and the uncomfortably accurate description of him by Janet Annenberg Neff. He would not take the chance of another identification.

He saw the headlights of the Cadillac emerge at the intersection and stop for the red light. Comfort ground his cigarette into the ashtray. Sammy put the car in gear, pulled away from the curb, turned left, and headed slowly east across Fiftieth Street.

Snow had begun to fall. Tiny flakes appeared on the windshield, hardly enough to warrant wipers, but Sammy, ever meticulous, flipped them on.

"I hope it doesn't start falling harder," he said. "It'll be a bitch if we gotta plow through snow to get back."

"Snow wasn't forecast," Comfort answered.

He watched the snow fall like fine dust in front of the headlight beams.

The beginning was always the most dangerous part of any job, Comfort knew. The possibility existed that word had leaked out, that City or Doc might have accidentally said something to somebody. He looked out the window, not sure of what he was looking for. Something was different. Something was strange. Why did he have this feeling? Was there an ambush being set up for them? Was a detective in that parked black car? Was that a plainclothesman on the corner signaling, or was it a man simply waving?

Comfort thought of the robbery a year earlier in which he had

174

"lost" his friend Hank. Hank, Bill Komis, and two others had planned to rob the palatial home of a member of the board of Reynolds Aluminum. Comfort had been asked to join, but refused. It was Komis's job and Bobby didn't trust his judgment. Bobby's instincts were correct. When Komis's gang entered the mansion, they were ambushed by a hundred cops who came from every-where—off the roof, out of the bushes, from the closets.

Tonight they too could be greeted by an ambush in the Pierre. Even after the most careful planning, something unexpected could happen.

Driving across town they were soon beyond the sleazy rows of Hell's Kitchen tenements, and across Broadway, brightly lighted even at a quarter to four in the morning.

In less than seven minutes they'd be there. Comfort's .38 was on the floorboard of the car where he had placed it. He picked it up and put it in the waistband of his trousers. Through his dress shirt he could feel the cold steel of the heavy weapon. He had never fired a gun during a robbery and had no intention of doing so tonight. To Comfort, guns were tools—like hammers or chisels. He wanted no part of them, other than the utilitarian purpose they served for him. They were the real convincers.

The piece of cold steel reminded him of something his mother often said. She had, at times, defended him to friends and family. "Well," she would say, "Bobby might have caused trouble, but he never killed anyone. That's one thing he'd never do. Stealing is wrong, but killing is evil. And for all of my Bobby's faults, one thing he's not, is evil."

But he knew that if he were cornered, if he had to, he'd use the gun.

The car went past sprawling Rockefeller Center and past majestic St. Patrick's Cathedral, still lighted by floodlights. Then they drove through the canyon of glass-and-steel skyscrapers on Madison Avenue. Both Sammy and Comfort were silent.

"This is like a fight," Comfort thought. "You're all wound up before the bell—and you want to get the start over with." His stomach felt queasy, almost like he had to throw up.

"I hope Doc's okay, I hope he's not too jumpy," Sammy said.

"Yeah," replied Comfort.

175

Sammy continued north on Madison and drove to just below Sixty-first Street. He pulled up to the curb. The Pierre was around the corner to the left.

The Cadillac had slowed down a few blocks south on Madison to allow Sammy to park, and to give the leaders time to walk close to the hotel entrance.

Comfort and Sammy left the car and walked around the Sixty-first Street corner and up the block. There it was: the Pierre. The well-lighted square canopy looked like an oasis on the dark, deserted street. Not a single car was on the block. Not a light burned in any of the brownstones across the street.

Comfort thought, one limousine parked for two hours at the hotel entrance without a waiting chauffeur—it might draw interest from a squad car. But, it's a risk we've got to take.

The two men moved along the shadows of the buildings and drew closer to the Pierre. They stopped about ten feet short of the entrance. From this vantage point they could see the guard sitting at the locked door, the same elderly, gray-haired, pouchy-faced man who had sat there most of the nights that Comfort was posing as Dr. Wilson.

Comfort looked back up the street. Empty. The Cadillac should be turning the corner about now. At least two minutes had elapsed since they had parked the Ford.

"Goddamn it, where are they?" Sammy rasped.

Comfort didn't reply. They stood there and waited silently. Comfort could feel his heart beating. Both men watched the corner for sight of the limousine.

Comfort pulled the flap of his glove back and looked at his watch: 3:58.

"Finally!" Sammy muttered.

The long limousine turned the corner, its headlights piercing the darkness of the street. The driver, City, glancing about, spotted his accomplices against the building. He looked for the signal, for a wave which meant "Don't stop, we're not doing it," or an upraised fist—"It's on."

Comfort brought up his fist.

The Cadillac pulled in front of the entrance of the Pierre, and stopped.

176

The sleepy security guard hardly stirred. His face was expressionless. He had seen so many limos, town cars, Fleetwoods, six-door Mercedes, even at four o'clock in the morning. He was not at all suspicious of this car.

City triggered the trunk release and then got out of the car. He moved around to open the rear passenger door for Doc and Country to emerge. Comfort watched as City then stepped to the trunk, raised the lid, and removed four suitcases, exaggerating their heaviness. City slammed the lid shut, then lifted two suitcases. Doc and County each picked up one and, following City, walked to the hotel entrance.

Comfort, still in the building shadows alongside Sammy, heard City call out, "Reservations—Dr. Foster's party."

He watched the three men standing quietly for a moment. The guard, as he had seen him do many times during his stay, called the registration desk to confirm the name.

Comfort had called ahead and made the reservation. There couldn't be any kind of problem, unless—Comfort heard the door being unlocked. He caught his breath. He saw City enter through the door, then Country, followed by Doc. Without a word Comfort stepped out of the shadows, pulled on his ski mask, and in just a couple of strides was on Doc's heels. Sammy followed immediately behind.

As soon as City got through the door, he dropped the suitcases, drew his gun, and stuck it in the door guard's bewildered face. "Huh," the guard grunted, blanching.

"Turn around. Keep your mouth shut and you won't get hurt," ordered City.

Country and Doc had moved rapidly through the door and dropped the luggage.

Country grabbed the guard, swung him around, handcuffed him, and pushed him forward toward the desk area. The men moved swiftly but remembered not to run.

City and Sammy headed straight to the security office down the long lobby leading to the Fifth Avenue entrance. They passed another security guard moving out of the executive office alcove. The guard hesitated, looked curiously at the two men, then a voice from behind him commanded, "Don't move." The guard turned quickly, and stared at the man in a ski mask brandishing a .38. Bobby brought the guard to the alcove and sat him down facing the wall. He handcuffed him, then taped his mouth and eyes.

City and Sammy went directly to the front desk. The desk clerk moved out from behind the cabinet partition and greeted the two men.

"Reservation for Dr. Foster," said Sammy.

The room clerk turned to check his reservation book. City said, "We're taking over. Don't move." Sammy leaped over the desk to prevent the clerk from pressing any signal button. At gunpoint, Sammy led him to the alcove, where he was taped and handcuffed.

City hurried past the concierge's desk to the cashier's window. He peered in. The vault was open. The auditor was inside at his desk. When he looked up from his papers, City stepped to the door before the auditor could move to lock it.

"Don't look at me or you're dead," said City, rushing to the vault. He jammed his foot into the door, then walked the auditor to the alcove and returned to search for other people.

Doc went swiftly around the corner into the long hallway toward the Fifth Avenue entrance. The hostages were herded into the large alcove beside the registration desk. Country stood guard over them. The others fanned out to capture anyone else in the area. Thus far, there were seven men hostages.

A burly bellman appeared in the main lobby. Sammy stepped out from behind the wall. "Come with me," he snapped. The bellman looked unbelieving.

"*Qué pasa?*"

Sammy poked a gun in his belly. "Move over there."

Comfort stepped up to the elevator operator. "I've got a gun, follow me." The elevator operator's eyes riveted on the pistol in Comfort's hand.

"No one's gonna get hurt. Just get down the hall fast."

Another security guard had finished making his rounds of the rotunda area outside the Cotillion Room. He walked down the marble staircase and noticed a young blond man in a tuxedo on a settee. As the security man approached, the young man jumped up. "The manager wants to see you," Doc said sternly.

178

"What? The manager's not here."

"We've taken over. Move it and be quick." He showed his gun. The guard threw up his hands. Doc frisked him. The security men were without weapons.

Comfort went into the basement and spotted one of the cleaning men. "Where's your helper?" asked Comfort.

"I don't have one," the cleaning man said.

"Upstairs, let's go," said Comfort. "This is a holdup."

His gun out, Doc searched the kitchen and pantry. Satisfied that no one was there, he pushed through the kitchen door and hurried back to the lobby.

Meanwhile, Doc had intercepted another of the elevator operators returning from his break.

Another porter was captured in the employees' washroom. An elevator operator and a security man were caught exiting from an elevator; another porter was taken in the manager's office.

In all, fourteen employees had been marshaled into the alcove and forced to sit down facing the wall.

Country stood guard over the hostages as the gang combed the lobby area for anyone they might have missed. They searched behind the columns, and in and out of the nooks and crannies of the main floor.

Comfort looked over the captives and whispered to Sammy, "We're missing three guards. There's usually seven. We've only got four."

Comfort pulled the tape off the room clerk's mouth. "There's supposed to be three more guards," Comfort said. "Where are they?"

"I don't know what you're talking about," the clerk responded.

"You know what I'm talking about."

"They're not here tonight."

Comfort pulled the tape off the mouth of one of the guards. "Where're the other guards?"

"They're not here tonight. It's a skelton staff for the holidays," he said.

Comfort had no choice but to accept it as fact. He retaped the men's mouths.

"Is that it?" asked Doc.

"Looks like it," Comfort said. "But do another check." After the hotel was secured, Doc took up his position as sentry inside the Fifth Avenue entrance.

Comfort looked at the ornate clock behind the reservations desk. The time was 4:15.

They had captured the most elegant and, Comfort hoped, the richest hotel in New York City in just fifteen minutes. They were in complete control. No one could enter or leave without their knowledge.

City and Sammy went back to the vault to begin cracking the boxes.

Country stood in front of Comfort, waiting for instructions.

"Take the guard's seat at the Sixty-first Street door," Comfort said, "and don't open up until you check back with me."

He sat down in the assistant manager's chair. From there he could be at "control center." He was just ten feet from the front desk and would have responsibility for all calls, could handle anything unusual that might come up, and still keep an eye on the hostages.

Comfort felt the sweat under his mask dripping down his neck. His hands were moist inside his gloves. The nervousness would diminish soon, he thought, it always did.

For a brief moment his attention focused on the handcuffed hostages in the captured alcove.

They were trapped and in total fear, he thought. I'd be scared, too. They don't know what to expect, but they know they're in trouble. He walked up behind the hostages and reassured them that no one would be hurt or robbed. He said he and his men would be gone as soon as possible. He returned to his chair.

Everything had fallen into place. The lobby was calm now, but not quiet. Hammer striking metal in the vault some sixty feet away was heard.

In the vault the battery of safe-deposit boxes against the wall numbered 208, and ranged in size from small doors, which measured two and one half inches by five inches, to the larger boxes at the bottom of the vault, which were five times that size. The steel door covers on the individual boxes were an inch thick. However, the hinges were exterior ones, little knurled knobs. City and Sammy used hammers and chisels on them.

Less than fifteen minutes had passed when Country, from his chair at the Sixty-first Street door, called out, "A car's pulling up." Comfort peeked around the corner. He didn't want anyone outside catching a glimpse of a man in a mask.

"Ask them what they want, then let 'em in," Comfort said. "I'll get them from behind."

A white-haired man appeared, rapped on the glass and held up his key.

Country unlocked the door. As the man walked toward the alcove, Comfort stepped out.

"We're robbin' this place," he said. "Step in here."

"Oh no, please don't do this to me," the man cried, "I've got a bad heart . . ." His face was stricken with terror.

"There's nothing to worry about," Comfort said. "No one's going to be hurt."

The man seemed about to collapse.

"Just come over here with the rest of the people."

"I don't want to go anyplace."

"Sir, you've got to."

"I can't move, I don't think I can move," the man said.

"Look, I'll help you."

Comfort took him by the arm. The man was shaking. Comfort guided him slowly into the alcove, then pulled up a chair. "Sit down," he said. "Nobody's going to cuff you, nobody's going to bother you."

"Are you going to blindfold me?" the man asked.

"No," said Comfort. "Just look at the wall, don't look at us. Do you need a glass of water or something?"

The man shook his head, and Comfort moved toward the desk again.

All was quiet except for the noise coming from the vault around the corner.

Comfort smoked cigarette after cigarette. Minutes ticked by.

Comfort pulled his sleeve back and looked at his watch: 4:50.

The woolen ski mask was itchy. He had no idea what was being taken from the safe-deposit boxes.

Calling to Country to cover the hostages, he walked around to the vault.

He found Sammy and City, kneeling like sculptors, chiseling the hinges off the strong boxes.

Twenty to twenty-five steel boxes had been strewn haphazardly in a corner. The four suitcases were on the floor, behind the men. One suitcase was already half-filled.

Comfort knelt and sifted through some of the stuff. There were a few diamond bracelets and earrings, but mostly stock certificates, passports, wills, and bankbooks, nothing *gigantic*, nothing like he had imagined. Not the *real* jewels. He estimated the worth at four hundred thousand dollars. Nothing like the fifty million dollars they had dreamed of—nothing like *one* million.

"What's going on?" Comfort said to Sammy. "Is this it so far?"

"Yeah," Sammy replied. "Nothin' else. I thought there'd be more than this by now."

"It's there," said Comfort, swallowing. "I *know* it's there. It's still early. It'll come."

Sammy turned and pulled out another box. This one contained one gold Dunhill cigarette lighter.

Sammy tossed the lighter in the suitcase.

"What are you taking that for?" asked Comfort. "That can't be worth more than a hundred dollars to us."

"I'm taking everything," Sammy replied grimly.

If anybody was going to find the treasure, Sammy would. Comfort could see the determination in his eyes. This was Sammy's specialty; and Comfort considered him the best in the business.

Without a word, Comfort motioned Sammy to follow him to the alcove. When they came around the corner to where Country and the hostages sat, Sammy suddenly stopped.

"What is it?" Comfort asked.

Sammy stared at the old man in the chair.

"Why ain't that guy cuffed?" asked Sammy. "Why ain't he blindfolded?"

"It's okay," Comfort said, breathing easier, "he came in through the door. He was going to have a heart attack."

182

"But goddamn . . ."

"You're tense."

"I'm not tense!"

"Why don't you just take care of what you've been doing? I'll handle it out here."

"Okay, what did you call me out here for?"

"To get the auditor. He's got the list of who owns the boxes, so we can pick out the women, or the married couples. They're sure to have jewelry. This way's too hit-and-miss."

"That's right," said Sammy.

The man in the brown suit, Comfort remembered, was the auditor. Comfort led him back to the vault.

When Comfort asked him for the list of boxholders, he said there was no such record.

Comfort said, "You're the auditor. You have to know who owns each box. It's nice of you to try and protect these people, but you'd better give me the list."

Sammy moved over to the auditor, picked up his pin hammer and tapped the auditor on the head with the rubber end.

"I don't wanna have to hurt you," Sammy said. "I want the list."

The auditor took a key from his pocket and, with a trembling hand, unlocked his desk drawer. He pulled out a set of typewritten index cards.

"Which one belongs to the princess?" asked Sammy.

"I don't know of any princess."

Sammy tapped him on the head again with the hammer.

In another situation the short man in a curly wig and false nose would have seemed comical. Now he was deadly frightening.

"I don't *know* of any princess. I swear to you."

"What princess are you talkin' about?" City asked.

"I don't know," Sammy said. "I figured there must be some duchess or princess staying in this place."

City bound the auditor with his own necktie. "Sit him down on the chair, we might need him again," ordered Sammy.

Sammy shuffled through the index cards.

"Here's one," he said. "Box 44—Thomas Yawkey, he owns the Red Sox. Hit that one," he said to City. "And here's Harold

183

Uris, the real-estate guy, Box 178. Oh Christ"—Sammy was glowing—"Calliope Kulukundis, the Greek billionaire—"

City gingerly began cracking Box 44. "How do you know who all these people are?" he asked.

"Reading—the library. Don't you ever go to the library?" Sammy didn't wait for a reply. He read the next card. "Lagerwall, I'll be damned! She's the one I read about who goes to the opera loaded down with all those jewels—well, next year I think she'll be going there naked. See this," he said to City, "she's got two boxes, 154 and 194."

Sammy picked up his hammer and with renewed vigor broke Box 154.

He opened Lagerwall's box and pulled it out from the wall. "This is more like it!" he said. The box was heaped with jewels. He emptied the contents into the blue suitcase and City, who had never seen anything like this in his life, watched in disbelief. Sammy began hammering furiously on Box 194.

Meanwhile, Comfort, curious to find out how helpful the auditor's file cards were, left the alcove and went back to check in on the vault. He took one step into the small, stuffy room and stopped short. The room was aglow with the reflection of gems. It was as though he had come upon a treasure chest in a cave. On the floor two suitcases were filled with a profusion of bracelets, watches, rings, pins studded with sparkling stones—rubies, sapphires, diamonds. A rainbow of jewels.

Sammy and City were obviously using the house "list" to good advantage. The men were sweating profusely as they worked; the closed-in room, without ventilation, gave off a stale odor.

"Now *this* looks beautiful," said Comfort.

"It's the list—I just see a good name, and boom," said Sammy, pulling out another strongbox. "Look! Diamonds like this in every box!" There was that familiar excitement in his voice now. Comfort reached into the box and withdrew a diamond necklace with about four hundred diamonds set in platinum. Each stone was at least a carat. Comfort removed his glasses from under his mask to better scrutinize the diamonds. He held the necklace to the light. He wished he had a loupe to determine the value. Each diamond

184

looked flawless. He estimated each to be worth a couple of thousand dollars.

Gently, Comfort dropped the necklace onto the stack in the suitcase. He put his glasses back on under the mask and returned to the alcove.

It was 5:05.

All of the hostages sat quietly, except for periodic movements to adjust body weight. The white-haired man, although no longer gasping, still seemed nervous. Comfort was unraveling his second pack of cigarettes when he was startled by the ring of the front desk phone.

At the third ring Comfort moved to pick up the receiver. Before a voice came on, he spoke into the phone. "Hold on a minute, please, we are a little busy here." He hit the hold button.

Comfort went to the alcove for the night manager. With some effort he helped the heavyset man to his feet. Then he guided him to the front desk, cupped the phone in his hand, and shouted to Sammy in the vault.

"Knock off for a minute, we've got a call here."

Sammy instantly appeared, his .38 in one hand, his hammer in the other.

"What's going on?" he asked.

"I want the manager to answer this call, just in case it's someone familiar with the hotel," said Comfort. He turned to the manager. "Just say hello."

The frightened manager slowly lifted the phone and meekly spoke into the mouthpiece. "Front desk." He listened, and then said, "You better talk to him."

"Me?" Comfort said, looking at Sammy.

Comfort grabbed the phone and heard a man with a foreign accent. The caller was angry.

The man complained he had been ringing for an elevator for ten minutes and none had come.

"I'm sorry, sir," Comfort said. "You can't imagine the trouble we've been having. The elevator operator had a heart attack—we had to rush him to a hospital."

"I hope he's all right," the voice said, softening a little.

185

"We'll send someone up for you immediately."

Comfort nestled the phone onto its cradle. "It's okay," he said, motioning Sammy to return the night manager to the hostage area. He then went to get Doc, at the far end of the lobby.

"Did you hear an elevator buzz?" Comfort asked.

Doc rose out of his chair. "What elevator buzz? The elevator never rang," he said.

"A guest is bitching that he's been ringing for ten minutes. You're the bellhop, go up there and take him where he wants to go. We have to give them service."

Comfort returned to the alcove with Doc and undid the handcuffs from the larger bellhop, removed his jacket, and handed it to Doc. The gold-button beige jacket was too short in the sleeves and too full in the chest but it had to do.

Doc hurried to the bank of high-floor elevators. He entered, pressed the close button, and was on his way up.

Five minutes passed. Comfort waited at the elevator door. He lit another cigarette.

What's taking Doc so long? he wondered.

Suddenly, the phone rang again. Comfort didn't need the night manager. He picked up the phone.

"Front desk," he said without hesitation.

"I'm stuck up here."

It was Doc.

"What do you mean 'stuck'?"

"The goddamn elevator crapped out on me. The door won't close. I have people with me. How the hell am I getting down?"

"Where are you?"

"On thirty-seven."

"Where are you calling from?"

"A suite."

"Whose?"

"I'm in the guy's mother-in-law's room. She lives here. They're from Brazil. This guy's here on his honeymoon."

"Where's his wife?"

"She's up here, too. Their room's on twenty. They've been up here awhile, sayin' good-bye to the old lady because they're takin' an early plane back today."

186

"I'll send someone up there. What's the room number?"

"3702."

Comfort motioned Country back from the door and explained the setup to him.

"And take the guy's wife and the old lady, too, and bring the three of them down," said Comfort.

In short order the second elevator door opened at the lobby level. Doc and Country brought the Brazilians to Comfort in the alcove. Of the three captives only the man was fully clothed. The mother and daughter wore dressing gowns and silver slippers. Comfort saw that the women looked pale and nervous. Comfort explained to the three Brazilians that no harm would come to them as long as they cooperated with him. When he turned to look at the bride, she wrapped her robe tightly about her. In so doing she unintentionally revealed a shapely figure, and a very large square-cut stone on her ring finger.

Sammy came around the corner. "What's all the noise about?" he asked. Comfort told him. Sammy's eyes went to the bride's glittering solitaire.

"Let's get that piece before you cuff her," Sammy said to Comfort.

Comfort ignored him and turned to the Brazilians. "We aren't going to rob you," he said. "It's unfortunate that you're trapped in this. If you have a safety box, give me the number and we won't break it open—unless we already have. In that case, it's gone."

The man gave Comfort the number. The threesome was moved in with the rest of the captives. Sammy returned to the vault, City and Country to their respective entrances.

Once again calm descended on the lobby of the Pierre, except for the hammering in the vault.

City appeared in the lobby alcove and motioned Comfort to follow him.

"What is it?" asked Comfort.

"You'll see," said City.

Comfort waved Country over to cover the desk, then followed City into the vault. Sammy was sorting through one of the large safe-deposit boxes. It was filled with neatly piled stacks of packaged cash. The bundles were all in hundreds, fifties, and twenty-dollar bills wrapped in paper bands, which were stamped "$10,000," "$20,000," "$30,000."

"How much do you think's here?" Comfort asked.

"Half a million, easy," Sammy said.

"Who in hell would keep cash in a box instead of a bank, and lose interest?" City asked.

"People who don't want anyone to know they've got this kind of loot," said Comfort. "Scheming businessmen who have other concerns besides bank interest."

"Crooks, huh?" City said. "Or politicians. Shit, this is campaign headquarters for Nixon, isn't it? I wonder—"

"Wonder on your own time," said Comfort. "This isn't a coffee break. We don't have all morning here."

The men dumped the packaged money into one large suitcase. It was now completely filled.

Comfort returned to his position at the front desk. The time was 5:58.

Bobby calculated that the two suitcases brimming with jewels, and the one suitcase overflowing with cash, were worth millions. And they still had another half-hour, with one empty suitcase remaining to be filled.

He lit another cigarette. He looked at the ashtray and, using his gloved finger, counted thirty-two stubs.

A rapping at the Sixty-first Street door brought him back. It was the newspaper delivery service. The truckman was carrying the morning papers in bundles for the hotel newsstand.

Comfort signaled Country to open the door.

The truckman moved in, saw Country with his gun drawn, and instantly dropped the bundles.

He was taken to the alcove, handcuffed and taped with the rest of the hostages. It was 6:05. Bobby went back to the vault. "They're starting to straggle in. We'll go in a few minutes," he said, urgency in his voice.

"There's at least a hundred good boxes we haven't hit yet," said Sammy.

188

"We're sure not taking *these* boxes with us," Comfort replied. Sammy shrugged.

"Oh Christ, no," said Comfort. "We've got enough to carry. There's four suitcases filled."

"We can get another suitcase from the bellman's closet."

"We don't need it! Jesus! Lock up the cases."

"He's right," City said. "We've been here too long."

"Twenty people will be walking in here in about fifteen minutes," said Comfort. "We can't handle an entire new shift."

"Five more minutes," Sammy said.

Bobby nodded. "Five more minutes."

In the alcove Comfort was nervously taking a drag on his cigarette when he heard Country call, "Squad car! Coming up the street!"

Comfort jumped out of the chair. He poked his head around the corner.

"Is it stopping?" he called back.

"I don't know. What should I do?"

"Nothing. Maybe it's just cruisin'."

Comfort waited. He watched Country's reactions. He saw Country's head turn slowly from right to left following the movement of the squad car.

"They passed, Bobby," said Country.

Comfort raced over and snatched Country by the lapels.

"What's wrong?" asked Country.

In a hissing whisper Comfort said, "Don't ever call me by my name in this place. Do you understand?"

"Shit, I'm sorry. The cops. I got nervous."

Comfort dropped his hands. There was no way the hostages could have missed hearing Country shout his name. Well, it's history, he thought. I just hope we don't do anything else stupid.

At 6:25 Comfort returned to the vault. "That's it," he said. "We're outta time."

Even under the false beard, Comfort could see Sammy's drained face. City looked tired, too. It had been an exhausting two and one-half hours of labor.

"Last one," said Sammy. "Maybe this one belongs to a princess."

He cracked it open and slid the drawer out. Fumbling around, he came up with one gold loop earring. He held it in the palm of his hand.

"One earring?" Sammy said.

Comfort spread his palms. "Maybe the princess only has one ear."

The three broke into laughter.

In the vault each suitcase was stuffed to the brim and difficult to close. Just as City was closing the last one, Bobby said, "Hold it."

He took his gun from his waistband and tossed it on the heap of jewels.

He nodded to Sammy. Sammy pulled out his .38 and dropped it alongside Bobby's weapon. City shut the case and picked it up. "Goddamn," he grunted, "heavy."

Bobby went to the long hallway and motioned Doc that they were leaving.

The bags were carried to the entrance door at Sixty-first Street. It was exactly 6:32 A.M. Still dark outside.

Comfort stopped at the alcove. Country, City, and Doc—once again, the two gentlemen and their chauffeur—moved out the door with the suitcases. As calmly as possible, they took the suitcases to the rear of the limousine. City opened the trunk, deposited the bags, slammed the lid closed, and opened the door for his two passengers. He went around to the driver's side, got in, and drove away for the short trip across town to the West Fiftieth Street hideout.

From inside the Pierre Comfort watched the shiny black limousine disappear from view. He looked at his watch: 6:34.

Sammy moved out of the door of the hotel to get the yellow Ford and return for Comfort.

Bobby remained to make certain that no hostages would get to a phone before the Cadillac was safely across town at the hideout. They needed another six minutes.

Once he and Sammy left, it didn't matter if the police were called and they were picked up. There was no incriminating evidence: they had neither jewels nor guns in their possession.

His partners gone, he was alone, unarmed. The hostages, al-

190

though unaware of these facts, knew something had changed. The incessant banging from the vault had come to a stop. There was complete silence. The tension seemed transformed into a dreaminess, an unreality.

Comfort looked at the still backs of the hostages, like a row of stone figures. He recalled vividly what it was like to be cramped in a cell, unable to move freely, fearing the unknown. He looked at the auditor, the hefty night manager, both of whom had exhibited a kind of loyalty in trying to protect the hotel by briefly withholding information from him. He looked at the Brazilian mother and daughter, who had calmed down after their initial fright. The Brazilian man was contained through it all. Even the old man had not collapsed.

He walked over and stood a few feet from the captives.

"We're leaving here in fifteen minutes," he said. His voice startled a few people. "I want all of you to remember that nobody was hurt. We never intended to hurt you. If you think about becoming a star witness, about identifying anyone you happened to see, you'd better reconsider. Don't help the police in any way. If you do, your wives, your kids, your mothers—anything in the world you value—will never be safe again.

"I'll come back," he continued, "or send somebody back. If you put us in prison, you'll get what's coming to you. If you don't, you've got nothing to worry about. I hope you understand."

He looked at his watch: Sammy had been gone for four minutes. He looked to see if the car was in front. It wasn't.

Comfort now pulled out a roll of bills, bent forward and began placing a twenty-dollar bill into the pocket of each of the eight uniformed hotel employees. "I know this won't make up for the inconvenience and the scare, but at least you can go out and buy yourself something," he told them.

As for the guests, they didn't need his money, and certainly Bobby was not going to tip the security guards.

He walked from the alcove toward the desk. His watch showed 6:41. It was exactly seven minutes since the Cadillac had gone. The three accomplices should be at Fiftieth Street by now.

Bobby grabbed his coat from the desk and put it on just as he

191

heard a short horn-blast outside the door. He walked around the desk for the last time and stopped abruptly. Reaching across, he picked up the ashtray that was spilling over with his butts and carefully poured them into his raincoat pocket. Then he strode across the lobby, peeled off his ski mask, wet with perspiration, stuffed it into his other pocket, unlocked and pushed open the lobby door, and walked out, the cold air hitting his face sharply.

"What took you so long?" asked Comfort, climbing into the car.

"The goddamn car wouldn't turn over," said Sammy. "It's okay now."

Comfort wiped his sweaty face with the sleeve of his coat.

Sammy had removed his wig and false beard. "Looks like everything's all right."

"It's too early to celebrate," Comfort said. "We're not off the streets yet."

"Yeah, I know," said Sammy.

The light snow had stopped, but the sky was beginning to lighten.

Southbound, they stopped for a red light at Fifty-seventh Street. Westbound, they stopped for a red light at Sixth Avenue, and again at Seventh Avenue. As they came up to Eighth Avenue, the light there turned red, too.

Comfort laughed.

"All that planning, Sammy, and we're still making every red light in the goddamn city."

"Fuck you," said Sammy.

They hit the red lights at Ninth, Tenth, and Eleventh avenues, too.

It wasn't until he turned south at the green light on Eleventh Avenue from Fifty-seventh to Fiftieth Street that Sammy's mood brightened. By the time he turned east on Fiftieth and dropped Comfort off at the apartment, Sammy was glowing. They had a lot to look forward to upstairs.

192

◆ 25 ◆

Bobby Comfort climbed the stairs to the second floor of the seedy tenement building, and made his way carefully down the long dark hallway. When he approached the last door, he knocked. He was feeling strangely hollow. This should have been a time of complete exhilaration, but it wasn't. When the door opened, he was greeted by a big bright grin.

"Mornin'!" said Country.

Comfort entered without smiling. The light from the tilted table lamp lent a yellow cast to the shabby room. Doc was sitting in the middle of the floor near the four suitcases. He had removed the tie and jacket of his tuxedo and was drinking beer.

"City tells me it was a good haul," Country said. Country and Doc had never entered the vault during the job and had no idea of the contents of the suitcases.

"We did all right—I know we did," said Comfort. "I'm not sure what we got in jewelry. One thing I do know, we've got one suitcase filled with cash."

"Filled with cash?" asked Doc. "City didn't mention anything—"

"Loaded with big bills—couple hundred thousand," said Comfort.

"Let's open one of 'em," he said. "Just for a look."

"We'll wait for Sammy and City to get here," said Comfort. "This way no one thinks someone is putting anything extra in his pocket."

Country walked to the window and anxiously peeked out from behind the torn shade. He came back and sat down on the old velvet sofa, sending a cloud of dust floating up.

Comfort was out at the refrigerator when he heard a knock. It was City, returning from having parked the limousine several blocks away.

"So that's it," City said, nodding toward the suitcases, "our personal little treasure."

"Yeah, look at 'em," said Country. He stood up and walked around the suitcases, like a wolf circling his prey. "They look like nothin'—like they could be empty, could have rags in 'em or something." He took a long gulp of beer.

They heard a key slip into the locked door. It was Sammy.

"Well," said Sammy, closing the door and hooking the chain, "let's open 'em up!"

"Sammy, why don't we give Doc and Country a surprise and open the blue one. They'll be happy with that," said Comfort.

Sammy laughed. He knew Doc and Country had no knowledge of jewels and that they were more "cash guys than jewel thieves."

"City," said Sammy, "put the blue suitcase on the table."

"Happy to," City said as he lifted the bulging suitcase and hoisted it to the kitchen table. The table creaked under the weight. They all gathered around as City fumbled with the latch. The lid sprang open and bundles of green cash burst out with the force of a gusher; money spilled onto the table and fell all over the floor.

"That's gonna buy some ton of hog feed," exclaimed Country, picking up some of the packages and tossing them into the air.

"I've got other plans for mine," said Doc.

194

Comfort looked at the men. Doc, Country, and City had never seen that much money in their lives, he thought. This was their biggest score, and this was only the money suitcase.

"Let's get the other stuff," said Comfort.

Sammy walked over to the three remaining brown suitcases, turned one over, and opened it. Jewels tumbled out. He opened the next and more jewels spilled onto the floor. He undid the third suitcase—it was overflowing with the sparkling gems, along with a variety of the usual wills and documents people place in vaults. The apartment was filled with money and jewels.

Comfort recalled: "Everybody was saying, 'This is it for me.' I think each one of us meant it for the moment. We knew we had enough money never to do another job."

There was a great deal of work still to be done. Not only did they have to count the money, but all the gems had to be removed from their settings.

The nonnegotiable stock certificates, bonds, and other papers were to be stacked in a pile on the floor, and then stuffed into a garbage bag and burned.

Comfort recalled that the first thing he had to do was count the money. "I had no inclination to do it. I was tired. I didn't know why. I was depressed. All the tension was gone. My head ached. I tried a Coke and felt nauseous. This was the biggest score of my life—it was the thing that would let me live the rest of my life like a millionaire, and I was sick. I couldn't explain it. They wanted to count the money. 'Go ahead,' I said, 'count it. Just tell me how much we've got.' They scooped up all the bundles and brought them in the living room. They sat on the floor counting. I leaned against the table, watching. Maybe I'd get two million on this one. I couldn't get thrilled. Maybe I was disappointed that there'd be no reason to rob anymore. Maybe I wanted to keep stealing. There was the excitement—it made me feel good. It made me feel—well, it's like a drug—it made me feel superior to other people. I hate to say it, but it's true, knowing I had the balls to do what other people only dreamed about.

"The guys were counting and clapping. Even Sammy, who always tried to be cool. 'Ah, we got it now. I told you—I told you we'd get the money,' he said. I had to laugh.

"I looked at Doc and remembered how I had to talk him into doing it with us.

"The cash was all in denominations of twenties, fifties, and hundred-dollar bills. Each guy was taking money and stacking it in piles of ten thousand.

"We had found cash in several boxes, but nothing like the bundle in that one safe-deposit box.

"Sammy was sitting there cross-legged on the floor and slapping bills into piles, and City said, "Sammy, whose box do you think that was with the half million or so?'

" 'Probably some friend of Nixon's,' he said. 'He's got guys all over the country twisting arms for reelection contributions. I heard they got so much money they don't know what to do with it all.'

"Country said, 'We should have checked the name on the list with the box,' and they all went back to counting the money."

Comfort spotted the small radio on the window ledge. He switched it on and turned the dial until he heard the news. He listened, but nothing was said about the Pierre holdup.

"Too early to be reported yet," said Sammy.

Comfort nodded. He kept the radio on and leaned against the table, watching his partners. He wished they'd hurry with the counting so they could go through the jewels. But he knew that the money came first. They'd split it up right here. The jewels would have to be worked on for at least several days and the value decided before the proceeds would finally be split up.

Daylight entered the room in thin shafts through the drawn, torn shades. It was early Sunday morning in the city, and now the sound of an occasional truck on nearby Eleventh Avenue became more distinct.

Suddenly, the voice of a radio announcer broke into the music. Everyone stopped. "This just in. What police say may be the biggest hotel robbery in U.S. history occurred just hours ago at the prestigious Hotel Pierre on Fifth Avenue. . . ." The men on the floor stopped counting and listened. "Four or five men with masks and guns burst into the hotel at four this morning, rounded up nineteen hostages, and emptied the hotel vaults of what is believed to be a million dollars in jewelry. . . ."

196

"And cash," added Country.

"Quiet," said City.

"Police are interrogating the hostages. So far, there are no clues. More on this later. Now back to music."

"They aren't going to find no clues, either," said Sammy, returning to count the money.

The robbery had been a complete success, thought Comfort, just as he had dreamed. It was the perfect crime. No one in the hotel could identify them because of their disguises. Except for Doc, who wore no disguise, and had been seen by the Brazilian family face-to-face. But Doc was leaving town immediately.

After nearly two hours the cash was finally sorted out. It came to $887,000. Sammy and Bobby got 10 percent off the top for expenses and for the planning.

City, Doc, and Country took $171,000 each, while the two bosses got $187,000 apiece.

"After we split up the money," recalled Comfort, "Sammy seemed a little sad.

"I said to him, 'Something wrong? Aren't you satisfied?' He said, 'Nah, I'm okay. We still have a lot of work to do, getting these stones out.' But I knew him. I knew there was something going on in his mind, some scheme. It made me uneasy.

"I let it pass. Sammy and City set about taking out the jewels. Since Country, Doc, and I were from out of town, we'd agreed to leave the city and get back home to establish an alibi as fast as we could."

Comfort, Doc, and Country changed from their tuxedoes into street clothes, and City changed out of his chauffeur's uniform. They stuffed the clothes into a large black plastic garbage bag. Later City would take the sealed bag to the Forty-sixth Street pier area, where he would place the contents into one of the many oil-barrel fires that usually burn along the waterfront. These fires usually keep the drifters warm during the winter daylight hours. No one would be suspicious of the bag's contents, and the flames would do the rest.

Sammy had placed one of the suitcases of jewelry on the table and begun taking stones from their settings.

"It didn't bother Sammy that I wasn't going to help," said

Comfort. "He'd joke about me not being good with tools. 'You couldn't get out of a screen door,' he'd say. He said it to me a thousand times. Prying out stones was too much like work. But Sammy enjoyed it like a kid playing with toys.

"There was no way all the jewels could be separated in one day. There were too many pieces. It's hard to get at some of them, and you don't want to scratch them. It was tedious work. It would take about a week for Sammy, depending on how much help he got from City."

Comfort emerged from the bedroom dressed in a sport jacket and tie. Sammy and City were at the table, working at both ends of a necklace at once with jewelers' pliers. As the stones were loosened from the prongs, they were gently placed on the table. Comfort estimated that nearly a hundred stones were lying on the white-topped table. They included rubies, sapphires, two large green emeralds, and diamonds in graduated sizes ranging from one to twelve carats.

"When Doc and Country were changed and ready to go, I offered them each a couple of stones in case they wanted them for their women," Comfort recalled. "I said I was taking a few. I was surprised when they turned me down. They said they'd take the money after the jewels were sold. But I don't think they even cared about getting anything from the jewels now. That was my immediate impression. They just seemed satisfied with the cash for the time being."

Comfort's final responsibility required that he contact a friend, a smelter, who would take the separate bags of gold, platinum, and silver settings. The man would have to be called for the eventual pickup instructions. The precious-metal scale was in the kitchen, and once the weight had been determined, the cash would be paid, and then split with the partners.

Sammy was to keep all the stones from the job in the black satchel in his own "safe deposit" niche in the floor of the bathroom at his Forty-fifth Street apartment.

This niche was so well hidden that it would take the total demolition of the building to find it. The New York City building code requires that all bathrooms, because of bathtub weight, be set in cement. It was in this cement floor that a hole had been chipped out and covered with the commode.

"I told Sammy to stash the satchel until we decided how and when to sell the stuff," recalled Comfort. "There was no hurry. We had enough cash to last us for a long time.

"I had complete faith in Sammy to do the right thing. I trusted him—we all trusted him—with what looked like at least ten million dollars in jewels alone.

"I told Doc that I would give him the numbers later. He said that would be okay. I said, 'You won't be able to find us again if you don't want to take the jewels with you.' He said, 'No problem.' I said, 'We'll get in touch with you.' I would also be in touch with Country, and we both knew how to reach City."

Country and Comfort initially had planned to return upstate together. Comfort, however, decided that it was best if they traveled separately. Country would drive home alone. Comfort would take the train. So would Doc. Comfort recalled, "I had too much money on me to take a plane. At the time, airline security required a passenger search before you boarded a plane."

Having discarded his raincoat—old cigarette butts included—into the trash bag, Comfort put on his blue cashmere coat. The three men, ready to leave, began stuffing the cash into their pockets.

Doc was the first to leave. Five minutes later Country departed. Comfort looked at his watch: 11:15. He walked over and put a hand on Sammy's shoulder. "Give me a call when things cool down," said Comfort.

"Okay," said Sammy, grimacing as he struggled to loosen a stone.

Comfort could tell that Sammy's interests for the moment were solely on his work.

"Don't forget about throwing those garbage bags out," said Comfort, "and any other stuff we might have left—cigarette stubs, beer cans, anything."

"Right—and I'll be in touch in a month or so," Sammy said.

Out on the street, Comfort saw a cab turn the corner and come down Fiftieth. My lucky day, he thought. He hailed the empty

Checker, but it took effort to raise his arm because of the weight of the cash in his coat pockets.

Inside Grand Central Terminal holiday travelers stood in extended lines at the ticket windows. Comfort purchased a reserved seat for Rochester and then checked out the newsstand, though he knew it was still too soon for the papers to have the story. He stood in a remote corner of the cavernous terminal until the loudspeaker announced the departure track for his train.

Finally, Comfort boarded the train and nestled into a seat beside a window in the parlor car. The train soon began to move, and after a while Comfort looked out at the Hudson River, and watched the towns and woods of New York State pass by.

He was weary, but he knew he couldn't sleep. Relaxing with a couple of drinks, he thought about Millie and how she'd react when he walked in the house.

The train carrying Comfort arrived in the old soot-covered, high-vaulted brown brick Central Avenue station in Rochester at 8:42 that evening.

Bobby grabbed a cab, and twenty-five minutes later he was home.

Millie was rearranging groceries on a shelf; her mother, who now lived with them, sat at the kitchen table.

"Hi, Mom," said Comfort. "Mill—come on upstairs for a minute, I want to show you something." She hadn't yet looked at him.

"Just a minute," she said, placing a can in the rear of the cabinet.

"Mill," he said, "don't you think that can wait? I have something to show you."

Millie gave her husband a leveling glance. "Do I have to drop everything the minute you want something?" She put another can in, closed the cupboard doors, glanced at her mother, then walked past and up the stairs.

Bobby closed the bedroom door behind them, leaning against it until he had Millie's full attention.

She turned and looked at him strangely. "What's going on?" she asked. "You look like a big toy balloon."

200

"I do? Well, watch me deflate."

He stood beside the king-sized bed, put both hands into the pockets of his coat, yanked out handfuls of money, and tossed them on the bed. He dug into his inside coat pockets and extracted more money and threw that on the bed. He shrugged off his coat and dropped it on the nearby recliner.

Millie looked at the money, then back at Bobby in amazement.

"Bobby!" she said.

Comfort began to pull bills from his jacket pockets and then removed the jacket. He dug out the money in the pockets of his pants, opened several buttons of his shirt, and scooped out bills that were padded in next to his body. He shoveled them onto the bed.

Millie stared at the money, which covered the entire bedspread. Then she slowly turned to Bobby.

"You got the Pierre!" She was staring at him.

He smiled and nodded. "How did you know?"

"How dumb do you think I am? Where else could all this come from? It's all over the news. All day long! My God!—"

"There's almost two hundred thousand right there, and we've got—who knows—two, maybe three million more coming."

"This is unbelievable! Bobby, there's going to be *some* investigation. They're not going to give up."

"It was absolutely perfect."

She sat down on the bed. "How did you get home?" she asked apprehensively.

"I took the train," he said, "and grabbed a cab to the house."

"A cab? Why did you do that?"

"Why not?"

"The cab driver could identify you. Why didn't you call me? I would have come to get you!"

"Calm down. There's no way they can connect me with it. All the cops know is, an unknown gang has vanished into thin air."

"Are you sure?"

"I'm sure."

"I hope you're right," she said. She looked at the money. "I'm glad you have it. I'd be lying if I said anything else."

"This'll be enough to take care of us for the rest of our lives. I'll never have to do another job. Never. And this is your money— you can do anything you want with it."

Bobby now was standing in front of Millie, and enjoying her turn of mood. His eyes took in his wife.

He watched her as she reached out and picked up a handful of bills and let them flutter through her fingers. "If the bank was open, I'd run right down and put all this in the vault—every single dollar of it," she said.

"I guess you'll have to wait until morning," he said.

He playfully pushed her down on the bed. She tried to wriggle from him, half teasing, and as they tossed about, he managed to pull the sash of her dress. After a moment he had her pinned. She gave up willingly, and laughingly.

"Bobby," she said, coyly tilting her head to the side, "do you mean it this time? Is all this money mine?"

"I said it was, didn't I?"

She reached up and brought him down to her. The money crackled beneath them, and the fifties and hundreds danced all over the bed and fluttered to the floor.

Bobby Comfort wanted to be seen in town that night. It was important to have people know that, on the day of the crime, he was safely ensconced in Rochester—even if it was as long as fifteen or more hours after the crime. It was still January 2. And it was more than three hundred miles away from the plush lobby and the steel vault of the Hotel Pierre.

He showered, shaved, and drove with Millie to the Fontaine-bleau, a restaurant owned by a friend in downtown Rochester.

The Pierre robbery was the major topic of conversation among Comfort's friends at the restaurant.

He recalled them saying, "Did you see the score they pulled off in New York? The news said they got five million."

" 'I wish it had been me,' I said.

"I remember one guy saying, 'Bob, you're good, but you'd never get one like that. That's a once-in-a-lifetime job. Nobody'll ever get it again.'

"It was big news. I was feeling good. No clues, nothing. Of course, I didn't believe everything I heard, but I knew they *shouldn't* have any clues. We had been extremely careful.

"I hadn't planned on selling any of the Pierre stuff for maybe a year. Then I'd sell only a piece whenever there was a need for money. We had five guys, and probably five hundred stones apiece. I could put them in a small bag and use them for the rest of my life. And every year the value increases 15 percent. I'd never have to go into business; I'd have my business right in that little bag in the basement. I had a hundred and eighty thousand in cash on hand, and two million in gems. What could possibly go wrong?"

◆ **26** ◆

Bobby Comfort slept the sleep of a contented man. He rose at noon, put on his navy blue silk monogrammed robe and slippers, and went downstairs. He was anxious to read of his exploits in the morning paper. Millie had been up for hours with Nicole and was now at the stove preparing eggs; the coffee was perking. Nicole was sitting on the floor coloring in a book. Bobby leaned down and kissed her.

He looked up at Millie. "Coffee smells good," he said.

"It'll be ready in a minute," she said.

The paper was lying open on the kitchen table, and the bold headline told of the daring Pierre theft. Comfort picked up the paper and scanned the story—nothing new or different from what he had heard on the radio and TV reports. He was about to turn the page when his eye fell upon a small headline at the bottom of the front page:

POLICE FIND A CLUE IN
ROBBERY AT PIERRE HOTEL

Comfort started. He pulled off his glasses, and brought the paper closer. The story read:

> . . . Spreading a dust used for detection of fingerprints, the police came up with a stray print. There was a flurry of excitement. But things calmed down when the fingerprint was discovered to be that of one of the technicians dusting for fingerprints.

Bobby laughed, more relieved than amused. He called to Millie. She had just dropped two slices of bread into the toaster.

"Take a look at this," he said, pointing to the headline at the bottom of the page.

She padded over in her slippers and picked up the paper. She smiled. "I know, I saw it."

"That's just the way the cops work," said Comfort. "They're so damn careless. We all wore gloves. Fingerprints! You know the only way the cops ever catch anyone is by informers. Did you ever hear of them actually tracking down a criminal?"

"There are good cops like there are good mechanics or good teachers," she said. "The point is whether they catch the criminals—that's what their job's all about. So they use an informer. So what? The criminal still winds up behind bars, doesn't he?"

She didn't understand law officers, he thought, how could she? She didn't know their mentality as he did. He was feeling too good to argue, and returned to the paper.

When the robbers left the Pierre, he read, one of the captives who was not handcuffed ran to Fifth Avenue, where he hailed a passing squad car.

Finding the foyer full of bound captives, one of the policemen radioed to the 19th Precinct for assistance. Within an hour the hotel was swarming with detectives and cops, and, before much more time had elapsed, newspaper reporters, photographers, and TV crews crowded the premises of the hotel. Members of the police laboratory spent the entire day dusting the lobby furnishings, the vault doors, safe-deposit boxes, and the elevators for prints. The FBI was also called in, since it was assumed that the loot might have been taken across state lines.

Each of the hostages was interrogated to the point of weariness. The captives, including the security guards, said the action had been so quick they were unable to get a good look at the thieves. Most of them had been taken by surprise from behind. Of all the victims the Brazilian lawyer, Helio Fragas, seemed the most articulate. "I was so scared," he later told reporters. "They kept telling me not to look at anyone, so I didn't. The people in the room were sitting on the floor, very quiet. One man, obviously the leader, sat at a desk, a gun in his hand. He kept repeating, over and over, 'We don't want to hurt anyone. Don't look at us.'"

The first police alarm, an all-points bulletin, described at least the first three bandits (all armed) as

1. About 5-feet-5, 145 pounds, late 30s, clean-shaven, well-dressed, wearing gold-rimmed glasses and false nose.
2. About 5-feet-11, 180 pounds, 30 to 35 years old, dark hair, bushy sideburns, neatly trimmed mustache and beard, dark suit and topcoat, hat pulled down to eyebrows.
3. About 5-feet-6, slim, swarthy, softspoken, wearing dark hat, black suit, topcoat.

A fourth member of the gang was described only as being six feet tall with a swarthy complexion.

One of them was described as having a Southern accent. That can only be me, Comfort thought; it's like the Annenberg woman at One Sutton Place who told the cops that I had a foreign accent.

"Mill," Bobby said, looking up, "do you think I talk funny?"

"You *look* funny—does that count?"

Rubbing elbows with wealthy dowagers in the Pierre corridors were detectives from three new specialized police units: the Fourth Detective Division Robbery Squad; a forty-man major-crime unit set up recently; and a new unit whose specialty was the detection

206

and pursuit of criminals whose chief targets were New York hotels. Comfort and Sammy, who by this time had robbed some forty hotels, were the specific reason that the hotel unit had been formed.

The old precinct detective squads had been disbanded, and specialized detective squads were being used to investigate major crimes.

Chief Albert Seedman announced that for the Pierre case his forty-man force had been augmented by twenty-five FBI agents from the New York office. When a special hot-line number was established, the cops were inundated by phone calls. Every tip had to be investigated.

"One man had been standing at a bar," Deputy Police Commissioner Robert Daley would write, "and the man next to him withdrew money, and out flopped a rubber nose. The two stared down at the rubber nose on the floor, then the guy picked it up, rammed it into his pocket, and left the bar.

"There must have been dozens of calls referring to rubber noses. Every person in the city who owned a rubber nose became a suspect."

Chief Seedman told interviewers, "This job was not performed by virgins." The thieves were characterized by police as "seasoned professionals." "Their pictures are somewhere in our files," said another senior police official.

Detectives went through the hotel, knocking on doors, asking questions, scouring for clues.

A full accounting of all stolen property had to be made, in order that reports could be circulated to major-city police agencies.

The original police estimates of the losses ranged from between $1.2 million and $4 million. "But some Pierre residents," reported Eric Pace in the *New York Times*, "have said that the total value of the loot might reach $10 million."

Out-of-town Pierre residents were called in Palm Springs and Palm Beach, the French Riviera, the Costa del Sol, and Acapulco, and advised of the theft of their safe-deposit boxes. Inventories of the contents that had possibly been in their boxes were registered.

Detectives, accompanied by owners of the looted boxes, checked out Cartier's, Tiffany's, Harry Winston, Van Cleef and Arpels, and other jewelry stores in Manhattan. The detectives sought photographs of all specially designed jewelry pieces that could be secured.

The police were well aware that gems could be transported swiftly out of the city or the country.

From long experience the police knew of jewel thieves' "travel points"; booty could be shipped from New York to Miami or Puerto Rico, then on to South America or Europe, all in ten hours.

Of all the victims the biggest loser seemed to be Gabriele Lagerwall, the café-society figure. Mrs. Lagerwall estimated her loss in the neighborhood of two million dollars. Deputy Police Commissioner Daley in his memoir, *Target Blue*, described the scene in her apartment shortly after the robbery: "The detectives sat around a coffee table on which reposed photos of her fabulous jewels. Some were missing. Some she thought might be in a safe-deposit box elsewhere. One piece, originally reported missing, had turned up in the pocket of her bathrobe. She was a woman somewhere over forty, with very white skin and an opulent bosom. Although it was the middle of the afternoon, she was wearing an extremely low-cut dress. . . . The detectives couldn't take their eyes off her. . . ."

The crime did not seem to outrage the public; rather, people appeared amused, even titillated by each new development. "Possibly not a soul in the city felt sorry for Mrs. Lagerwall or any of the other 'victims,' and to many spectators this seemed an almost benign crime," wrote Daley. "All that seems lacking is proof that the robbers intended to endow a research hospital, or a home for delinquent boys. Once this proof came in, the applause could commence.

"Unfortunately, however, the rape of the Hotel Pierre was a callous, cold-blooded crime, perpetrated by vicious men. It was not the kind of thing which, in the movies, would be engineered and carried out by some courtly, bungling actor such as Peter Ustinov; and it did not seem likely that the criminals would be brought to justice in time for the next popcorn break."

In a few days Comfort read newspaper stories that confirmed his ideas of people admiring and delighting in the obvious success of the daring bandits.

A *New York Times* news summary read:

PIERRE CAPER: CRASHING THE GATE AT A JOLLY STOCKADE

... The place is a sort of jolly stockade for the old rich, the new rich, and the would-be rich as well. ... For years, the hotel's most obvious security worry was keeping uninvited youths from crashing its debutante balls. ... The greatest gate-crashers of all passed through the portals at four A.M. last Sunday [and] had a ball. They were well-dressed, youngish-looking fellows, and, as hotel founder Charles Pierre might put it, they showed a certain *savoir* at their *metier.*

In the *New York Post*, columnist Pete Hamill wrote:

The holdup at the Hotel Pierre was beautiful. Nobody got hurt. The pre-war amenities were scrupulously observed. The robbers got away with something like ten million dollars, and maybe more; and when it was over everybody in New York felt better, except the people who got robbed.

In a time when junkies hit old ladies in elevators for fourteen-dollars-and-change or come in the back window looking for the silverware you got one piece at a time at the RKO Prospect in 1951, something this well organized, so minimally violent, and so grand in scale could only be applauded.

With tongue in cheek he went on to suggest that these crooks should work for the city and start the "Robin Hood Division of the Controller's Office": to rob from the rich and give to the poor to alleviate some of New York's financial burdens.

"After all," Hamill continued, "Washington and Albany have been robbing us blind, anyway, taking much more in taxes than they give in services."

One of the situations that developed in the aftermath of the robbery centered around John Keeney, the Pierre's security chief, a former New York City detective. He had not been on duty that fateful night.

Keeney felt compelled to defend himself and his security guards. He had to have been distressed, and tried vainly to maintain a brave front.

"This hotel has the best security in the city," he told reporters who had hurried to the scene. "We have more men per square foot than any other hotel, but if guys get the drop on you, well, there's really nothing you can do."

Keeney, standing in the anteroom at the exact spot where the employees and guests had been held captive by the gunmen, said that one boxholder had called from Rome and was told his valuables were untouched. "They were happy over there, dancing down the Via Veneto because they didn't get hit," he said jauntily.

When asked to estimate the dollar loss to the victims, Keeney joked half-heartedly: "It's like the market—flexible. And at the moment, it's going up."

Observing Keeney's banter with the newsmen were the president and vice-president of the hotel, both looking extremely glum. And behind *them* was NYPD Lieutenant Edward O'Connor observing them watch Keeney with distaste. O'Connor, head of the new hotel detective unit, felt sorry for Keeney who, he realized, was trying to slither out of a difficult situation gracefully. O'Connor shook his head and walked away.

Within a few hours Keeney was summarily fired.

Jimmy Weeda, the security guard who had opened the door to the robbers, was a softspoken, dreamy-eyed man in his late fifties, with white hair, reddish face, double chin, sloping stomach, and muffled speech.

When a reporter asked him a question about the robbery, he lowered his eyes. "I'm not allowed to give any publicity," he said. "I don't want to lose my job."

The reporter persisted. Weeda, seemingly intimidated, began to offer some information, when another security guard came up behind him, yanked him by the arm, and pulled him away, berating him for speaking with a reporter. Weeda nodded and accepted the reprimand.

On late Monday morning, January 3, while the Pierre was besieged by press and law-enforcement officials, FBI man Joe Holliday and his wife, Linda, were leisurely driving back to the New

York area after a long Christmas vacation in New England. As they moved along the highway, he turned on the car radio. Within minutes they heard the news of the robbery in Manhattan.

Riveted, they listened to the sketchy details. At the conclusion of the report, she looked at him and asked, "Who do you think did it?"

"I don't know," he replied, "but I have a pretty good idea what I'll be doing for the next couple of weeks."

What the lean young FBI agent and Syracuse University graduate understood was that he, like the other twenty-five men in his Major Theft and Fugitive Investigation Section, would drop all activities and concentrate on this sensational multimillion-dollar hotel robbery.

When Holliday reached New York, he called headquarters. "Get some rest," he was told, "because tomorrow we've got a lot of work for you. Nothing else gets done until this thing is resolved."

The next morning, even before sunup, Holliday was ready and eager to start on the case. It was this kind of energy that had influenced his boss, Leo McGillicuddy, to put Holliday on another notorious jewel robbery, the Sophia Loren case. He had been in the section only a few months when McGillicuddy had passed the word to "give the ticket to Holliday." Both flattered and apprehensive, Joe Holliday had continued to pursue leads since the Loren robbery a year and a half before. He had been in touch with the actress whenever new evidence surfaced.

A highly dependable FBI informer had tipped Holliday to two New Jersey hoods as suspects who, the source said, had been involved in the Loren robbery. Vincent Morris and Joseph Fernandez had been apprehended by Holliday and held over for possible identification, awaiting Loren's arrival from abroad.

On her return to New York, Loren was shown mug shots of the two suspects. Later, at the line-up, the actress, her secretary, her maid, the hotel bellhop, and the night manager all concurred that Morris and Fernandez were two of the participants that early Sunday morning in November.

Despite the pleadings of the two men, they were held over and subsequently indicted by a federal grand jury for the robbery; but months later the charges against them were quietly dropped when other sources revealed the names of "Sammy the Arab" and his partner, "Bobby," as the actual perpetrators. The ultimate crime for Morris and Fernandez was their close resemblance to the men who did the job. Holliday, with no evidence to justify an arrest, did not want to make another mistake.

Obviously, the misidentification by Loren, her entourage, and others, was the result of their desire to cooperate with the authorities who seemed so enthusiastic about having caught the jewel thieves.

Holliday now climbed into his car and began the drive to the FBI's East Side office. He went over in his mind the list of some thirty jewel thieves he had been tracking for the last two years. Perhaps the Pierre gang was in that file of thirty, and perhaps this time they had made the slip that would finally nail them.

◆ 27 ◆

Wednesday morning, January 5, 1972, Rochester

The blue wall phone in the Comfort kitchen was ringing. Bobby, seated at the table only a few feet away, stirred his coffee and let the phone ring.

"Don't you hear something?" asked Millie, taking a carton of orange juice from the refrigerator on the other side of the room.

"Uh-huh," said Bobby.

"So why don't you just pick it up? You're closer to it."

"I'm sitting, you're standing," he said.

"So stop sitting."

"I'm comfortable."

She walked to the phone, shaking her head.

"It's for you," she said. Comfort immediately became aware of an uneasiness in her tone. She had recognized the voice on the other end and knew better than to mention the name. Stretching the long, coiled cord, Millie handed Bobby the phone.

"Hello," said Comfort, looking questioningly at Millie.

213

"Take down this number." It was Sammy.

"Wait a minute."

One of Nicole's crayons was on the table. Comfort grabbed it, then said, "Go ahead." He wrote the number down on the margin of a page in his daughter's coloring book.

"Call me in fifteen minutes," Sammy said.

Comfort looked at his watch: 10:40.

"Okay." Comfort handed the phone back to Millie.

She looked at him inquisitively.

Neither had expected Sammy to call.

"He wants me to call him from another phone," Comfort said.

"Didn't he sound a little strange?" she asked.

"No stranger than usual," he said, smiling.

"I hope you're right, Bob," she said.

"I'll be back in a little while," he said, "there's nothing to worry about."

But Comfort was concerned. What the hell did Sammy want? He went upstairs, dressed, and drove to Perinton Plaza, a few miles away.

At the Star supermarket in the shopping mall, he changed five dollars into coins, anticipating that the phone call might not be a short one.

Six phones were lined up side by side on a brick wall in the quiet enclosed mall. Comfort went to the end phone and waited a few minutes. At 10:55 he began to dial.

Sammy picked up on the first ring.

"Yeah?" said Sammy.

"Sammy?"

"This isn't Sammy, this is Mike. Sammy's my cousin."

"Okay, Mike," said Comfort. "What's the problem? I thought I wasn't going to be hearing from you for a while."

"I gotta get rid of some of the ice. I owe the Shylocks."

"Jesus Christ! Didn't you take care of that shit with what you got?"

"It wasn't enough," said Sammy.

"What the hell do you want me to do?"

214

"I want you to come down."

"Are you nuts?"

"I'm in trouble. I don't want to unload any of the stuff without you."

Comfort rapidly considered the risks involved in a trip to New York. Even though no clues had been found, it would be sheer stupidity to return so soon. Yet Comfort was confident his partner wouldn't jeopardize their situation needlessly; he was too cautious for that. Sammy's situation had to be serious.

"When do you want me?"

"Today?" Sammy asked. His voice was plaintive.

"How are you going to dump it?"

"I already made a connection." He outlined his plan and assured Bobby that the fencing exchange would be handled smoothly.

"You don't waste any time, do you?"

"I can't afford to," said Sammy. "The guys are after me, and I've gotta give." Then after a moment. "Well? . . ."

"All right," said Comfort.

Sammy said, "See you later," and hung up.

The last thing on Comfort's mind at this point was to be around those jewels, even if they were loose stones. It was too soon after the robbery, and they were too hot. Although neither he nor Sammy had been dealing directly with fences since the Sophia Loren job, Comfort wondered why Sammy had asked him to come down with a "go-between." It could be that Sammy's contacts suspected the jewels came from the Pierre robbery, were too nervous and had turned down the deal to fence the gems. But if Comfort brought a messenger with him, there'd be no hassle.

Comfort stopped speculating and drove to Dom Paulino's apartment on the north side of the city. Paulino was a close friend of Comfort's.

Comfort rang the bell. Dom, built like an ambulatory fireplug, answered the door in his pajamas, his curly hair uncombed.

"Gee, Bob," he said, squinting, "don't you realize you're waking people up in the middle of the day?"

Comfort smiled. He enjoyed Paulino. "Well, it's important. And you can make some easy money."

Inside the apartment, over a fresh pot of coffee, Comfort explained that he had been behind the Pierre hit, that there was an urgency now, and convinced Dom to accompany him to New York at once. He readily accepted the 5 percent fee Comfort offered him for the transfer of the gems as a good deal for himself.

Comfort finished his cigarette and headed out the door for home.

"Pick me up at twelve-fifteen, we'll make the one thirty-two to LaGuardia," Comfort told Dom, clapping him on the shoulder.

Comfort arrived home, walked into the kitchen, and told Millie that he was heading back to New York for a few days.

"You're going where? New York? Now? You just got home!"

"Mill, wait a—"

"Are you out of your mind?" she said.

"I've got to, Mill, Sammy—"

"Sammy, shit! The only thing you've got to do is stay home. Sammy calls and wants you to risk everything. He calls and you go. You can't take the chance. Don't be a fool."

"Millie, look," he said calmly, "Sammy's my friend, he's got a problem."

"You always choose your friends over your family. They'd sell you down the river for a buck. Sammy's no different."

"Sammy's been a good friend . . ."

"If he's such a good friend," she countered, "he wouldn't be asking you to go back to New York."

He had seen her angry before, and he knew that the storm would pass. He rose from his chair and gathered her into his arms. Stroking her soft hair, he said slowly, "Millie, listen, there's nothing they can pin on me. I'll just be a guy in the city on a little vacation."

He cupped her chin in his hand and forced her to look directly at him. "Millie," he said, "don't ever think that anybody in the world is more important to me than you and the baby."

Millie stepped back slowly, willing herself to be calmer.

"Bobby," she said, "I'm worried, I don't like it, I don't like the feel of it. Call it woman's intuition or anything you like. I'm asking you not to go."

"Mill, I've got to go. Everything is going to be all right. Look, after it's all over you come on down and meet me, and we'll spend a few days with Joe and Rosie. Mom can take care of Nicole. It'll be good for you, and we'll be alone for a change—okay? Look at me. Okay?"

She gave him a long look. His words had deflated her. The argument and the venom had all been spent. She shook her head, took a cigarette, and lit it.

Comfort went upstairs to pack.

◆ 28 ◆

Wednesday, January 5, 1972, New York City

From the moment the plane landed and hummed to a stand-still at LaGuardia, Bobby Comfort had an uneasy feeling. He couldn't quite pinpoint it, but it was there. He mentioned it to Paulino in the cab that was taking them through the marshmallow-white Queens Midtown Tunnel.

"You're a private citizen," said Paulino. "You can come and go as you please in this town or anywhere else."

"I know that, but I'm having second thoughts about coming," said Comfort quietly. "I've got to be a suspect. The FBI's got to be thinking about me—maybe not primarily about me—but I've got to be on their minds."

"Relax, Bob," said Paulino. "There's no clues. You read that in the papers."

"And something else is bothering me."

"What's that?" Paulino asked.

"Millie. She really gave me hell for coming down here. Never saw her that mad. It was like she knew something."

They emerged from the tunnel onto Thirty-seventh Street and continued across town to the Royal Manhattan Hotel on Forty-fifth Street and Eighth Avenue, close to Sammy's midtown apartment. They moved into the lobby with their bags, and Dom signed the register D. Paulino and R. Paulino, New York. They proceeded to the elevator and ascended to 1553, a large double room overlooking Eighth Avenue.

Sammy Nalo, Dom Paulino, and Bobby Comfort had lunch later that afternoon and organized the scenario for the exchange that was to take place the following day if every detail could be arranged.

In a series of calls from a pay phone on the windy corner of Forty-fifth Street and Ninth Avenue, arrangements were coming together for the fencing of some fifty stones.

Comfort recalled:

"Sammy phoned his contact, Bertram Stern. I didn't know him, but Sammy had had previous business dealings with him. Stern had rented space in the jewelers' exchange with a hot-shot international operator whose name was Harry Towson. Sammy had been told by Stern that Towson had excellent overseas connections for unloading gems. It sounded easy. Stern had contacted Towson. Towson said he'd talk to his people and get back to Stern as soon as possible the next day.

"In the morning we walked to the corner of Forty-third Street and Eleventh Avenue, near the Market Diner, one of our hangouts, and waited in the cold public telephone booth for the call from Stern. Sammy had given Stern the number.

"The call came in at about twelve," said Comfort. "Stern was to meet Towson at the Cattleman restaurant for lunch at one o'clock. Towson's friend, Tom somebody-or-other, would be along. Tom was the broker for the buyer, and wanted to meet with Stern for easy recognition on the next day. The arrangements were to be worked out then.

"After lunch Stern was to come to the Royal Manhattan and meet us at four o'clock to tell us what the arrangements were for the sale."

Comfort still had a strange premonition that he could not shake. As he walked down Eighth Avenue with Paulino later that day, he would stop and furtively peer over his shoulder to see if they were being followed. He lingered at store windows and watched for reflections.

There was justification for Comfort's anxiety. The Pierre story was still prominent in news coverage, and remained of great interest around the city.

As agreed, Towson met for lunch with his messenger, Stern, and the buyer's man, Tom, at the Cattleman at one o'clock. In a booth beside a frosted-glass partition, they discussed the arrangements that would culminate in the exchange of the jewels on the following day.

Bert Stern left directly after lunch and walked across town to the Royal Manhattan Hotel bar to give the final details to Sammy.

Stern was to arrange for an appraiser to accompany him, and meet with Towson in the lobby of the Summit Hotel at Fifty-first and Lexington Avenue at noon the next day.

Stern, a tall, thin, long-necked man of about thirty-five, wearing a shiny blue suit, moved through the revolving door of the Royal Manhattan Hotel's street-side bar and grill. He recognized Sammy, who sat with two other men in the shadows of a booth. There were brief introductions. Comfort and Paulino remained silent, while Sammy discussed the plan for the next day. After the time and place had been delineated, Sammy pointed to Paulino and told Stern, who was nervously arranging and rearranging his napkin, that Paulino would be the "carrier" bringing the stones. Everybody understood the roles they were to play.

When Stern departed, Comfort turned to Sammy.

"I don't like it," Comfort said. "This guy is scared shitless."

"This guy is good," Sammy countered. "I'm tellin' you, it's safe. Don't get so excited. For a change you're the one who's too conservative. Looks like you've picked up some of my habits."

The partners left Paulino at the bar and walked out to Sammy's white Ford Galaxie parked at a meter on Forty-fifth Street.

Before Sammy got in the car, he said to Comfort, "I'm gonna call City and have him hold the rest of the jewels until the business at the Summit is finished."

That surprised Comfort.

220

"Why give it to him? The stuff is safe in your place, isn't it?" he asked.

"I don't know. There's never been this kind of heat for any of our other jobs—you never know what they could come up with. They've had their eye on us since Loren. I just don't want anyone ripping my place apart and finding the satchel. So I'd just like to get it out of there, until we know everything's okay after the Summit. Unless"—and Sammy paused—"unless *you* want to hold it. It's only a few days."

"I don't want to hold it! Okay, there's no heat on City, that's what you're saying. He's clean."

"Right," said Sammy. "We'll go together. I'll call him, then call you later."

Sammy climbed into his car and pulled away. As Comfort began the walk back to the hotel, he thought he saw two men watching him from across the street. He walked past the Royal Manhattan, and one of the men moved as he did. They're following me, Comfort thought. He quickened his pace and, upon turning the corner, dashed down Forty-fifth Street, cut through Shubert Alley, crossed Forty-third Street, then on to Times Square. There he was swallowed up by the crowds. He knew that no one could follow him through that maze.

Just before midnight Sammy and Comfort, in the white Ford, pulled up in front of Stark's coffee shop on Madison Avenue. A black Chevy Impala stopped right behind. It was City.

The three men entered the coffee shop, seeking out the farthest booth to settle into.

"You gotta hang onto the ice for a while," said Sammy.

"Why?" asked City. When it was explained, he said, "I don't want to hold this stuff. I don't live in the best section, maybe somebody robs me. Are you going to believe it? You'll come around and kill me."

"Look," Comfort said, "we're not worried. We're giving you the bag because we know it's in good hands."

"It'll just be for a while—tonight and tomorrow morning. Then we'll pick it up," said Sammy.

"I don't like it," City said. "But okay."

They finished their coffee and walked out. Sammy opened his car trunk, removed the heavy black satchel, and deposited it in City's trunk. He slammed it shut. They watched City drive off, the red taillights receding in the uptown traffic.

◆ 29 ◆

Friday, January 7, 1972, New York City

His face grim, Sammy entered Comfort's Royal Manhattan Hotel room to deposit the stones. They were wrapped in tissue paper and folded in a handkerchief.

"This is worth about a quarter of a million," said Sammy, placing the packet on the dresser top.

"I just want this over with as soon as possible," Comfort said.

Sammy looked around. "Where's Dom?"

"In the john."

"Okay. I'm leaving now. I'll call you later." And Sammy was gone.

Around eleven o'clock Paulino went down to the lobby, walked to the desk, and advised the clerk that they'd be checking out before four that afternoon. He paid the hotel bill and pocketed the receipt.

He figured that would save time on his return; he realized that the sooner they left New York the faster Comfort's uneasiness would dissipate.

Earlier Paulino had called Stern to make certain no changes had occurred since the day before. It was on. The exchange would go as scheduled.

Paulino hailed a cab. Knowing crosstown traffic in New York was uncertain, he preferred to arrive a little early.

Left alone to wait out the events, Comfort, with time on his hands, went downstairs for cigarettes and the papers. He returned to the room, read the latest Pierre news, then settled back to watch TV and wait for Paulino.

On his arrival at the Summit, Paulino greeted Stern, who was standing and talking to two men on the sidewalk. The man in a black coat and hound's-tooth hat was Benjamin Fradkin, the appraiser. With rounded shoulders, and stooping slightly, he appeared to have spent a lifetime working over a diamond cutter's wheel. The other man was Harry Towson, middle-aged, with glasses, and wearing a camel's-hair coat.

The four men entered the lobby of the hotel and were introduced by Towson to Tom Jones, the contact for the buyers.

Jones gave the key to Room 1544 to Stern and told him to go upstairs and check to see if everything was okay. Stern returned in five minutes and nodded. Jones walked toward the bank of phones in the lobby to make his call, advising his "money people" that everything was ready for the exchange.

Upon his return Jones instructed Paulino and Fradkin to go up to the room to await his people. Fradkin relinquished the key to Paulino, and then, accompanied by Jones and Towson, disappeared into the Cork 'n' Bottle bar for a short drink, their mission accomplished.

Paulino and Fradkin walked through the lobby, entered the elevator, and went to the fifteenth-floor room.

Ten minutes later Stern, Towson, and Jones came out of the bar toward the Summit's Lexington Avenue entrance. They said perfunctory good-byes and parted, leaving Jones in the lobby.

Instantly, two policemen came up behind Stern, grabbed him, pinned his arms, handcuffed him, and forced him into a waiting unmarked squad car. The arrest took fifteen seconds. It was handled so deftly that it went virtually unnoticed by noontime passersby. As the terrified Stern was unceremoniously dumped into the rear seat of the police sedan, he glanced wide-eyed out of the car window. In amazement he saw Harry Towson walking blithely up Lexington Avenue, oblivious to his plight. The shaken Stern was utterly mystified as to why this was happening to him.

Looking out from the lobby, Jones saw the arrest. He went immediately to a house phone and placed a call. It was to Room 1546. Two FBI agents and two plainclothesmen were there, and had been listening with an electronic bugging device to conversations emanating from Room 1544. They were awaiting the call from Jones to make their move to the room next door.

"Okay," said Lieutenant Edward O'Connor, putting down the phone, "let's take 'em."

With guns drawn the four officers burst into Room 1544. "Everybody's under arrest!" one cop shouted.

Paulino and Fradkin shot their arms over their heads as if released by springs. In shock, they stood stiff as robots.

The blood had drained from Fradkin's face. "I—I don't know—I'm just an appraiser," said Fradkin. "God almighty— what is—"

"Where's the rest of the gang?" hollered one of the cops. "We know you robbed these stones—we know where they're from."

On the round table in the middle of the room was the open white handkerchief, revealing fifty-two sparkling stones. Beside it was Fradkin's loupe, his scale, his pad and pencil.

Both men were frisked thoroughly for concealed weapons. "I don't know what the hell this is all about," said Paulino.

Fradkin and Paulino were handcuffed and whisked downstairs, out into a waiting squad car, and driven to the FBI office on Sixty-ninth Street, headquarters of the joint investigation between the FBI and the New York City Police Department.

The capture had uncovered nothing conclusively linking the loose diamonds—which were unidentifiable—with the Pierre robbery. Towson had told the FBI that he was certain this was part of the Pierre loot. The authorities could only speculate that these stones had been part of the stolen jewelry.

The suspects were pushed into a small interrogation room

and searched. The lawmen deduced that the elderly Fradkin was an unlikely crook. He was soon eliminated from suspicion.

Stern appeared as though he could be part of the gang. They would hold him over.

Dom Paulino appeared to be a tough guy. His mannerisms suggested previous police confrontations. After giving his name, he said he knew nothing, and remained silent.

Paulino didn't have to speak. In his jacket pocket the room receipt from the Royal Manhattan Hotel was found. It was stamped "$60 PAID Jan. 7, 1972, Room 1553, D. Paulino and R. Paulino." Lieutenant O'Connor, examining the receipt, picked up the phone and hastily placed some calls.

To O'Connor this small detail, this one slip of paper, the receipt, could be the clue to lead the authorities to the mastermind of the Hotel Pierre robbery.

◆ 30 ◆

Within minutes two squad cars responding to a call from O'Connor pulled up in front of the entrance to the Royal Manhattan Hotel. They showed their shields to the fifteenth-floor chambermaid. Her eyes widened and filled with fright.

"It's okay," said Detective Joe Gannon, a burly Irishman, "nothing will happen to you. Just knock first and say you're bringing in towels."

Comfort was lying on the bed in shirt and pants watching TV. His sports jacket was draped on a chair nearby. According to Comfort, this is what happened:

"I heard some noise down the hall. There were shuffling sounds.

"In a minute there was a knock on my door. It was the maid with towels for the room. I said we didn't need any because we were leaving. Boom! The door came crashing open. Four guys rushed in. 'Don't move,' they yelled. Their guns were out. Two came over immediately and grabbed me by the shirt and threw me

227

up against the wall. Another guy searched me. 'What is this?' I said. 'Whaddya want?' One of 'em says, 'Shut up.' I see one guy is rifling through my clothes in the closet.

" 'Where is everything?' one guy asks me. I tell him, 'I don't know what you're talkin' about.'

" 'In that case,' he says, 'you're no use to us.' He calls to another guy, 'Hey, open the fuckin' window for this guy.'

"The cop opens the window wide and the cold air blasts in the room, and then they drag me to the window. What the hell is this? Then they lift me up—holy shit!—and they throw me out! But they were gripping me by the ankles. I'm flapping out the window. I'm terrified. I pissed so fast it shot out like a bullet. It must have flown straight past my face because I never remembered getting wet.

"I'm looking straight down, I see people and cars. Everything is swirling. I'm in a state of shock, I'm choking, I can't breathe, I'm scared stiff. One of the cops at the window ledge hollered at me, 'Start talkin'.' Talk? I felt like my vocal cords were falling out of my mouth. I'm struggling to get some words out. I squeaked, 'Talk about what?' He says, 'You know what, just start talkin' about your robberies and when you lie, we're droppin' you.'

"Now there's people down there and they see me and they're waving and hollering something up to me. I don't know what they're doing, I'm trying to save my life by talking normal. 'Talk, you asshole,' he said. I must have sounded like a girl, I don't know why I did it, but I said, 'Go fuck yourself!'

"When they heard that, they shook me like they were going to drop me, but then they pulled me in. They threw me up against the wall again. I'm shaking, I can hardly stand on my feet.

" 'What are these?' the short, stocky cop says to me. They had gone through my jacket in the closet and found two loose diamonds that I had in my change pocket—I was going to have earrings made for a gift for Millie.

"I answered him politely. 'Two diamonds, officer.' I don't think he liked that answer because he said to his buddies, 'Let's kill this motherfucker. Let's drown him in the bathtub.'

" 'We can't yet,' another cop said, 'we haven't read him his rights.' Another cop laughed. 'Yeah, okay. We gotta do that.' One of 'em takes out a little card and says, 'Okay, you asshole, you got a right to remain silent, you got a right to refuse to answer questions. Do you understand?' I nodded yes. I can hardly talk, I'm still breathing hard. He says, 'Anything you say may be used against you in a court of law. You have the right to an attorney. If you can't afford one, you'll have one appointed. Okay? Now, are you willing to make a statement without an attorney being present?"

" 'No,' I said.

" 'We know who you are,' he said. He was holding my I.D. 'This says you're Robert A. Comfort, P.O. Box 149, Attica, New York. You're a fuckin' ex-con, so we don't have to be nice to you.'

"I said, 'Is this what you call being nice to me, throwing me out a window? Who'd you think I was, a doctor? A judge? What kind of remark is that?'

"I was feeling better now. They weren't punching me in the face or kicking me. Obviously, they didn't want to mark me up. They grabbed my jacket. Then they ripped it up looking for more stuff in the lining, but nothing was there. One of the cops said, 'Look at these threads this guy wears. A real expensive sports jacket. Big shot, ain't you?

" 'All right,' he said, 'you think you're gonna get away with something. You ain't gonna get away with nothin'.'

"I said, 'I don't know what you're talkin' about, I don't know what you're here for. I don't know nothing except I'm in my room minding my own business.'

" 'You're pretty smart, ain't you,' the short, fat guy said.

"I said, 'How smart can I be if people are tossing me outta windows and throwing me around in here? I don't know what you're trying to do, but there's gonna be a lot of trouble over this. I want a lawyer.'

" 'You'll get a fucking lawyer, you asshole!' He turned to another guy. 'I told ya that we gotta kill this punk because he's gonna be tough.'

"I asked them, 'What did I do?'

" 'You know what you did.' "

For the next twenty minutes Comfort was questioned. Who

are your partners? Where's the other guy? Who's Paulino?

That was the first hint Comfort had that something was amiss. "He's a friend of mine, that's who he is," he said. "Why?"

The cop said, "When's he coming back?"

"Pretty soon," said Comfort.

But Comfort was confused now. If they were waiting for Paulino, then he couldn't have been arrested. Did they have Sammy?

"Then the telephone rang. One of the cops put a gun to my head and cocked the hammer. He said, 'You say hello. Don't say a fuckin' word except "Everything's okay." '

"He picked up the phone and held it to both our ears," Comfort recalled. "The voice at the other end said, 'How's everything goin'?' It was Sammy. I said, 'Get me a fuckin' lawyer.' And the cop slammed the phone down.

"The cop holding the gun was mad as hell. 'The cocksucker, I told you we couldn't trust him. Who was that?' he said to me. I said, 'Paulino. Maybe he won't come back, because he's going to get me a lawyer.' "

It surprised Comfort that he was taken to FBI headquarters. Why would the New York City police be taking him there? he wondered.

The FBI office at Sixty-ninth Street was a typical government setup, austere, with a dreary gray-and-green interior. Comfort was led past rows of desks and filing cabinets to a small room. They sat him down at a long table. The four plainclothesmen were joined by a police lieutenant, a captain, and several FBI men.

"Looks like we found 'Bobby,' " a police sergeant said to Lieutenant O'Connor.

"It's a start," the hefty officer replied.

One of the interrogators asked Comfort what he did for a living.

He told them he played cards.

"How much do you make a year?"

"Forty to fifty thousand," he replied.

"You must be a skillful player," the FBI man said.

"I'm a skillful cheater."

The FBI agent was intrigued. He produced a deck of cards from the desk, and motioned Comfort to show them how to deal

230

seconds and bottoms and perform the invisible shuffle. They seemed impressed.

Then the grilling took a tougher turn.

Comfort recalled, "A cop named Cohen said, 'We gotta beat the shit out of this guy. When I'm done with him, he'll talk.'

"Then Cohen, this fat little guy, threw me up against the wall and said, 'You gonna start talkin' or what? You lied before, saying Paulino was on the phone. Paulino was in the fuckin' jail when that phone rang. Who was that on the phone?' His face was right up to my face when he said that, and I looked down at him, he was shorter than me, and I spit in his face.

"I said, 'Go ahead, start punching, you asshole. You gonna beat me up and make me talk?' I got mad. I got real mad. There were now three other cops and three FBI guys in there, and I was sure every one of them was going to start beating the hell out of me. My hands were cuffed behind my back. I felt I was in for it. Then this cop named Gannon said, 'C'mon, he'll see reason in a little while—let's not get all excited.'

" 'I've got nothin' to say. I want a lawyer,' " I said. Then I told them I had to go to the john, and two agents escorted me back out into the large outer offices toward the men's room. I broke away, handcuffs and all, and dove under a desk, and began shouting at the top of my lungs. 'They're killing me, they're beating me up. I want a lawyer.' "

The agents scrambled after him and wrestled Comfort from under the desk. Squirming, he was lifted onto his feet. The clerks and typists sat looking aghast at the wild scene. "Everybody's going to be subpoenaed," screamed Comfort. "You're all going to have to swear under oath that this never happened. You're going to have to say that I didn't ask for a lawyer under oath. One of you will tell the truth, and the others'll be perjured."

One of the FBI men plunged a handkerchief into Bobby's mouth. Kicking and mumbling through the gag, he was dragged back to the interrogation room, and the door was slammed shut.

Soon after, Comfort was transferred to the 19th Police Precinct station, where they removed the handcuffs and he underwent more questioning.

Around 7 P.M. one of the cops suggested that they send out

for some food and cigarettes in preparation for a long night session. The others agreed. One of the cops jotted down the food orders and asked Comfort if he wanted anything. He said coffee and a ham cappicollo sandwich.

Half an hour later a delivery man was ushered into the interrogation room, and the sandwiches were distributed to the hungry cops. Gannon called out, "The bill's twelve bucks plus tip." He then proceeded to enumerate individual charges.

"One guy said, 'Hey, I don't owe that much,'" recalled Comfort, "and another guy started arguing with him. They were fighting over this guy owing two cents more, and this guy owing a penny more. I reached into my pocket. I had a roll of a couple hundred on me, so I said to the delivery boy, 'Here, this oughta do it.' I gave him twelve dollars for the bill and a five-dollar tip.

"So Gannon smiled and said, 'See, he's not such a bad guy after all.'"

A natty young black man with reddish hair leaned forward in the rear seat of his official car, and asked, "Isn't there a faster way?"

"I'm sorry, Mr. Lowe, you see the traffic," said his service driver, glancing at him in the rearview mirror. In ten minutes they had traveled barely half a mile uptown from Lowe's downtown office. It was rush hour—and Manhattan traffic was typically snarled. At this rate they wouldn't get to the 19th Precinct on East Sixty-seventh Street for a good hour! The man in the back seat was in a simmering rage.

Richard Lowe was the assistant district attorney in charge of the Pierre robbery case, and the police and federal agents had not advised him of the arrests that had been made until *five* hours after the suspects had been brought in.

And they had arrested them contrary to his direct orders.

For the past forty hours, since they had learned about Stern's meet at the Cattleman restaurant, Lowe had felt the only way to proceed was through a wiretap of Stern's home phone. Lieutenant O'Connor was courteous but remained unconvinced and reluctant to agree. And when Lowe argued with him on the phone, O'Connor said, "Maybe we're stretching the search and seizure, but what are we going to do? What's there to wait for? If we don't move now, we'll have lost them."

What *did* they need to wait for? Evidence, thought Lowe. We've got none. Just a bunch of loose stones, and no way to trace the ownership.

There was nothing concrete on which to build the case. His initial plan was to isolate Stern, who, he presumed, was the one link to the Pierre thieves. He firmly believed he needed this evidence because the feds would be understandably uncooperative were he to request that the FBI produce their informant as a witness, or, at the very least, the FBI undercover agent who had been at the meeting. If these important people were removed from testifying there would be no basis for any arrests.

Why did cops and feds have to go charging ahead like gang-busters? lamented Lowe as he watched the tangle of traffic and listened to the blare of horns.

Arriving at the 19th Precinct, he was ushered into a room where he would interview the defendants individually.

"Do you want to make any statements?" he asked Comfort.

"Yeah, I don't know what's going on," Comfort replied. "I've been asking for a lawyer, and I've been physically abused, and no one has charged me with a crime."

"Do you have anything else to say?" asked Lowe.

"No."

"That's all."

Paulino struck an equally innocent pose, and Fradkin and Stern were so upset, they obviously were dupes of some kind, and surely not daring hotel robbers.

While Lowe was talking with Stern, a patrolman opened the door and called the assistant district attorney outside. "The cop tells me they're holding a press conference downstairs," recalled Lowe. "They're telling reporters that the Pierre robbery case is cracked. I couldn't believe it! Here I am upstairs interviewing the defendants and everyone is telling me to take a flying fuck—and I'm sweating blood because I've got nothing, bubkis—and now they're announcing to the world that it's over!"

233

He rushed downstairs. In a room filled with TV cameras, lights, and photographers snapping shots, Police Commissioner Patrick V. Murphy was standing behind a table with his double chin held high. On the table were fourteen pairs of handcuffs, taken from the Pierre hostages, and several opened cloth pouches containing about fifty small diamonds, taken from Room 1544 of the Summit Hotel. On either side of the table was a shotgun-toting patrolman guarding the table.

"I'm happy to announce that the jewel robbery case at the Pierre Hotel has been broken," said Murphy. Lowe closed his eyes and shook his head.

Murphy said he had "high praise for the FBI's development of leads that led to the arrests."

Lowe muttered to himself. From what he could gather, only one, or maybe two, of the four arrested were in on the Pierre robbery—Comfort and perhaps Paulino. There was no physical evidence, and only a quarter of a million dollars' worth of jewels was uncovered. Where was the other five to ten million, whatever the figure would turn out to be? Now that the cops had moved so swiftly, would *those* jewels disappear with the two, three, or four other robbers still not apprehended? Some arrests! Some press conference! Lowe walked out. He stopped a patrolman in the hallway and asked if anyone had any aspirins around here.

Bobby Comfort was allowed one phone call. He used it to contact Millie. She was expecting to hear from him, but not under these circumstances.

"I've got a little problem here, Millie. Don't say a word, just listen," he said. Briefly, he explained the situation. Before he hung up he said, "Call Rosie and tell her to get me a lawyer. And one other thing." He paused. "If anyone calls and says they want to deliver a package, let me know. It'll help everybody."

She knew that was a caution signal. She assumed it meant that if Sammy called, she would warn him to be careful.

Millie hung up, then dialed Rosie in Yonkers, and relayed the information.

234

* * *

Rosie dressed, hurried to her car, and drove into New York. At the 19th Precinct there was the usual buzz of activity, and she wandered around the offices looking for assistance. She found herself in the doorway of a detective's office when she heard her brother's name mentioned. Speaking on the phone at his desk was Detective Joe Gannon. His back was to her, and he was unaware of her presence.

As Rosie told Bobby later: "He was telling someone, 'No, Comfort's not saying anything. He absolutely refuses to answer any questions. The other guy? The little fat guy, Paulino? All he does is laugh. Neither of 'em are sayin' a word. We haven't got a case.' "

Rosie continued, "When the cop hung up, he turned around and saw me and said, 'Yes, ma'am, can I help you?' I told him, 'I'm Bobby Comfort's sister.' You never saw such a look on anybody's face in your life."

Rosie and Bobby met briefly, and she assured him she would be getting him the best available lawyer.

After being held for over twenty hours, Comfort was finally booked on a charge of first-degree robbery for the two stones found in his jacket pocket. He was taken to the Tombs, the city prison, to await a lineup the next day. Comfort wondered if any real evidence had turned up, or if identification had been made. He was totally unaware of what had transpired at the Summit Hotel, and of what had happened to his friend Paulino and the stones Paulino had carried to the Summit.

He wondered where Sammy was—and if he had left town. And he wondered about City who—he hoped—was holding the black satchel worth as much as $10 million in gems.

◆ 31 ◆

Despite Police Commissioner Murphy's press conference, the FBI and O'Connor's squad were wrestling with a still-uncertain case. However, the FBI and the NYPD Robbery Detail knew they were onto something.

The arrest of Bobby Comfort and the three others with the fifty-two stones at the Summit gave heart to the authorities. They theorized that *Comfort* plus *diamonds* plus *Pierre* could equal *"Sammy the Arab."*

This reasonable extension was fortified by the FBI informant who had identified "Sammy the Arab" as a participant in the Loren jewel robbery with a partner known as "Bobby from Rochester." The police now had Bobby Comfort from Rochester in custody. This was the plus side of the ledger.

The minus side? Well, the elusive "Sammy the Arab," a.k.a. Richard Farmer, Ralph Ballo, Ronny Horowitz, and others—the authorities did not know his true last name—had no known police record, therefore no prints, no mug shots; and information had it that he used as many disguises as aliases.

236

A four-man detail consisting of FBI special agents Joe Holliday and Milt Graham, and NYPD detectives George Bermudez and Ed Fitzgibbons, was assigned the task of tracking down "Sammy the Arab."

Bermudez, a thirty-five-year-old Puerto Rican, spoke Spanish fluently, knew the Bronx and Manhattan intimately, and had numerous contacts in the area.

The FBI insisted upon its continued presence in the ongoing hunt, and this met with no resistance from O'Connor. Having been instrumental in uncovering the fencing at the Summit, through its paid informer, the FBI was "in" to the end. Furthermore, if a capture occurred across state lines, it meant a federal arrest, with all the attendant publicity that would be favorable to the FBI.

The following day, after the orders came down, two unmarked cars with both pairs of investigators pulled up in front of 305 West 45th Street. Holliday had a hunch. Agents had trailed a man fitting Sammy's description to that address and then had lost him. Therefore, Holliday suggested that this should be their first stop.

Bermudez and Holliday entered the vestibule, checked the mailbox for some of his known aliases, or for Middle Eastern names. No luck.

They rang the superintendent's bell. An elderly man appeared.

Bermudez flashed his badge. Holliday described the man they were looking for: short, black hair, dark skin, good dresser.

The super thought for a moment, then nodded. "It's Mr. Farmer."

"What's his apartment number?" asked Holliday.

"4-A."

The officers took the elevator to the fourth floor, knocked on the door, and waited.

A woman's voice answered the door.

"What do you want?"

"We're looking for the man in this apartment."

"He's not here, nobody here but me."

The door opened.

A young dark-haired woman let the men in. She identified herself as Amelia Lemos, from Colombia. She explained that she stayed at the apartment occasionally when the owner was out of town.

She had met the man through her girlfriend.

"When did you last see him?"

" 'Bout a week ago. Sammy is very nice to me."

This was the first time the name Sammy had been mentioned.

"Who is your girlfriend?" asked Bermudez.

"Elena Sorentino."

"Where does she live?"

"On Forty-seventh Street—310 is the number."

"Are you sure?"

"*Sí, sí*, 310 West 47th Street."

The lawmen left and headed to the apartment of Elena Sorentino who, they hoped, would shed more light on "Sammy."

It was 6:30 P.M. In the car, the radio news was full of the arrest of Bobby Comfort and the others as suspects in the Pierre robbery. Bermudez was fully aware that Sammy had to be listening to these same accounts. If Comfort and the others had been caught, he realized that it would be a race to catch Sammy before he left town, or the country, if indeed he hadn't done so already.

The door of the brownstone apartment on Forty-seventh Street was opened by Patrice Sorentino, Elena's sister. Patrice was clad in a halter and short shorts that showed off her well-endowed body. When she learned what Bermudez and Holliday wanted, she called Elena, who emerged from the bedroom in a silk robe. Both girls, as aliens without papers, feared the police and were very cooperative. Bermudez learned that Patrice and Elena had moved from Brazil to New York several years before and were topless dancers at the Metropole on Seventh Avenue. They had come to know Sammy since he frequented the topless-bar circuit. Sammy was a big spender. They liked him.

Bermudez asked Elena if she knew how to reach Sammy.

"No," she said. "I never know, only see him when I dance. Maybe Diana does."

Diana DePeña, another topless dancer, was a friend. Elena called Diana's home. No answer. Then she phoned the AP Talent Agency, their booking agents. She was told that Diana was working at the Circus, a topless bar on Sunrise Highway on Long Island; Holliday asked Elena to call her. Diana was there; she would be finished with work at eight, and, yes, she'd meet Elena at ten o'clock at her own apartment. The conversation between the girls was in Spanish. Bermudez indicated to Holliday that no alarm had been voiced.

At 10 P.M. that night two unmarked cars departed from West 47th Street. Holliday and Bermudez were with Elena in one car, and Fitzgibbons and Graham were in the other car with Patrice. They drove down to 36 East 3rd Street, where Diana DePeña lived.

The two girls got out of the cars and went upstairs to get Diana. The officers reasoned that the girls would help relax Diana, and perhaps get information from her that she might otherwise keep from them. In effect, they enlisted the women as their agents.

Twenty minutes went by. No Diana, and no Elena or Patrice. Holliday climbed out of his car and walked over to Bermudez's car.

"That's enough time, don't you think?" asked Holliday.

Bermudez said, "Yeah, let's get up there."

The front door of the apartment building was locked. They rang the DePeña bell. Nothing. They rang again. The buzzer opened the door. Bermudez and Holliday entered.

The two men climbed three flights of stairs to Diana's apartment. She let them in. Classy-looking, Bermudez thought, especially for a stripper. The other two girls were sitting at the kitchen table.

She was questioned about Sammy.

"I don't know much about him," she said. She seemed scared.

Bermudez said, "Can we talk privately with you for a moment? Just want to ask some routine questions. Nobody will get into any trouble."

Diana and the two officers went into the bedroom and closed the door. Bermudez and Diana sat on her unmade bed; Holliday pulled up a chair. Bermudez said, "We've got to talk to Sammy. It doesn't involve you, you've got nothing to worry about. No one has to know you helped."

Diana said, "Okay, but no one can know."

Bermudez took out a notebook.

"How did you meet Sammy?" Holliday asked.

"Elena," she said. She was trembling slightly.

"Relax, honey," said Bermudez, lighting her cigarette.

"What's Sam's last name?" he asked when the cigarette was lit.

"I don't know," she said.

"When did you see him last?" This was Holliday.

"About two weeks ago. He gave me a beautiful silver fox coat."

"Did you meet any of his friends?" Holliday asked.

"Someone named Bobby and his wife, Millie."

"Anyone else?"

She inhaled her cigarette and added, "I met Walter Leavitt. He made my coat on Seventh Avenue."

Bermudez asked, "Where did you go with Sammy?"

"Lot of clubs, track . . . I don't know his business except he say he is going to open a nightclub. And I've been to his place on Forty-fifth Street."

"Do you know where he is now?"

"No, I was supposed to have dinner with him on Wednesday, but he never showed up. But that's like Sam. He's mysterious. He disappears for days—weeks . . ."

"Did he say anything to you about leaving town?"

"No."

Bermudez said to Holliday, "What now?"

Holliday turned to Diana. "How often have you been to Sam's other apartment? I don't mean the one on Forty-fifth Street," he said.

"Just once," she said. "About six months ago."

Bermudez wrote that down without acknowledging his surprise. Neither of the men had known that Sammy had another apartment; Bermudez immediately realized that Holliday had taken a wild guess—and it had paid off.

Holliday said nothing, knowing that silence could sometimes be the best catalyst for gaining information. Bermudez stopped writing and slowly looked up.

"Do you know the address?" Bermudez asked.

"I'm not sure where it is," she said. "Somewhere in the Bronx."

"Do you know the area?" asked Bermudez.

"It's on a hill. But I don't remember nothing else."

"Would you mind if we drove you around the Bronx? Maybe you'd recognize the building."

"I don't want to hurt nobody and I don't want to be hurt," she said. "Sammy knows rough people."

"No harm will come to you, Diana," said Holliday. "You're safe. We promise you that."

She got her coat, the silver fox. They called in for a squad car to drive the other women back home. It was 11:45 P.M., Saturday, January 8.

Fitzgibbons and Graham in their car followed Bermudez with Holliday beside him and Diana DePeña in the back seat. Speaking in Spanish, Bermudez continued trying to jog the girl's memory for the location of Sammy's apartment. As they approached the Major Deegan Expressway, Diana said, "I remember a firehouse near his place."

"A firehouse near a hill," said Bermudez, brightening. "I think I know the area you're talkin' about."

He was thinking of "Hollywood Harry." "Harry's factory was near a firehouse," Bermudez said to Holliday, "and it was hilly."

Hollywood Harry, or Harold Munger, had been a major dope dealer operating out of a warehouse in the Woodcrest section, by far the hilliest area in the Bronx.

Bermudez had helped break the Hollywood Harry case, and had spent several weeks driving around the area.

They now turned onto the Major Deegan Expressway; in a few minutes they pulled off at the 161st Street ramp, near Yankee Stadium. In the night shadows Yankee Stadium, under reconstruction and with the seats torn out in the grandstands, looked more like the ruins of the Colosseum than a great ballpark. They drove past the stadium, onto the Grand Concourse, then turned around at Macombs Dam Park.

The first side street they came to was Anderson Avenue, and there they turned right. Some areas of the Bronx have hills that are as steep as those in San Francisco. Bermudez now felt the strain on the car as it made its way up the sharp incline of Anderson Avenue.

241

"Tell us when you see something familiar," Holliday said.

"Nothin' yet," she said. "It's too dark to see here."

They drove to the firehouse that Bermudez had remembered. Diana looked at it blankly.

They went up and down several more streets, slowing up, sometimes stopping, turning the headlights off to enable the woman to see outside more advantageously. They turned and looked at Diana for some hint of recognition. Nothing.

This was an exercise in futility, thought Holliday. They had come this far, so close, yet Sammy the Arab was still eluding their grasp.

They had been driving for over an hour when they decided to call it quits and head back to Manhattan. As they came down 162nd Street to the dead end at Anderson Avenue, a street they had previously driven on, Diana leaned forward and exclaimed, "There it is! That's where he lives!"

"Which house?" asked Holliday.

She pointed. "With the two lights in front."

Bermudez pulled over to the curb. Fitzgibbons and Graham stopped alongside them.

Bermudez leaned over and said to Graham, "She thinks this is the place."

"Let's go up and let her show us the apartment," said Holliday. It was 1:20 A.M.

No. 946 Anderson was a six-story red-brick building in a quiet, still-respectable neighborhood.

The three people in the front car got out and walked into the dim vestibule. There was one small bulb overhead.

"I think I remember where the apartment was," Diana volunteered. Her voice quivered.

They took the elevator up to the fifth floor. Very quietly, they turned left. She stopped and pointed down the hall.

Holliday motioned for the others to stay right where they were. Quietly, he walked to the end of the hall and noted the number on the door: 5-D.

They took the elevator back to the ground floor.

Walking out the door, Holliday told Bermudez that Fitzgibbons should drive Diana back to Manhattan, and that Graham should wait in the remaining car.

"The two of us will wait here and stop him," Holliday said.

Bermudez nodded, but he had an uneasy feeling that Holliday was trying to take over. Bermudez had some fifteen years more experience than Holliday. He wasn't going to be told by any smart-ass FBI guy, or anyone else, how to handle a collar. However, he thought better than to create a furor at this point.

Bermudez and Holliday returned to the building and checked the listing for the name of the superintendent. It was Rotten-bucher, 1-A.

They knocked at the first door on the right. Soon a woman with a German accent asked who was there.

"FBI," said Holliday.

A tall, big-boned woman in curlers, visibly frightened at being awakened like this, opened the door. She said she was Mrs. Rosa Rottenbucher.

She told them that apartment 5-D was leased to a Mr. Sam Kelly, who had been living there for about a year.

Description? "Oh," she said, "he is very much a gentleman."

"How does he *look*?" asked Bermudez.

"Not high," she said, raising a hand to the level of her chin. "And mit hair on the face, bushy."

"Did he ever have visitors?"

"One," she said, "a tall dark woman mit long black hair."

She told them that Mr. Kelly always dressed nice, usually in suits. She thought he traveled a lot because he'd be gone for days at a time, and when he returned, he'd be carrying a suitcase.

"Anything else?"

"His rent he pays always on time."

Her husband, white hair tousled, came to the door and sleepily asked what was going on. He was told. Holliday asked Mr. Rotten-bucher to show him the back entrance of the building.

The two lawmen and the super—throwing on a coat—walked outside and through a darkened passageway lined with garbage cans to the rear of the building. Three apartment houses, each six stories high, encircled the black courtyard. They were surrounded

243

by hundreds of darkened windows—except for one. The super looked up and pointed to that lone lighted window and said, "That's Mr. Kelly's bedroom."

The three men returned to Rottenbucher's apartment.

Bermudez and Holliday decided to call headquarters to advise of their moves.

The detective and the special agent were continually in touch with their superiors; since this was an important, widely publicized case, both agencies obviously wanted to hold a tight rein on it. Any contravention of legal technicalities could injure their case and embarrass them in court and in the press.

Suddenly, the two lawmen and the Rottenbuchers turned toward the door of the apartment. Footsteps echoed in the hallway outside. Then the front door opened and closed. Holliday motioned for the woman to step to the window, and parted the Venetian blinds for her.

Peering out onto the street, she whispered, "That's him—that's Mr. Kelly."

Holliday started for the door. So did Bermudez. Holliday stopped. "You stay here," he said to Bermudez, "and cover me." Bermudez stayed, and watched from behind the Venetian blinds.

"The suspect was carrying a brown paper bag and a black shopping bag," recalled Bermudez. "He was partially in the glow of the streetlight. I watched him turn left and take a few steps. He was right below us. He dumped the paper bag in a garbage can—in front of the building—then he started walking down the hill with the shopping bag.

"I saw that the other FBI agent had pulled the car up to the curb across Anderson Avenue. Holliday crossed over to the car and stuck his head in the window and said something to his partner. Then Holliday walked rapidly and caught up with Kelly, then passed him. When he did, Kelly turned around and began walking back *up* the block. He tossed the shopping bag under a small van parked at the curb. That was when I decided to run out. I had visions of all the Pierre jewels in that bag."

Bermudez continued, "I grabbed the bag and opened it. There was a hammer and a crowbar in it—burglar's tools. But no jewels.

The suspect hadn't seen me. Holliday turned back up the street after he had reversed himself. I watched the guy pass the entrance, with Holliday at his heels. I met Holliday at the entrance to No. 946 and told him what was in the bag.

" 'That's enough to stop him,' said Holliday. 'The guy is definitely goosey.'

"I felt for my gun. I was keyed up. So I took my gun out, and if there was trouble, I'd blow him away."

In front of them the short man with the curly hair and dark coat turned and looked over his shoulder. The two men came up behind him.

In a few quick steps they were at his heels.

"Don't move, motherfucker, or I'll shoot," said Bermudez.

The suspect stopped and turned. He looked down at the gun in Bermudez's hand. The steel glinted in the dim overhead light from the streetlamp.

Holliday's gun remained on his hip.

"We got ya, Sam," said Bermudez.

"I'm not Sam. My name is Ricky. Ricky Roberts."

"We know who you are, don't bullshit us."

"What do you want from me?"

Holliday frisked him for weapons. Finding nothing, he stepped back.

Bermudez said, "Let's see your I.D." He motioned with his gun. As he did so, his gun accidentally brushed against Holliday's temple.

"Get that goddamn gun out of my ear, you asshole!" shouted Holliday. "You trying to kill me? Jesus Christ! The guy's not armed. Put it away."

"Yeah, geez, tell this guy to keep cool," said the suspect.

Bermudez stuck the gun back into his shoulder holster.

The suspect's wallet revealed a New Jersey driver's license in the name of Richard Roberts.

They hustled him into the lobby of the apartment building, searched him further, and found several rolls of bills totaling nearly six thousand dollars. There were also several keys, including two sets of car keys.

In the top pocket of his jacket were two white-gold ring settings, but no stones. They also found three sets of safe-deposit-box keys.

"We know you have an apartment here, Sammy," said Bermudez. "We know who you are, and we've got Comfort."

Without blinking, Sammy said, "I don't know any Comfort."

"Sammy, you're wise enough to know we're not fooling," said Holliday.

Sammy looked at the two men and nodded.

"Okay, I live here," he said. "Let's go up, but let's be quiet."

In the bedroom of Apartment 5-D were two suitcases open on the bed. In one was a passport with the name Sorecho (Sammy) Nalo, born October 20, 1932, Detroit, Michigan.

The law officers looked at each other. Now they were certain. They had finally captured "Sammy the Arab."

Bermudez called O'Connor at the precinct. O'Connor said he'd be right up with a search warrant. That was the letter of the law. Unless there was solid information or evidence, suspects could not be arrested on the street; their homes could not be invaded. They did not want the case damaged in court.

However, there was no one to prove that Sammy's apartment was being searched. Bermudez and Holliday handcuffed Sammy to a chair, and "patted down" the place, waiting for O'Connor's arrival.

They found a stack of newspaper clippings, primarily from the society pages, and in particular the "Suzy" columns of the *New York Daily News*. Newspaper photos were found in an envelope in a drawer; they included Anne McDonnell Ford, Sophia Loren, Maria Callas, Merle Oberon, Lady Sarah Churchill, Princess Diane von Furstenberg, and many others. It was subsequently learned that most of these women either lived at or had visited the Pierre at one time or another. There was also a detailed, full-page *New York Times* listing of every social and charity event in New York for the 1971–72 season.

A confidential Manhattan telephone directory of all unlisted subscribers was uncovered from a pile of photo albums.

Also in the apartment were a manual for a shortwave radio, a photo collection of female nudes, model folders, and party photographs taken at various nightclubs.

In the bathroom cabinet were plastic vials of prescription drugs, including Valium, and pills for digestive ailments. The names on the bottle labels were Ballo, Horowitz, Kelly, Fisher, and Roberts.

A newspaper ad for a Natural Hair growth formula also turned up.

Three gold ring settings, one silver bracelet, twenty-four assorted keys, one scale, one hammer, one crowbar, and a man's black wig were also found.

A little red notebook with hundreds of entries was discovered, including names like Rocky Midnight, Count Nicholas, John Phoney, the Gemological Institute, as well as Elena and Patrice Sorentino and Diana DePeña. Also there was a phone number for someone in Fairport, New York: "Bobby Comfort."

"You told me you didn't know any Bobby Comfort. What's this?" Bermudez asked.

"I don't know what you're talking about," replied Sammy.

"We know you did the robbery," said Holliday.

"I'm no robber, I owned a donut shop 'til it folded," he said. "I'm on unemployment. I got canceled checks to prove it."

Casually and unexpectedly, Sammy, one wrist handcuffed to the chair, reached out with his free hand and rubbed the lapel of Bermudez's dark brown suit between his thumb and forefinger. "Nice stuff," he said with genuine admiration, "real nice."

"Thanks, Sammy," said Bermudez, obviously flattered. "I like some of your stuff, too, it suits my taste."

In fact, Bermudez was tempted to appropriate a pair of gold cuff links he had found in Sammy's drawer. He could have easily switched them with the pair he was wearing. He took the cuff links out, held them in the palm of his hand, then decided that there was going to be enough heat on this case and it wouldn't be worth the risk. He placed the gold cuff links back in the drawer.

When O'Connor arrived, he asked Sammy questions pertaining to the Pierre. Sammy answered impatiently, "Look, let's go downtown. We're just wasting time here."

247

O'Connor smiled and said to Bermudez, "He's right. Let's make him happy. Book him."

Assistant District Attorney Lowe had been following the tracking of Sammy the Arab by hourly phone calls from O'Connor. When Sammy was finally brought in, Lowe was at the precinct. It was four hours into Sunday when he began his interrogation. He received the same lack of cooperation from Sammy that he had got from Comfort.

After the suspects had been arraigned, Lowe called for the hostages from the Pierre robbery to appear at the police lineup the following morning.

Fifteen of the nineteen hostages had agreed to appear. The Brazilians, including the mother, now back in Rio, refused to return to New York. It was an American problem, Lowe was told; they would have nothing more to do with it.

Lowe believed that they would have been his best witnesses. Helio Fragas had had a long look at two of the suspects, and he was one of the few hostages who had not been taken from behind.

The fourth hostage who would not appear was the old man with the heart problem. He had disappeared between the time the robbers departed and the cops arrived.

The witnesses, all men, were mainly hotel employees: middle-aged security guards, Puerto Ricans who spoke little English, and some blacks, who all told Lowe they feared for their jobs and their lives. A positive identification of any of the suspects could cost them either or both. Lowe was aware of one of the robbers' parting admonition to them, threatening them and their families if they talked. Yet Lowe believed that a positive identification was his only hope of salvaging the case.

248

◆ 32 ◆

Monday morning, January 10, 1972, New York City

On the seventh floor of the New York State Criminal Courts Building at Foley Square, in the brightly lighted, compact lineup room, Bobby Comfort and five other men sat on wooden folding chairs against the smudged white wall. Pinned to Comfort's striped shirt was a large tag with the handprinted numeral 6. The five others sat to his right, each wearing a tagged number: Paulino bore 3, Stern was wearing 5. Three plainclothesmen filled out the lineup—numbers 1, 2, and 4 respectively. This was the first time Comfort had seen Paulino since he had walked out of their room at the Royal Manhattan Hotel three days before. Comfort was anxious to find out what had gone wrong, but no talking was permitted in the lineup.

Comfort absently ran a hand over his neatly combed black hair and stared straight ahead. Across the room a policeman sat at a desk with a phone at his elbow. On the desk was a clipboard

249

holding a typewritten list of names. To the cop's immediate right was a darkened window the size of a chessboard, made of one-way reflecting glass, standard in police lineup rooms. The men in the lineup were being observed from the dark room on the other side of that window.

Dick Lowe stood at the window inside the viewing room, waiting. Also in the room were Assistant District Attorney Kevin McKay and Deputy Police Commissioner Robert Daley.

Each witness was led individually from the waiting room outside into the viewing room, where identifications would be attempted.

It was 8:30 A.M.

The first witness brought forward was Charles Figueroa, the newspaper delivery man. Lowe would repeat to each witness as he entered the darkened room:

"The men on the other side of this window cannot see you. Each one will walk up to the window. Do not attempt to make any identification until you have looked at all of them. Do not speak or make any sign until I speak to you."

Lowe picked up the telephone intercom on the wall and spoke to the desk officer in the lineup room. "We're ready in here."

The cop hung up and pointed to Number 1, a detective. Number 1 stood up and walked to the window and looked directly into it. Then he turned in profile.

The delivery man asked, "Could he put on a pair of glasses? The man in the ski mask was wearing glasses." (Comfort himself was not wearing glasses now. They had fallen off his face when he had been held dangling out of the window at the Royal Manhattan.)

The detective was given a pair of glasses, and slipped them on. He looked straight ahead, and then in profile.

"Need any more?" Lowe asked Figueroa.

"That's enough."

"Next man," said Lowe into the phone. He repeated the process until Number 6.

Comfort, awaiting his call, sat and wondered which of the hostages was looking at them. He had worn the ski mask—what

250

could they have seen? He felt confident that a positive identification was highly improbable, but there could always be an old-fashioned frame-up.

A sparring of wits had developed between Connor, the cops, and the D.A. Since his arrest Comfort had been attempting to build a solid defense in the event the case went to trial.

He would attempt to maneuver the prosecutors into making as many technical and procedural errors as possible. He knew the law, and he knew some of its loopholes. In this regard, an incident earlier that morning, outside the lineup room, might help enormously.

Comfort had protested in the Tombs hallway that he would not submit to a lineup without his lawyer present; he said he knew he was entitled to one. One of the policemen, handcuffed to him, had said, "You're not entitled to anything." Nearby stood three lawyers involved in other legal matters who overheard Comfort's complaint. One of the three turned and walked over to Comfort and said, "My name's John Russo. I'm a lawyer. I heard every word said here. I heard you object. Do you have a lawyer?"

"Thanks," said Comfort, "but I'm getting a lawyer soon."

"Fine," said Russo. "If you want me to testify in your behalf, I'll be happy to do so. Here's my card."

Comfort was lying. A lawyer was not coming, because he did not want one. He had told Rosie to delay hiring one. And so this unlawful lineup procedure could be one of the technicalities in his favor.

"Number Six," called the cop at the desk. Comfort rose. He walked to the window, looked at the glass square, then was told to show his profile. The cop, the intercom phone to his ear as he took instructions from Lowe, now said, "Here, put these glasses on."

"Oh no," Comfort replied, "I'm not putting on any disguises."

"Yes you are," said the officer.

"I'm within my rights not to put that disguise on. But if I'm forced to, I want you to know that I'm doing it against my will."

Comfort slipped on the glasses. One more technicality.

He repeated the procedure in front of the window again.

"Okay," said the cop at the desk. "Sit down."

251

"Do you recognize anyone in that room?" Lowe asked Figueroa.

"No, sir," said Figueroa.

"Are you sure?"

"Yes, sir."

"Want to look at any of them again?"

"No, I'm sure."

The next man ushered in was James Weeda, the Pierre Hotel security man who had been on duty at the Sixty-first Street entrance at the time of the break-in.

He remain silent until Number 3 walked up. "He looks like the short guy who came through the door with the gun," said Jimmy Weeda.

"Are you sure?" asked Lowe, looking at Dom Paulino.

"No," said Weeda meekly. "No. I'm sorry."

One of the porters, a black man named Robinson, said Comfort looked familiar. "I wish he had a chauffeur's cap on."

A chauffeur's cap was placed on Comfort's head.

"Is that better?" asked Lowe.

"No," Robinson said.

Lowe cleared his throat to hide his disappointment. "Okay, thank you. Next."

The manager, Benjamin O'Sullivan, thought Number 1 was the man with the bellman's jacket. Lowe nodded. Number 1 was Detective Higham. The hefty bellman named Louis Rabon thought Comfort was the same size and build, but couldn't recognize the face.

"We had nothing," recalled Lowe. "One witness after the other could not identify any of the three suspects.

"I kept asking, 'Do you recognize anyone?' 'No, no, no.' We had gone through fourteen witnesses. Now it was up to Weathersby, my last witness. I was getting weary. We had no evidence, and I kept thinking about the police commissioner's press conference. The case was going from bad to worse. It was becoming embarrassing."

Also, none of the witnesses would recall any of the robbers calling one of the gang, "Bobby," as Country had done.

252

Lowe had kept his strongest witness for last: Elijah Weathersby. From interrogation immediately after the robbery, it was determined that this middle-aged black porter had had the best look at the robbers of any of the witnesses. Yet he had told the cops and the prosecutors that he would not view the lineup.

Lowe called Weathersby into his office.

Weathersby, a shy, reticent man, fixed his gaze on the floor as he sat before Lowe's heavy wooden desk.

"Why aren't you going to cooperate with us, Mr. Weathersby?" asked Lowe.

Hesitating, Weathersby said softly but firmly, "I don't want no mess with them Mafia. They the ones who done it, and I ain't gonna put my neck out so they come and chop it off. And why should I do that for them rich white folks? They don't give a damn whether I lives or drops dead tomorrow. And then I'll have the Mafia comin' after me? No-o-o sir."

"You know, these guys had nothing to do with the Mafia," said Lowe in gentle tones. "These guys are nothing but a bunch of white hoods. Okay, maybe those rich white people don't care about you. But here's a chance to get back at Whitey."

"The cops an' the courts never help no black man, so there's no reason I should help 'em now," said Weathersby.

"Look, Elijah, it's true what you say about the criminal justice system and how unfair it is to blacks. But hey, look, none of those accused of a crime is black. You got a bunch of white thugs, is all. I'm asking you to help a brother. I'm in charge of this case, right? I do well on this case, it helps my advancement. It's a feather in my cap. If I don't do well, the office won't penalize me for losses. It's a natural fact. But the higher I go, the more I can do to see that the brothers get just that much more justice in this system. We got to help each other, man."

Weathersby looked up. Lowe saw in Weathersby's softened eyes that he had made an impact.

"All I'm asking you to do," said Lowe, trying hard to keep the fish on the hook, "is to go to the window and look at the people, and if you recognize anybody, tell me who it is you recognize."

In the darkened viewing room, Weathersby peered through

the one-way glass. Lowe watched his lean, leathery face. Silently, Weathersby watched each of the six men in the lineup walk up to the window, look in, look sideways, walk away. Lowe could feel his body pulsing with anticipation. The little dark room was loud with silence. Finally, Lowe broke it. "Do you see anybody in that room you recognize?"

Weathersby stared into the lineup room for another moment, then raised the five bony fingers of his left hand. Lowe swallowed hard and waited. Then Weathersby added the index finger of his right hand to the five upraised fingers of his left.

Lowe was grinning. "Are you telling me that you recognize Numbers Five and Six?" Numbers 5 and 6 were Stern and Comfort.

"Yes, sir, that's right," Weathersby said.

"Thank you," said Lowe. "Now if you'll just go back into the waiting room. . . ."

As soon as Weathersby left the office, Lowe cheered.

"I'll never forget it," Lowe said later. "I acted just like a child, jumped up and down and hollered. After all this work, finally something broke right."

In a few minutes the identifying process would begin again, but this time Sammy would be in the lineup with five detectives. As Lowe looked out into the lineup room, he was astonished to see two large detectives tussling with Sammy Nalo. The detectives were attempting to slap a wig on Sammy's bald head. It was one of the two wigs that had been uncovered in his apartment in the Bronx. Hotel witnesses had described a short man wearing a wig. Now Sammy took the wig and ripped it in half. Lowe watched bemusedly as the detectives patched the wig with tape and safety pins.

"I went out to see him. 'Listen, Sammy,' I said, 'we have you cold. So why don't you make it easy on yourself. We can do it the easy way or the hard way. And the hard way is, I'm walking away from this, and these guys will make sure that you go into that lineup with your wig on your head. I also have a court order that says you got to wear that wig.'

"I'll never forget his eyes. They were cold, calculating—the iceman cometh. His eyes just pierced right through me. There was no bluffing Sammy, no bullshitting him. I tried to con him, and he looked at me with scorn, as if to say, 'You're not in my league.' And I guess I wasn't. Sammy eventually did wear the wig in the lineup, but it looked like a crow's nest—all patched up and scraggly."

Near the end of the second lineup, Louis Rabon, the swarthy, husky bellman, entered the room.

He looked at Sammy. "I was shook up, and angry," Rabon would recall. "The guy standing in front of me had a gun on me at a time when I couldn't do anything about it. It seemed like the same guy, but to be certain I asked Lowe to have him say, 'Don't turn around. Don't look at me. Put your hands up.'"

Sammy droned the words. Rabon turned to Lowe and said, "Un-fucking-believable. That's him. I'd know the voice anywhere."

Lowe was too tired to do anything but thank Rabon. There was no jumping for joy. He opened the door to let him out.

It was close to five o'clock. Lowe had been going for nearly two full days on no sleep. The lineups were all over. As Lowe buttoned his collar and slid up the knot of his paisley tie, he watched the men walk out of the lineup room, Nalo leaving just before the last detective. Lowe had a case now, though he still wondered how the identifications would hold up under cross-examination by a skillful defense counsel. But he'd have to worry about that later. Tomorrow—or whenever he woke from the deep sleep for which his body now ached.

◆ 33 ◆

Tuesday morning, January 11, 1972

In a long, windowless gray room in the Manhattan House of Detention, more commonly known as the Tombs, Bobby Comfort met Leon Greenspan, his attorney, for the first time. They sat on stiff brown wooden chairs in a booth. Guards hovered nearby. A dim fluorescent light burned overhead. Although Greenspan's law practice in White Plains, New York, concentrated on civil actions, he had represented a few clients in criminal cases that resulted in noteworthy publicity. He had come to the attention of Rose Gustino, who then recommended the attorney to her brother.

Comfort now mentioned that he had been reading about Greenspan's defense of Jersey City Mayor Thomas Whelan, charged with extortion and income-tax evasion. Greenspan was surprised and flattered that Comfort was aware of the case. But in his direct manner he went immediately to the business at hand.

"What's this all about?" Greenspan asked.

Comfort summed it up quickly. Before asking the next question, Greenspan glanced around the room. Aware that it could be bugged, he asked quietly, "Up or down?"—that is, guilty or not guilty?

Comfort turned his thumbs down: guilty.

"That's what floored me," Greenspan recalled. "Comfort told me that what he was hoping for was the lightest possible sentence. He said he was prepared to do his time, get out, and, I imagine, reap the benefits of what he had accomplished.

"Comfort had told me he didn't want a criminal lawyer representing him," continued Greenspan. "And the interesting thing was, Sammy Nalo was represented by one of the really fine criminal lawyers—Jim La Rossa, a former assistant U.S. attorney. The problem with him, in my judgment, is that he *looked* like a criminal lawyer. He looked sharp and gave the impression of being slick. The jury would have to watch him and really examine with a grain of salt everything he said. Yet he was an exceedingly competent attorney.

"Neither my partner, Joel Arnou, nor I reflected the criminal-lawyer impression, I think. We were both young—neither of us had hit forty—and we were rather conservative, suburban-type dressers. I guess that's what Comfort wanted."

Because Arnou was ill, Greenspan would handle the entire case himself.

"I admired Comfort's candor," Greenspan said. "He doesn't try to be something he isn't. He doesn't try to justify or explain his actions—well, I came from a poor background, which he didn't, and it's all society's fault, or anything like that. He is what he is, and you can take him or leave him.

"I think, though, that Bobby Comfort was completely amoral. He didn't find anything morally wrong in what he did. He recognized that what he was doing was wrong by somebody else's standards, but not by his. He was going to get what was out there by his own means, because he was good at doing it."

If found guilty Comfort knew that with his prior record he could get twenty-five years to life imprisonment. Perhaps the best he could hope for, with that result, was release at age sixty-five.

257

After the meeting with Greenspan, Comfort was returned to his cell.

The Tombs is the holding tank for men held over for trial, or about to be sentenced after conviction. It received its dreary epithet, obviously enough, because of the deathly atmosphere of the place. To Bobby Comfort it was the filthiest jail he had ever been in, and that included the miserable Monroe County Jail in Rochester. There were bedbugs in the mattress, roaches crawling the walls, and rats scurrying loudly about on the overhead pipes.

And the noise in the Tombs was so loud that one had to shout to be heard by the person next to him. The din was like the roar inside a steel-mill foundry. Prisoners hollered, screamed, and argued; bells rang incessantly; radios blared rock music; and iron doors clanged constantly.

On a catwalk outside the cells were picnic-type benches, where the prisoners gathered, talked, and played cards. It was here that Comfort and Sammy discussed their future during daytime breaks.

Neither knew the circumstances surrounding their capure, nor did they have any knowledge of the kind of case the D.A. had. Nor could they speculate on what had transpired in the lineup room, whether they had been identified and, if so, by whom and by how many.

And what of the evidence? Three platinum ring settings had been found in Sammy's apartment. Bobby asked him if they fit the stones uncovered in the Summit. Sammy didn't know. If the stones and settings did match, their case could possibly be hurt. Not destroyed, but hurt. The D.A. still had to have witnesses to prove robbery. Comfort wondered whether the cops knew about City, Country, or Doc. If they were nabbed, would the three turn state's evidence?

Newspapers were sold at the Tombs commissary. Comfort was never a more avid newspaper reader than now.

Later that morning of January 11, Comfort, sitting on a bench on his tier, was reading the *Daily News*. A story about a cop killing dominated the front page. Comfort turned the page and was astonished to see the headline:

258

$750,000 IN PIERRE
GEMS RECOVERED

He read the story carefully: A man in Detroit had come to the FBI with a package containing jewels. One of the Pierre suspects had given it to him. The Detroit man was not identified in the article, but the jewels were. They belonged to Gabriele Lagerwall. Records checked with Harry Winston jewelers on Fifth Avenue established that fact.

Comfort was stunned. He knew nothing about this package of jewels. All the jewels but those found at the Summit were supposed to be in the satchel guarded by City.

Detroit, thought Comfort. Now what the fuck are those jewels doing showing up in Sammy's home town?

At the other end of the bench, Sammy was talking with a couple of other inmates. Comfort caught his eye and beckoned him. Sammy broke away and came over.

"I want to show you something," Comfort said.

"Sure." Sammy sensed something odd in Comfort's tone.

They walked to the far end of the tier, not saying a word, Comfort clenching the rolled newspaper in his hand. When they were far enough away from everyone, Comfort stopped beside a barred window. He coolly handed the paper to his partner.

"Read this," he said. "Ain't that somethin'?"

"He read," Comfort recalled, "and he began to turn white. Then I knew for certain what he had done. And he knew that I knew.

"Sammy said, 'There might be a little mistake here.' He looked up at me. He's scared shitless. Now he thinks he's dead. We were alone, and he knew I could squash him right on the goddamn catwalk before anyone could come to help.

"I said, 'Let's not go through all the mistakes. I want you to know that our ten million or twelve million or eight million is right down the fucking drain. You know it, and you caused it.'

"He said, 'Those Detroit stones were our ace in the hole, Bobby. That was for me and you.'

"I said, 'You don't steal money from me, Sammy. You don't

259

steal from any of us. We all had that money coming. Everybody that was there earned it. Everybody risked the same thing we risked.'

"He said, 'You never want to think of me and you—I couldn't tell you because I knew you'd do just what you're doin' now. You want to give everything to those punks.'

"I said, 'They're not punks when they walk in there with us, and they're not punks when we leave. And a guy like City, he was smart enough to handle the Pierre with us, and now, after he reads this, he'll be smart enough to fink off with the stuff we gave him. Why the hell should he hold anything for us now? He's got me robbin', too, ain't he? Me and you are the bosses. The two bosses have to be doing the robbin'. We've lost three or four million apiece because you tried to rob a lousy million for yourself.' "

Comfort stared at Sammy, then turned and walked away. "I didn't threaten Sammy and I decided never to bring it up again," Comfort recalled. "Why should I? What was done was done. I couldn't change it. I also knew why he raked the money off the top for himself. He always needed money to pay his gambling debts. He lived in fear of a contract on him. He was desperate all the time. He couldn't help himself. I mean, he probably had a good reason in his own mind for what he did. Sammy figured, 'No one's gonna miss the Detroit jewels, so what's the big deal? Bobby's still gonna end up with a few million dollars for his split. I need more than he does.'

"Nobody could ever have been a better friend than I was to Sammy. If he would rob me, he'd rob anybody. I trusted Sammy completely, I let him hold everything. I didn't count one piece. I never once questioned him.

"After this a lot of guys would have wanted to kill him," Comfort continued. "I just figured that it's my own fault. I judge people by myself. What I would do, I figure they would do. It might be a mistake, but that's how I live with myself.

"And I figured that I could take being robbed for a change. You're not going to hear me make a sucker's holler. Why shouldn't I be able to take it? I've been robbin' all my life. So I had done to me what I had been doing to others.

260

"Sammy's robbin' me hurt me more than it made me mad. I felt that I had been betrayed by a friend. Funny thing is, I couldn't hate him. I liked him too much to hate him now. We'd had too many good times, went through too many dangers together. It's like being in a war with a guy, sharing the same foxhole. No matter what happens, you can't forget all that.

"I didn't stop talking to him. After all, we were still fighting the case together.

"And we talked about the case coming up. I told him as long as everyone keeps his mouth shut, there'd be no problem. Just don't admit anything. Tell them nothing, and we'll be all right. That was the whole case. They had nothing on us.

"But all this time Sammy knew how I felt about his move. And he knew that whatever I was doing—being nice and calm and all that—was all bullshit now."

It was Detective Bermudez who succeeded in uncovering the manner in which the jewels had landed in Detroit. On the Tuesday after the Pierre robbery, Sammy had called an old friend, a tavern owner in Detroit named Louis Peppo, and persuaded him to fly to New York. Peppo came. In New York Sammy talked about himself and Peppo opening a bar-and-grill in Detroit, with Sammy financing it. It was something Sammy said he always wanted, a good little business. Then Sammy gave Peppo two packages to take back to Detroit. "This one's for your wife," he said, "perfume." The other package was wrapped in a brown pouch bag. "I'll pick this one up next time I'm in Detroit," Sammy said. Peppo later told Bermudez that he'd thought nothing further about it.

Peppo stayed overnight at Sammy's Bronx apartment.

The following morning Sammy told Peppo, "I'll have to drop you off early at the bus station"—snowstorm warnings in Detroit had forced a plane cancellation—"because I have to meet someone." (In a few hours Comfort and Paulino would be flying in to New York.)

When Peppo arrived in Detroit, he took the brown bag Sammy had given him to the basement of his bar. Curious as to its contents, Peppo decided to open it in that dark basement, and when he did, it stunned him. Dazzling jewels filled the bag: four sets of earrings, a diamond-and-emerald necklace, a diamond-and-emerald bracelet, and a diamond brooch.

Peppo heaved an appreciative sigh, rewrapped the package, and tucked it behind some wine cartons in a corner.

On Monday, five days after he had left Sammy, Peppo read of Sammy's capture in a Detroit newspaper.

Now he remembered Sammy "dwelling on the front page and the second page of the newspaper" when he was in New York. The stories on those pages dealt with the Pierre robbery. Peppo said Sammy never told him about the robbery and certainly never mentioned what was in the brown pouch bag he had given him.

Upon reading of Sammy's capture, and fearing that he could inadvertently become involved for withholding incriminating evidence and possession of stolen property, Peppo phoned the FBI office in Detroit.

Agents rushed to the tavern, and Peppo handed over the brown bag.

A week later, flown to New York under guard, Peppo told Lowe that he could not cooperate because he feared his life might be in danger—if not directly by Sammy, then by friends of Sammy.

In the Tombs, Comfort grew increasingly confident as more time passed because of the D.A.'s delay in setting an early trial date. Usually, it is the defendant's attorney whose strategy it is to stall, hoping that something will turn up to help his case. But it was the defendant now who insisted on the trial; Comfort pressed Greenspan to force the issue. He asked the lawyer the reason for the standstill. "Why am I being kept? Nobody ever said I stole anything. Nobody ever said I committed any crime. There's no evidence to point to my involvement in the Pierre job. Yet they keep me here and I get no trial."

In addition, Bobby Comfort—like Sammy the Arab—was being held without bail. Lowe had insisted that any amount of bail short of ten million—the estimated take of the robbery—might result in the defendants skipping out. The two suspects remained in the Tombs while the authorities tracked down all possible leads, attempting to bolster their weak case.

The three sets of safe-deposit-box keys found in Sammy's

apartment were thought to be important. They might lead to the depository that contained stolen jewelry. Both Sammy and Comfort refused to cooperate.

Holliday and Bermudez were assigned to check out the keys.

Two of the three sets of keys were identified. One belonged to the First National Bank on the West Side; the other to the Chase Manhattan Bank in Mount Vernon, a suburb north of the Bronx. Neither of the banks listed Sammy's name, nor any of his aliases, in connection with their roster of safety-deposit-box depositors. One name did look familiar, however: it belonged to a friend of Sammy's who owned the Plaka restaurant. Holliday and Bermudez sought him out. The man admitted they were his boxes, kept in a joint name, in case anything happened to him (he suffered from a bad heart), so that Sammy could assist his wife.

"We'd like to see the boxes anyway," Bermudez said.

In each of the banks the contents were as described: some stock certificates, insurance policies, and a few bundles of yellowing Armenian currency which were kept as memorabilia.

But there was still another set of bank safe-deposit keys without stamped identification.

With literally a thousand or more banks in New York City and tens of thousands of safe-deposit boxes, it might take years if an attempt were made to locate the boxes these keys fit.

The keys' identity, therefore, became highly significant—or had the potential to be—to the police department and the FBI.

Sammy and Comfort, when questioned about the keys, refused to divulge any information concerning the location of the bank. The authorities attempted to convince them that a solid case existed, and lighter sentences might be considered if they cooperated and revealed the location of the boxes. It sounded like a fair exchange.

Lowe, however, was opposed to this device. He reasoned that if the loot was in those boxes, the men weren't stupid enough to reveal that information, even for lesser sentences.

The FBI's contention was that whatever they could get would be helpful.

Lowe finally agreed. Comfort and Sammy were brought to his

office with Holliday and Bermudez present. Lowe told the suspects he was prepared to offer bail if they would reveal the location of the deposit boxes.

For one hour they negotiated the amount of bail. Comfort held out for a time until Lowe, in desperation, offered bail to be set at ninety thousand dollars.

The suspects were then permitted, at Comfort's insistence, to discuss the offer privately. After an animated few minutes in a corner of the office, they agreed to the proposed arrangements.

"It's the Manufacturers Hanover Trust, on Broadway just south of Canal," Comfort told Lowe.

The boxes were in the name of "Meyer," one of Sammy's aliases.

Lowe said, "Thanks, fellas. I'll keep my word. My word is my bond."

Taking a squad car, Bermudez and Holliday sped to the branch bank in Lower Manhattan, on the outskirts of Chinatown.

They entered the bank and presented their identification and the authorization to a bank officer on the platform.

The officers waited impatiently for twenty minutes, until the president of the bank finally authorized their request.

Down the gray rows of steel boxes they were led until they came to the three key-matched, numbered boxes. Two keys are used to open safe-deposit boxes. The vault guard opened one lock in the box and Holliday opened the other. Holliday anxiously pulled the box out. In it he saw one sealed white envelope—unmarked—no name, nothing.

Holliday withdrew the envelope and carefully opened it. Inside there was a folded piece of white-lined notebook paper. Bermudez asked, "What's it say?"

"Nothing. Blank."

The second box yielded the same.

Holliday tried the third box. In it was still another white unmarked envelope. He ripped it open.

"Well?" asked Bermudez.

"Same damn thing," Holliday replied. He slammed the box shut in disgust.

The men stood there looking at each other.

264

"They conned us," said Bermudez, verbalizing what Holliday was thinking.*

They returned to the Criminal Courts Building and told Lowe what had transpired in the bank vault.

Lowe shook his head. "Those slippery bastards," he muttered.

His assistant, Kevin McKay, asked, "What are you going to do about the bail promise, Dick?"

"I gave 'em my word, so they've got it," he answered unhappily.

Sammy's mother, who owned a parking lot in Detroit, produced the bail bond that released her son. But friends capable of supplying bail for Comfort kept their distance. They felt that they might be harassed by the authorities for information concerning their money sources. Bobby's relatives simply did not have it, and certainly Millie, holding over two hundred thousand dollars in cash, was not about to volunteer to make bail for her husband. He had spelled that out in no uncertain terms.

So, for the time being, Bobby Comfort remained in the Tombs.

---

* During the interrogations no satisfactory explanations were forthcoming from either Comfort or Sammy regarding the three safe-deposit boxes. It remained an unsolved mystery to the police.

In August of 1971 Comfort had been contacted by a "friend" who had suggested (for a percentage) that a branch of the Manufacturers Hanover Trust at Canal Street and Broadway in lower Manhattan was an "easy score." Comfort had been told that every Thursday, sometime after noon, four bags containing five hundred thousand dollars in small bills were delivered by armored carrier to the bank's vault, located in the basement of the building. The money was to be used for check cashing on payroll accounts every Friday. Comfort's source also assured him that security was lax: only one guard was on duty after the bags were delivered and the money had been counted.

The partners "cased" the bank on five successive Thursdays and were satisfied that their information was correct.

Comfort's plan called for them to be in the vault at the time of a regular delivery, wait for the completion of the counting, then overtake the lone guard, repack the bills in their own bags, walk upstairs and out the bank entrance situated ten feet away from the top step of the vault.

In September, Nalo sent a friend to the bank to rent three safe-deposit boxes, using a fictitious name. This done, the keys were turned over to the partners. This ensured their rightful access to the vault. As instructed by Nalo, the friend had placed a white envelope containing a blank sheet of note paper in each of the boxes to make it seem that they were being used for legitimate purposes.

Later Comfort and Sammy agreed that the bank heist would be their backup insurance job in the event the Pierre was canceled.

$$* \quad * \quad *$$

Numerous leads in the Pierre case were pursued by the police and the FBI. All of them fizzled.

Bert Stern was detained for a period in the Tombs. Comfort spoke at length with him to try to piece together how the police and the FBI had tracked them down. He wanted all the details. One never knew when a small bit of information could help the case. Also, he was curious as to how the plans for the fencing of the jewels could have been so bungled after the robbery had been planned and executed so perfectly.

Comfort would eventually learn what happened:

Paulino's call from the Royal Manhattan to Stern on that Friday morning had set off a chain reaction.

Stern had first called Towson to say Paulino was coming to the Summit.

Towson, as Comfort eventually learned, then called the FBI to confirm that the fencing was coming down on schedule.

At FBI headquarters on Sixty-ninth Street, Agent Robert Hartman took the call in the noisy operations room on the eleventh floor. He was told that the transaction would take place in two hours.

Special Agent "Tom Jones," acting as the go-between for the buyer, called headquarters, and that precipitated the moves by the FBI and the city detectives at their assigned positions at the Summit Hotel. Room 1544, where the fencing was to take place, had been rented by the FBI, as was the adjoining room, 1546, where two detectives and two FBI men waited. It was established that the FBI, having paid for the rooms, had legal right of entry.

The FBI and the NYPD had been working closely together for three days, ever since the Tuesday afternoon when the FBI undercover agent referred to as "Tom Jones" had received a call from Harry Towson. Towson had informed "Jones" that he had just been propositioned by an acquaintance to "handle" a sale on a small collection of gems. Towson, an FBI informant, had indicated that the cache might be from the Pierre robbery.

With this tip the FBI summoned NYPD Lieutenant O'Connor to its headquarters, divulged its information, and laid down the ground rules for making O'Connor the joint commander along with Special Agent Hartman in the case.

Although the FBI had no jurisdiction, it was the FBI's informant who had made the connection, and that valuable source had to be protected by the bureau.

O'Connor had misgivings. But no alternatives had been presented, and it was a reasonable request, providing the Pierre robbery case could be solved.

O'Connor had a hunch that the police department shared secrets with the FBI, but the FBI shared few, if any secrets, with the NYPD. The FBI was known to seize the glory in joint investigations. Its use of informants had always been a source of contention between the two law-enforcement bodies.

The New York Police Department also had its informants, but they were kept on an informal basis. The police could not begin to compete in dollars with the feds, who had substantially more to spend for information. FBI informers were kept on retainer. The police department was envious and considered the FBI arrogant about it.

Before noon, in the downtown office of the Manhattan district attorney, Assistant District Attorney Richard Lowe had been assigned the case and was supposed to be kept abreast of all developments. He cautioned that no arrests were to be made without his authorization. The problem was a delicate one, for if the suspects were arrested too quickly, the remainder of the jewels could disappear. There had to be enough evidence to support a strong case.

On Thursday, when Stern had met with Sammy, Comfort, and Dom Paulino in the Royal Manhattan, he was watched by two FBI men who had followed him there from the Cattleman restaurant.

When Comfort and Sammy walked outside to the white Ford Galaxie, Comfort's instincts had been correct. They were being followed.

New York City police covered the area on foot and by car. All were equipped with special radio frequency. Parking lots and garages were checked. O'Connor and Hartman were continually being called with any leads. Nothing concrete developed.

Suddenly, the white Ford Galaxie was spotted. Three men were driving in it. Behind the wheel was a dark "Latin-looking man." An unmarked police car moved in behind, but the drive appeared aimless, and lasted so long that O'Connor and Hartman, following the whole situation by shortwave radio, called it off because they believed the suspects had noticed the tail.

They had no choice but to wait for Stern to make contact with his "seller" again.

Lowe then instituted the long process for a court-ordered wiretap on Stern's home phone in Queens. Affidavits had to be drawn up, each supported by evidence. Ultimately, Lowe would appear before a judge to obtain the order to make it all legal.

While awaiting the judge's approval, the decision was made to stay clear of the Royal Manhattan Hotel. Once the tap was in, Stern might phone the hotel, revealing the room number. That was Thursday. By Friday a report from District Attorney Frank Hogan's office advised Lowe that the wiretap order had not yet been signed.

When Towson called FBI headquarters on Friday morning to say that the meet was on, O'Connor, Hartman, and Capt. Richard Nicastro agreed that arrests would have to be made that day. If this was a solid lead, they felt they had to move immediately, since it might be their one and only chance. They could not wait for the tap order.

Assistant District Attorney Lowe was not informed of this decision. He was still seeking the wiretap order when the FBI and police went smashing through the door of Room 1544 in the Summit.

◆ 34 ◆

Assistant District Attorney Richard Lowe used delaying tactics in hopes of gathering more evidence to strengthen his tenuous case. It wasn't until June 5, 1972, five months after the capture of the Hotel Pierre robbery suspects, that preliminary hearings began for motions to suppress evidence. Preliminary hearings are handled very much like an actual trial. Witnesses are summoned and cross-examinations are in order. Then, upon hearing the sworn testimony, the judge determines the evidence that may be admissible in the jury trial that follows. Missing is an empaneled jury and a courtroom teeming with spectators.

No mention of the preliminary hearings appeared in the press. The Pierre robbery was a flash that had faded from the headlines and public attention. Nixon, Watergate, Vietnam, the shaky state of the economy had again returned to the top of the news. So the hearing began in relative obscurity.

Yet the issues involved were crucial to each side: for the accused, freedom or lengthy jail sentences; for the prosecution, acclaim for a conviction or frustration and embarrassment if there was an acquittal.

The preliminary hearing was held in Part 35 of the New York State Criminal Courts Building in the high-ceilinged, wood-paneled Courtroom 1111.

Squares of dark brown tile covered the floor, and when a chair was pushed away from a table, it scraped noisily in the quiet courtroom.

To the right of the judge's bench, and beyond the bailiff's desk, was a door that led to the cellblocks of the Tombs. When the door opened, a spectator could see the first row of cells. It was from there that the prisoners entered the courtroom.

The attorneys for the defense sat at an oak table to the judge's right as they faced him. The defendants, Comfort, Nalo, and Stern (Fradkin and Paulino were to be tried separately), sat behind their counsels. Assistant District Attorneys Lowe and McKay sat at a table across the aisle from the defense.

The defense team was composed of Greenspan for Comfort, Michael DiRenzo—a stocky, bespectacled sixty-year-old criminal-courts veteran—for Stern, and James La Rossa representing Sammy Nalo. For the most part, the defense was to be guided by La Rossa, the former assistant U.S. attorney.

Trim, dark, six feet tall, La Rossa arrived at the courthouse in his chauffeured limousine. He wore a blue pin-striped suit and a flashy red tie. His demeanor was reserved, his voice deep but calm, his knowledge of the law impressive. Even to Lowe, his opposition, La Rossa was "smooth as silk."

Except for La Rossa's chauffeur, who sat in the rear of the twelve rows of spectators' benches, the courtroom was empty.

At precisely 10 A.M. Judge Andrew Tyler, the tall, imposing black presiding justice with close-knit eyebrows and prominent jowls, entered in his judicial robes and settled into his high-backed leather chair. On the wall high behind the seated judge was a large painting of the proverbial blindfolded woman, holding aloft the scales of justice in one hand and a small American flag in the other.

Comfort watched Judge Tyler as his bailiff handed him a sheaf of papers and exchanged a few words. He wondered what he could expect from Tyler. Greenspan had told him that Tyler could be as good a judge as he could hope for: capable, fair, and, most important, liberal. However, Comfort was curious about the possible prejudices of a black judge confronting white defendants, in addition to a black prosecutor and, certainly, some witnesses who were black.

Tyler, at fifty-six, had come a long way from his beginnings on the tough streets of Harlem.

His career was marked by controversy, however, and some sentencing imposed by Judge Tyler had been attacked by opponents as being "soft on criminals."

Tyler rapped his gavel. The questions and the ambiguities concerning the case, Comfort thought as he looked up at the judge, would not be sorted out quickly.

Detective George Bermudez, dapper in brown suit and burgundy tie, white hair combed and fluffed carefully, was called to the stand as the first witness. The question of the validity of the arrest of the defendants was paramount in determining whether the men should have been taken into custody at all; if not, then the case should be thrown out of court on the face of it. So the testimony of Bermudez, Sammy's arresting police officer, was crucial.

Bermudez was questioned in turn by La Rossa, Greenspan, and DiRenzo. Disputed points were raised that included whether Bermudez had read Sammy his rights, and whether Sammy's apartment was searched prior to a warrant having been obtained and served.

When Attorney La Rossa asked Bermudez if the contents of the black shopping bag—a hammer and a crowbar—that Sammy had thrown under the van were sufficient evidence to arrest the suspect to begin with, Bermudez answered yes.

Then Tyler leaned forward and asked, "Does a man possessing a hammer and crowbar seem to you to be in violation of the law?"

BERMUDEZ: No, but it was a person acting in a suspicious manner.

TYLER: Anything else convince you that this was your man?

BERMUDEZ: We found a passport in his suitcase, which gave us the impression he was fleeing the country.

LA ROSSA: I've got a passport at home. Will you arrest me for intent to flee the country, too?

That brought a smile to everyone's face in the courtroom, including Tyler and Bermudez—and Lowe.

Next witness was Detective Joseph Gannon, a tall, broad man in a conservative gray suit, in marked contrast to the modish Bermudez. With a strange mixture of respect and derision, Gannon was called by his fellow cops the "G-man," not because of the first initial of his last name, but for his reputation as a conscientious and "above-the-take" police officer. His testimony would completely contradict Comfort's version of the arrest.

Lowe asked if he was one of the detectives who arrested Comfort at the Royal Manhattan.

GANNON: I was.

LOWE: Will you describe to the court, please, the circumstances surrounding that arrest?

GANNON: Shortly before two-forty I was in an unmarked radio squad car when I received a call, radio dispatch would be 10–12, which would actually mean respond back to your command forthwith. And upon arriving at Sixty-eighth Street and Broadway, I was met by Sergeant [Norman] Cohen, also of the Fourth District Robbery Squad. At which time we picked up an additional detective, [Raymond] McDowell, also of the Fourth Robbery Squad. And I was with Detective [John] Barna at the time in the car. Sergeant Cohen informed us that we had to proceed to the Royal Manhattan Hotel relative to the Hotel Pierre robbery case and to arrest an occupant of Room 1553.

TYLER: Wait a minute. That's all he said to you? That you had to proceed to the hotel? And arrest an occupant of Room 1553?

GANNON: Right. That the occupant was wanted in connection with the hotel robbery.

TYLER: Detective Gannon, did he name the occupant?

GANNON: I believe he gave us the name of Comfort.

TYLER: That's all he said?

GANNON: Well, we were discussing on the way down there the procedure to use, because we had known that in the hotel robbery, weapons were used, and we were trying to determine the best and safest way of getting to whoever was in the room so there'd be no violence, no problems. And that was the main discussion on the way down.

272

TYLER: And you were talking this over with the sergeant?

GANNON: Well, it was a general discussion between the sergeant, myself, Detective Barna, Detective McDowell, as to the best procedure to use, how we were going to approach the room, once we found out where the room was. If there were any side entrances, who was going to cover them, and such and such.

TYLER: Did the sergeant tell you that he had a warrant for the arrest of this man?

GANNON: No. He did not, sir.

TYLER: Did he, in fact, have a warrant for the arrest of this man?

GANNON: No, he did not.

That was all for the prosecution at this time. Tyler had made an incisive point. Now La Rossa began the cross-examination.

LA ROSSA: Let us talk about that ride. How long did it take?

GANNON: Ten minutes.

LA ROSSA: During that ten minutes Sergeant Cohen told you they had arrested a Dominick Paulino; is that correct?

GANNON: Yes.

LA ROSSA: And he told you you were on your way to this particular hotel called the Royal Manhattan; is that correct?

GANNON: That's correct.

LA ROSSA: To arrest one Robert Comfort; is that right?

GANNON: I don't believe he used the name Robert. I believe he just said Comfort.

LA ROSSA: Just Comfort?

GANNON: I am not positive.

LA ROSSA: You knew the Pierre was robbed some six or seven days prior to this?

GANNON: Correct.

LA ROSSA: You were in the squad that was actually investigating that robbery, weren't you?

GANNON: Yes.

LA ROSSA: Were you given a physical description of Mr. Comfort in that car?

GANNON: No.

LA ROSSA: Were you told anything about Mr. Comfort in that car by the sergeant, other than what you have told us?

273

GANNON: Outside of the room and the location, no; physical makeup, no.

LA ROSSA: Did Sergeant Cohen tell you where he got the room number from?

GANNON: Yes, from Lieutenant O'Connor, the conversation he had with Lieutenant O'Connor.

LA ROSSA: Is that all you discussed in that vehicle, aside from pleasantries, or aside from your talk about how to effectuate the arrest, to protect yourselves?

GANNNON: Might have had a few other conversations, if there was a recovery, how that came about, or something like that, but nothing outstanding that I can recall.

LA ROSSA: As you walked into the hotel, am I correct you knew you were, one, looking for Robert Comfort; two, the room he was staying in; three, that a Dominick Paulino had been arrested, and nothing more than that about this particular case; is that correct?

GANNON: Right.

LA ROSSA: You told us that you went in and saw the registration clerk. Did you tell us you looked at the registration card?

GANNON: It was a yellow document.

LA ROSSA: Are you sure of that?

GANNON: To the best recollection, it was a yellow document that they produced.

LA ROSSA: You saw a Comfort's name down, an R. Comfort?

GANNON: I believe it to be on a right-hand angle, the name Comfort on the paper thuswise, and looking at it the name would have been like this, Comfort. [Comfort, listening closely, thought, Impossible, Dom registered me under the name R. Paulino.] And I am not sure if it said "Dominick Paulino" or "D. Paulino."

LA ROSSA: Are you absolutely sure that it didn't say "D. Paulino"?

LOWE: Objection.

TYLER: Overruled.

LA ROSSA: You are absolutely certain that that yellow card didn't say "D. Paulino and R. Paulino"?

274

GANNON: The one that I observed said—had "Comfort" written—it appeared like it was written in afterwards, after the "Paulino."

LA ROSSA: Am I correct, sir, that you went upstairs to the fifteenth floor?

GANNON: I did, right.

LA ROSSA: After the knob was turned, you opened the door, hit the chain; is that correct? You saw Mr. Comfort sitting on a bed and, with your revolver in your hand, you yelled out to him, "Police, don't move," or words to that effect; is that right?

GANNON: I yelled out his name and "Police, don't move!"

LA ROSSA: At that point, was he under arrest, Detective Gannon?

GANNON: Yes.

LA ROSSA: Is there any question in your mind about that?

GANNON: No.

LA ROSSA: Was he dressed at that time?

GANNON: Yes.

LA ROSSA: Did you frisk him?

GANNON: Up on the wall, yes, an outer frisk.

LA ROSSA: And every bit of his clothing; isn't that right?

GANNON: Right.

LA ROSSA: And you went through each and every piece of it, isn't that right?

GANNON: That's right.

LA ROSSA: Isn't it a fact you went through the dresser drawers?

GANNON: Right.

LA ROSSA: Isn't it a fact that you searched in the closets?

GANNON: Right.

LA ROSSA: Isn't it a fact that you searched the bathroom of that room?

GANNON: Right.

LA ROSSA: That you searched above the sills, and other places where people conceal things?

GANNON: Right.

LA ROSSA: Searched that whole room, didn't you?

GANNON: Right.

Comfort understood the point being developed by La Rossa: the cops had had no search warrant.

LA ROSSA: Am I correct, sir, that at that point you knew what you told us a few minutes ago about Mr. Comfort, plus the fact that in the inside pocket of one of his jackets you found some stones?

GANNON: Correct.

LA ROSSA: *Is* that correct?

GANNON: Yes.

LA ROSSA: Other than that, you knew nothing else; is that right?

GANNON: That's right.

Greenspan at this point took over the questioning for La Rossa.

GREENSPAN: Detective, you were armed when you came through that door, weren't you?

GANNON: Yes.

GREENSPAN: You came to the conclusion after examining physically the defendant Comfort that he was unarmed; is that correct?

GANNON: Yes.

GREENSPAN: At that time you also had another officer with you, didn't you?

GANNON: Three others.

GREENSPAN: Three different officers?

GANNON: Correct.

GREENSPAN: There were four of you in the room at that time?

GANNON: Correct.

GREENSPAN: And all four of you were armed, isn't that correct?

GANNON: Correct.

GREENSPAN: At the time you were questioning Mr. Comfort, did you have your weapons in your hands?

GANNON: When we were questioning Mr. Comfort?

GREENSPAN: Yes.

GANNON: No. After a search of the room established that there was nobody else present, the weapons were placed back in our holsters.

276

GREENSPAN: So all four of you were sitting there questioning Mr. Comfort and no guns were shown; is that correct?

GANNON: Right.

GREENSPAN: And you made no threat to Mr. Comfort, did you?

GANNON: Definitely not.

GREENSPAN: You didn't threaten to drown him in the bathtub, did you?

GANNON: No, definitely not.

GREENSPAN: Or to throw him out of the window?

GANNON: Definitely not.

GREENSPAN: As a matter of fact, in order to get Mr. Comfort to talk to you and cooperate with you, you promised that you wouldn't hang him out the window, didn't you?

GANNON: There was no mention of hanging him out or any type of violence on our part.

GREENSPAN: As a matter of fact, you threatened him with his life if he didn't talk; is that correct?

GANNON: Counsel, I have said we made no threats of any violence against Mr. Comfort at any time or in any gesture or in any manner.

GREENSPAN: That's all, Your Honor.

Louis Rabon was the first of the hotel witnesses to testify. The muscular bellman stepped onto the stand, his slick black hair gleaming under the ceiling lights.

LOWE: Now Mr. Rabon, were you employed at the Hotel Pierre on January 2, 1972?

RABON: Yes, sir.

LOWE: Were you present at the Hotel Pierre at approximately 4 A.M.?

RABON: Yes, sir.

LOWE: And did something happen, or something occur, at the Hotel Pierre on January 2, 1972, at approximately 4 A.M.?

RABON: Yes, sir. There was a robbery.

LOWE: And Mr. Rabon, I would like for you to look around the courtroom and point out to the court, if you can, anyone that

277

you see here today who was a participant in that robbery at the Hotel Pierre on January 2, 1972.

RABON: Yes, sir.

Rabon raised his hand and extended a finger.

RABON: In back of the three lawyers, the man in the middle, definitely.

LOWE [indicating the defendant]: Your Honor, Sammy Nalo.

TYLER: The man in the middle?

RABON: Yes, sir.

TYLER: With the bald head?

RABON: That's correct, sir . . . I'm not sure, but also *him.* I think he's the one that asked for Dr. Wilson, but I'm not sure.

Rabon's thick finger was pointing again.

TYLER: And you're indicating whom, when you say you're not sure?

RABON: The first one from my right to left . . . [indicating Bert Stern].

Comfort leaned over and said to La Rossa, "Would you mind asking that Spanish guy how he knew the three men sitting in front of Sammy are lawyers."

La Rossa turned to Comfort and smiled. "Thanks, but I don't think I'll need it." La Rossa then began his cross-examination.

LA ROSSA: When you arrived here at nine o'clock on the morning of the lineup, Mr. Rabon, and you came to the district attorney's office and met Mr. Lowe—

RABON: Yes, sir.

LA ROSSA: —did you have a conversation with Mr. Lowe?

RABON: No. Mr. Lowe was doing all the talking. We didn't have a conversation.

LA ROSSA: Go on.

RABON: Well, he started off saying he was in charge, that he would be the district attorney in charge of the case, and we were to view people in the lineup.

LA ROSSA: Did he tell you who the people were?

RABON: He just said we were to view people in the lineup.

LA ROSSA: Is that all he said?

278

RABON: Well, he described the procedure. We would go to the viewing room, and then we would leave there and go to the next office.

LA ROSSA: He told you how it was going to work; is that right?

RABON: That's right. Yes, sir.

LA ROSSA: He also told you how it was going to work here in the courtroom, didn't he?

LOWE: Again I object to the form of the question, Your Honor.

Judge Tyler doesn't reply.

LA ROSSA [to Rabon]: Did he tell you yesterday that you were going to testify here?

RABON: Yes, sir.

LA ROSSA: Did he tell you, sir, yesterday, the physical make-up of this courtroom?

Rabon moved uncomfortably in his chair and cleared his throat.

RABON: Yes, sir.

LA ROSSA: Tell me what he told you.

RABON: He said it would be a free-style, pretrial hearing, that there wouldn't be any spectators.

LA ROSSA: Did he tell you there wouldn't be a jury here?

RABON: Yes, sir.

La Rossa had seen Rabon's discomfort and, to make the bell-hop somewhat less defensive, softened his voice, and took on a more friendly air.

LA ROSSA: Did he tell you where the witness chair was going to be?

LOWE [interjecting]: Your Honor, I object to this fishing expedition. The line of questioning is irrelevant.

TYLER: Overruled.

RABON: The witness chair?

LA ROSSA: Yes.

RABON: No, sir.

LA ROSSA: Did he tell you you were going to be sworn in before you testified?

Rabon seemed relaxed now, and comfortable with the elegant attorney.

RABON: No, sir.

LA ROSSA: Did he tell you that the defendants would all be sitting at one table?

Lowe knit his brow.

RABON: They told me to look around.

LA ROSSA: Did he tell you Nalo was bald now?

Rabon was struck dumb, and looked around at Lowe.

LA ROSSA [sharply]: Did anyone tell you that yesterday, Mr. Rabon?

Rabon doesn't respond.

LA ROSSA: Mr. Rabon?

RABON: Yes, sir.

LA ROSSA: Who?

RABON: Mr. Lowe.

Lowe was expressionless. Judge Tyler hunched forward on the bench. Rabon hung his head.

LA ROSSA: Prior to the time you came into this courtroom; is that correct?

RABON: Yes, sir.

LA ROSSA: And did he tell you that Mr. Nalo was now bald and was the same individual you picked out in the lineup?

RABON: That's what he told me.

LA ROSSA: Before you came into this courtroom?

RABON: Yes, sir.

It was a blow to the prosecution, and it wouldn't be the last one. Rabon alone went on to muddy the case for Lowe. Rabon admitted that he had seen Bermudez before the lineup, and recognized him, which would render the authenticity of the lineup questionable. Also, Rabon testified now that every individual in the second lineup was clean-shaven except the stubble-bearded man with the wig.

LA ROSSA: You knew it was a wig, didn't you?

RABON: Yes, sir.

LA ROSSA: Were you told it was a wig before you came into the room?

RABON: No, sir.

LA ROSSA: Were you told while you were in that room that it was a wig.

RABON: No, sir.

LA ROSSA: But you visually can see it was a wig; is that right? Could you see that the wig was ripped?

RABON: Ripped, sir?

LA ROSSA: Yes.

RABON: No, sir.

LA ROSSA: Did it look shoddy to you in any way?

RABON: No, sir.

TYLER [interjecting]: How did you know it was a wig?

RABON: Well, it just didn't sit right on his head.

Lowe slumped in his chair as he listened to the testimony. Well, he thought, there's one more key witness, the man who identified Comfort: Elijah Weathersby.

Numerous delays, from legal questions that Lowe had to research to a brief illness of La Rossa, had put off Weathersby's testimony for about a week. Several other witnesses were called to the stand first, including several detectives involved in the lineups and in the arrests. Mrs. Rottenbucher, the landlady at Sammy's Bronx apartment, also testified. So did the attorney, John Russo, who had heard Comfort demand a lawyer outside the lineup room the morning after his arrest.

Virtually nothing was going Lowe's way. He continued his delaying tactics, trying to convince the FBI to allow their informant—whom they had refused to identify—to take the stand.

In consultations with Lowe and McKay, District Attorney Frank Hogan agreed that the U.S. attorney's office had to produce the FBI agent and/or the FBI informer if the state were to mount any kind of case. The U.S. attorney's office in New York refused. Hogan called Washington. FBI officials said the same thing, that they had good informants only because they guaranteed their anonymity. The D.A. was told that the informant and the agent were involved in other cases, and if they testified, those cases would be jeopardized.

Hogan fumed. "How much more important can other cases be than the biggest jewel robbery of all time?"

His exhortations fell on deaf federal ears.

The hearings wore on into July.

To be near Bobby, Millie was now staying with his sister Rosie in Yonkers.

Millie arrived at the courtroom each morning with their daughter, Nicole, now two years old. Bobby noted how pretty, demure, and trim Millie looked in her light summer dresses— and with her long black hair neatly brushed into a fashionable hairdo. He believed she was making a good impression on the judge.

As sometimes happened, Comfort and his wife were allowed to chat in the courtroom prior to the start of proceedings.

A wooden partition separated the judicial area from the spectators' gallery. A red leather chair was fetched and brought around the wooden separating barrier. The couple sat with their chairs facing each other alongside the partition. A security guard, gun on hip, billy club in belt, stood beside them, expressionless.

Comfort had grown a beard in the Tombs. When Lowe questioned him about it, wondering if he was growing the beard to change his appearance before the witnesses, Comfort retorted, "Would you shave there if you had to use the same blade after ten junkies and winos had shaved with it? When they let me have my own razor and blade, I'll shave."

But Comfort also knew that any edge with witnesses could be helpful.

Millie liked the beard. "If you had worn a beard when we first met," she told him, smiling, "I would never have stayed a virgin as long as I did."

"Now you tell me," he replied.

In his black-and-white-checked sports jacket and cream-colored shirt, he was once again her dashing husband.

Millie, of course, worried about the future, and made no attempt to hide her feelings.

"We've got it beat," Comfort said convincingly, hoping to please her. "They don't have anything to pin on me."

But neither of them knew for certain what—or who—the prosecution might present to the court that might change his optimism.

On July 18 Elijah Weathersby, the prosecution's star witness, finally took the stand. It was a torrid midsummer day, and the air conditioning in the courtroom had broken down.

Lowe fervently hoped that Weathersby's testimony would be the turning point for the state. Lowe, with patches of sweat showing on his white shirt, asked Weathersby to "give your testimony . . . in a loud and clear voice," for he knew Weathersby had a tendency to muffle his words.

WEATHERSBY: Yes, sir.

LOWE: Mr. Weathersby, on January 2, at the Pierre Hotel, did something happen to you?

WEATHERSBY: Yes, sir.

LOWE: Could you tell the court what happened to you?

Weathersby wiped his face with a handkerchief.

WEATHERSBY: I was tied up; I was bound, handcuffed, blindfolded, and told to be quiet.

LOWE: Mr. Weathersby, did a particular individual do this to you?

WEATHERSBY: Yes, sir.

Lowe could hardly suppress a little smile.

LOWE: Will you point him out to the court, please?

WEATHERSBY: Person over there.

TYLER: Which person?

WEATHERSBY: The center person.

TYLER: The center person?

WEATHERSBY: Yes, sir.

TYLER: Go down and point him out to me.

Weathersby unwound his lean body from the chair, rose, and walked over to where the defendants and the attorneys sat.

He walked unhesitatingly to directly behind Sammy.

Lowe couldn't believe what he was seeing.

LA ROSSA: May he put his hand on the man's shoulder?

TYLER: Yes.

Weathersby's long bony hand reached out and came to rest on Sammy's right shoulder. Sammy didn't move, and continued to look straight ahead.

So did Comfort, who was unaware that Weathersby had identified him, and *not* Sammy in the lineup. The judge and Lowe, on the other hand, were patently aware of the implications of this testimony.

Tyler, pointing to the court reporter, said, "Let the record indicate he has indicated the defendant Sammy Nalo." The judge then beckoned to Weathersby: "Come back to your seat."

When Weathersby returned, Lowe said, "Now Mr. Weathersby, would you tell the court if you see anyone *else*—"

WEATHERSBY: Yes, sir.

LOWE: —that you saw that day?

WEATHERSBY: Yes, sir.

LOWE: Will you point him out to the court, please?

WEATHERSBY: The first person sitting there.

He indicated Stern. Lowe was certain the shaken Stern was no daring thief. It was Comfort that Lowe wished identified.

Lowe was upset. "Mr. Weathersby, you have pointed two people out to the court as having been seen on January 2; is that correct?"

WEATHERSBY: Yes, sir.

LOWE: Do you see anyone else in this courtroom that you saw on January 2?

DiRenzo objected. Lowe spun around and almost shouted: "May I know the basis for that objection?"

Tyler put up his palms. "Mr. Lowe, just please keep your voice low."

Lowe said, "I'm sorry, Your Honor."

TYLER: Just a minute. I haven't ruled on that objection yet.

LOWE: I think you have ruled on that objection several times, Your Honor.

284

TYLER [annoyed]: Please, Mr. Lowe, take it easy. I don't wish to be told how to run this court.

LOWE: Sorry, Your Honor. [To Weathersby]: Did you see anyone else on the day of the robbery?

WEATHERSBY: Yes.

He pointed to Comfort.

LOWE: Does he appear any different to you today than he appeared to you on January 2?

WEATHERSBY: Yes, sir.

LOWE: In what way?

WEATHERSBY: He has a full beard.

TYLER: When and where did you see the defendant Comfort on January 2?

WEATHERSBY: I saw him when I first arrived at the desk, as he was the person that was giving the orders.

Tyler interjected and pointed out to Lowe that Weathersby had now identified three perpetrators in the robbery, but during the lineups he had only identified two.

Lowe considered that for a moment, and then decided it was time to request a recess.

He took Weathersby back to his office, and they consulted for a few minutes. Upon resumption of the hearings, Weathersby said that he wanted to withdraw a portion of his earlier testimony.

TYLER: In what regard do you want to change your testimony?

WEATHERSBY: In the identification of the person that held the gun on me as I was turning out the lights in the Café Pierre.

TYLER: Go ahead.

WEATHERSBY: The person I identified as being the person that held the gun on me was not the person. [He was referring to Sammy.]

TYLER: All right.

WEATHERSBY: The person that had the gun on me had reddish hair and a reddish mustache.

TYLER: Anything else?

WEATHERSBY: Which later on was black.

TYLER: [with eyes narrowed]: What do you mean by that?

285

WEATHERSBY: By the time I arrived in the area where I was handcuffed and blindfolded, his mustache had changed from red to black.

TYLER: And what appeared to be red a few seconds before, then suddenly became black; is that right?

WEATHERSBY: No, sir. The red had disappeared completely. It didn't change suddenly. The red had disappeared completely.

TYLER: And when you got to the corridor where this odd situation that you told us about happened, you turned around and looked at him?

WEATHERSBY: Yes, sir.

TYLER: And now he no longer had a reddish mustache?

WEATHERSBY: Yes, sir.

LOWE: That's all. Thank you.

As Weathersby left the stand, Lowe thought, Oh God!

The case for the prosecution was going from bad to terrible. People were identified, and then they were disidentified. Someone who was five feet tall became six feet tall, and a man with a red mustache became in an instant a man with a black mustache.

"The active facts that the police collectively relied on are before this court," said Greenspan in his summation to Tyler. "I will not parade them again, and Your Honor can readily see that a reasonable, prudent man would not arrest a dog for barking on this kind of evidence."

In morning proceedings throughout the hearings, Judge Tyler had heard the suppression motions; in the afternoons he convened the jury selection. Attorneys on both sides objected to this process.

"It's illegal," Lowe snapped to Tyler.

Greenspan agreed, and told the judge, "You're disobeying the law." The rules provide, Greenspan told Tyler, that the determination of admissible evidence must be made prior to jury selection: the picking of a jury officially commences a trial. Judge Tyler ignored the pleas.

Both sides had hoped that the other would capitulate before the case went to trial. Neither wanted to rush the situation, in the belief that the more the other side thought about the evidence, the more it would weaken.

What Tyler was attempting was to use pressure on both sides to force a settlement out of court as quickly as possible. It was apparent that he felt it incumbent upon his judicial position to dispose of cases rapidly. He obviously saw nothing improper in a judge assuming this to be his role, although it was considered a highly controversial legal posture.

Tyler acknowledged that the backlog of criminal cases in New York was staggering, and this sorry predicament was reason enough for him to proceed in this unusual manner. Expediting cases through plea bargaining before they came to trial had become common practice in recent times.

"I wasn't happy with what Tyler was doing," recalled Lowe. "He was trying to force a plea. I didn't fault him for it. But I thought I had a stronger case than he thought—or said—I did. Especially in regard to Sammy. I thought I had Sammy by the short hairs because the jewels that turned up in Detroit were identified as coming from the Pierre robbery, and Sammy was linked directly to those jewels. Tyler told me, 'Your case is a little weak. I may have to grant their applications to suppress all this evidence.' On the other hand he [the judge] told the defense, 'There's no way I'm going to grant your application to suppress this evidence. So you might as well cut your losses and take what you can get.' As I understood it, Tyler wanted to go on vacation, and so did the defense attorneys. It was mid-July, and I guess they didn't want this thing taking up their entire summer."

Comfort was convinced that not a single piece of evidence had been produced that could nail him as a perpetrator in the Pierre robbery. He had not been arrested with the jewels in the Summit Hotel, nor had he been caught with the settings, as Sammy had been. The stones found on Comfort when he was arrested could not be identified. The jewels that turned up in Detroit bore no connection to him. The Pierre witnesses had been virtually discredited by ambiguous, conflicting, and, at times, even ludicrous testimony.

Comfort, however, had other concerns relating to his jewel

287

robberies, which cost the victims somewhere between $20 million and $25 million in gems. He was still a suspect in the Sophia Loren case, as well as in the Regency Hotel robbery and other hotel robberies with *modus operandi* similar to the Pierre. As the *New York Times* would report, "The police investigation has focused on a number of highly skilled hotel robberies that occurred in 1970 and 1971 in an effort to determine whether the same group was involved. . . . To date, however, none of the defendants has been charged with these holdups." Also, Bobby realized it was only a matter of time before the Sutton Place robbery would emerge from the investigations. And Mrs. Neff had had a long, studied look at him; she had described him accurately in the newspaper account he had read after the robbery.

So when Greenspan told him that the judge was seeking a deal, Comfort was delighted.

Without question, Bobby Comfort would rather do a "little stretch" than go through all the other trials he saw looming ahead. But any sentence longer than four years would be unacceptable. With "good time," he would have two and a half years to serve on a four-year term; actually, only two years, in light of his stay in the Tombs for the six months prior to the hearings. That time would have to be applied against the ultimate sentence.

Since he felt he was in a strong bargaining position—and understanding that the D.A. wanted a conviction, but with meager evidence in his portfolio—Comfort put forward other demands to Greenspan: (1) complete acquittal for all previous crimes known and unknown; and (2) dismissal of any penalties for any and all income tax, state or federal, not paid.

Greenspan agreed to pursue this line with the D.A. and the judge.

When Comfort outlined the plan to Nalo, he was surprised at his reaction. Sammy was dead set against it. "Don't talk about no pleas, I'm not makin' no pleas," Sammy said.

"Sammy, you don't realize it, but we're not walking out free under any condition," Comfort told him. "You did your little steal, and you got caught. You can get at least ten years on a federal charge of interstate transportation of stolen property. I know the

288

law. They've got the merchandise, and they've got the guy out there who said you gave it to him; and he doesn't look like an accomplice because he turned it in."

"Okay. One year, I'll agree to that. But nothing more. After all the time you spent in prison, two and a half years would be like a weekend vacation."

"Look," said Comfort, "ask La Rossa. He'll tell you I'm right."

And La Rossa did. It didn't take long for the lawyer to convince Sammy that Bobby was right. Sammy accepted the four-year proposal that was still in the bargaining stages.

At one point during the plea bargaining, on July 19, 1972, Judge Tyler took Greenspan and Lowe to a Longchamps restaurant for lunch. It was the first time that Greenspan had ever known a presiding judge to invite the contesting attorneys to lunch; usually, attorneys would take the *judge* to lunch in an attempt to sway him to their side. This process by no means diminishes the relationship between the court and the counselors. It is a traditional and acceptable procedure in the adversary process—honest men of the court discussing the case together, fraternally and informally. But now it seemed Tyler was trying to win *them* over. Tyler insisted that he buy the lunch to maintain ethical propriety.

At lunch Greenspan drove home his particulars for length of sentence. The judge refused to give a commitment.

"Judge," said Greenspan, "unless I know what my man's going to get, unless I know what the parameters are, we are not going into any plea bargaining."

"Well, you've got to work it out with the D.A.," Judge Tyler replied.

"But whatever I say isn't binding on you, Judge," said Lowe.

Tyler said, "Well, each of you will have to tell me what you want, and then I'll decide for myself."

Lowe made it clear that he was appalled at the possibility of a short sentence. He insisted on a fifteen-year sentence in the event of guilty pleas. Greenspan rejected this proposal out of hand.

Judge Tyler then urged Lowe to make inquiry within the D.A.'s office to determine if a shorter sentence would be acceptable. That was where the lunch ended.

Ultimately, Tyler himself, according to Lowe, made a call to District Attorney Hogan in an attempt to work out the shorter sentence and resolve the case.

After consultations with the D.A., Judge Tyler supposedly received an agreement from Hogan that a sentence of zero to seven years would be acceptable to the people.

When Greenspan relayed this to Comfort, his client said unequivocally, "No. Four years, and no more."

During the hearings the next day, July 20, Greenspan passed on to Tyler his client's position. Tyler said he would make no promises, that no one could coerce him into any kind of sentence. He would not be threatened.

"Then we've got no deal," said Greenspan, and walked out of the judge's chambers.

A few hours later Tyler called the defense attorneys to his chambers.

According to Greenspan, Tyler said, "Okay, you've got a deal," and he held up four fingers.

Greenspan said, "Zip to four?"

Tyler nodded in agreement.

Greenspan then received guarantees from the IRS, FBI, and New York State that Comfort would not be subject to future prosecution for income-tax evasion, or charges of other crimes, if ultimately discovered by the authorities.

Greenspan assured Comfort he would receive a written guarantee from the state to that effect. As for the federal government, the agreement was made with a handshake. "My experience with the U.S. attorney's office in every place in the country is that when you make a deal with federal prosecutors, their word is absolutely immaculate," Greenspan said.

Late that afternoon of July 20, Tyler called the defendants and their lawyers into his chambers. It was a small, stuffy room with green paint peeling off the walls. Tyler sat behind his desk and puffed on his pipe.

"What will you two fellows want?" he asked Comfort and Nalo.

Comfort replied, "No more than four."

Tyler, recalled Comfort, said, "Okay. In the interest of expediting this case, I'll give you each four years."

"I want it in the record, Judge," said Comfort.

"We never put it in the record," Tyler said.

Comfort said, "I've been in jail quite a while, Judge, and I've been in a lot of different courts—and I don't trust judges, lawyers, or police. Are you going to give me four years or are you going to double-cross me?"

Tyler leaned back in his chair, pulled back his robe, and said, "Trust me, fellas. I have your best interests at heart."

Comfort said: "Okay, you've been extremely fair during the hearings. I'm going to trust you because of that. It's probably a mistake, but I'm trusting you."

When Lowe learned of the deal, he was infuriated. He did, however, convince Tyler to put off sentencing for six months so that it could be done in relative obscurity. Lowe felt that the publicity of a short sentence for a crime of the magnitude of the Pierre could be embarrassing to the D.A.'s office. It was far better that the public remember only that the authorities had captured the robbers and broken the case.

Between July and December of 1972—from the time Comfort was out on bail (his sister Rosie Gustino had put up her ninety-thousand-dollar house in Yonkers as his bail bond) to when he would report to the New York D.A.'s office to begin serving his sentence—he stayed home in Rochester with nothing more to do than ruminate on the past and anticipate options for the future.

One of his most frequently recurring thoughts concerned the whereabouts of the black satchel containing the jewels from the Pierre. The whereabouts of City, of course, would determine the location of that satchel. According to Comfort, this is the sequence of events that transpired after his arrest:

As soon as Comfort had discovered Sammy's end run, he contacted a friend, Carmen, to locate City, to make sure he didn't think that he, Comfort, had anything to do with the $750,000 in gems found in Detroit. Carmen learned that City had disappeared; but on July 21, 1972, the day before Comfort was released on bail, he was visited at the Tombs by Carmen.

Separated by a thick glass window, Carmen and Comfort spoke over the telephone intercom system. Carmen, a short, balding, crooked-nosed man with a froggy voice, told Comfort, "Meet me tomorrow around the corner from my place at three-thirty." "Around the corner from my place" meant the Plaka.

Carmen had done odd jobs for Comfort and Sammy. He had never gone on a robbery with them, but he had kept the work cars in good order during the winter months, helped case some hotels, and had looked after Sammy's apartments. He was a man-around-town who heard things, passed messages, and was known never to repeat anything confidential. He obviously had something important to relate to Comfort.

The following day Comfort was released from the Tombs. With time to kill before the meeting, Comfort arrived at the Plaka and sat in a booth, cooling off with a gin and tonic. He looked around at the few men seated at the bar in the semidarkness; he looked at the plants hanging on the separation between the bar and the booths, at the familiar mural of a Greek port on the wall above the booth, and he smelled the steaks broiling in the kitchen, remembering that this was the same place, the same booth in fact, where it all began three years before when he first met Sammy.

Carmen came in, sat down beside Comfort in the booth, and wasted no time. "Got a message from City for you," he said. "He called me. Wants to get in touch with you."

Comfort was surprised—happy, but surprised. Since he had not heard from City during the six months he was in jail, Comfort thought he had surely vanished with the Pierre jewels. Comfort had simply assumed that City, after reading about how the stones had turned up in Detroit, must have deduced that the two partners, Sammy and Comfort, had arranged a private deal to swindle the other three men.

"Where does he want to contact me?" asked Comfort. "When?"

Carmen said: "He's out of town—wouldn't tell me where. He says for you to be at the phone booth on the corner of Seventy-fifth and Broadway at seven-thirty tomorrow night. He'll call."

*   *   *

292

At 7:15 the next evening Comfort arrived at the designated corner. He had planned to occupy the booth for fifteen minutes to make certain the phone was free.

A fat Hispanic woman, with two bulky shopping bags at her feet, was on the phone. Although the glass door was closed, he could hear her chattering loudly in Spanish.

At 7:20 she was still on the phone.

At 7:26 Comfort looked into the booth again. The woman was still talking. At 7:28 he knocked on the window; she didn't hear him. He knocked louder. She looked up quizzically, still talking into the mouthpiece.

Comfort motioned for her to open the door. Annoyed, she did. The odor that emanated from the booth was overpowering. Comfort said, "Miss, there's something very important . . ."

"*No hablo inglés*," she interrupted. She slammed the door.

Comfort bristled but kept his temper under control.

He knocked again. She gave him a withering look.

Christ Almighty. His watch read 7:29.

In one swift move Bobby shoved open the door, grabbed the woman's two bags, and ran around the back of the booth.

She howled and ran out of the booth after him. Dropping the bags, he continued around the booth, jumped in, and slammed the door shut. A squeal from the voice on the dangling receiver sounded alarmed. Comfort hung up the phone.

The woman was beating on the door. The phone rang.

Comfort looked at the woman, opened the door, reached into his pocket, pulled out a fifty-dollar bill and thrust it into her hand—then slammed shut the glass door. She was fuming, then, glancing down into her hand, she suddenly broke into a gap-toothed smile.

"*Gracias, señor*," she called out, nodding her head vigorously.

Bobby, breathing hard, grabbed the phone.

"Hello!"

"Bob?"

"Yeah."

"Something wrong?"

"No, there was just a little inconvenience here. How you doin'?"

"Pretty good. Can I talk?"

"Yeah," Comfort said. "It's good to hear from you again. I thought you might have swung with the satchel."

"When the stuff showed up in Detroit, I figured you and Sammy cut us out of the deal."

"I was worried you would."

"But I got word it wasn't you. So it had to be that little bastard Sammy doing it alone."

"He did."

"All right. I'm planning to give you your split."

"What about the other guys?"

"Everybody'll get their split except Sammy. He gets nothing."

"I'm not going to stand here and defend a guy who robbed us, but there is something in his favor."

"What's that?"

"He hasn't talked—and he isn't going to."

"Fuck 'im. He gets not one red cent."

"That's up to you. When am I going to get my share of the jewels?"

"I'll be in touch. Talk to you soon." Click.

Comfort stood there thoughtfully for a moment with the buzzing of the phone in his ear. He had to trust City; he had no alternative. Slowly, he placed the phone back on the hook. He turned to open the glass door and recoiled in surprise. The fat Spanish lady was grinning weirdly at him.

When Bobby Comfort returned to Rochester, he was relaxed and content. It seemed that his life was in order—even with a jail sentence facing him. He had enough money to last him and his family for a long time, and he had the assurance from City that he would be getting a few million more. Now all that remained was a relatively short jail term. Judge Tyler had set the middle of December for sentencing. He was at liberty until then.

One late summer afternoon, as he and Millie sat in their backyard sipping beer, Bobby told his wife that he would not change a single day of his life—not a single minute.

"I remember reading this French writer, Balzac, who said, 'Behind every fortune there is a crime.' I believe it. How else could you become rich unless you do something illegal? A lot of rich people might not think they're doing anything wrong, just like I didn't think I was doing anything wrong. But business people, they'll double-cross you or trick you or destroy you to get money. Rockefeller did it, Henry Ford did it. You know all those people who got rich with the railroads and oil and Wall Street—they were called 'robber barons.' I've found that there's not a legitimate businessman—big or small—that's not going to do something crooked. I'm not so different from them."

"Bobby, I think you're crazy," Millie said.

"Why?"

"Because I think all your robberies were wrong. Even if it's true that when you got older you only stole from the rich. It was still their money. But more important, you were frightening innocent people in those hotels. How would you feel if someone put a gun to your face and was ordering you around, blindfolding you? Wouldn't you be petrified? Wouldn't you hate that person?"

"Sure I would," he replied, "but I knew I wasn't going to hurt them."

"They didn't know it."

"Look, I never killed anybody. Nixon, Johnson—presidents!— they sent kids out to Vietnam to get their heads blown off!"

"It's not the same thing."

"Millie, if you think I'm so bad, how come you stay with me?"

"Sometimes I wonder. But I think basically you're a good human being. I know you are. Even with all your stickups. I see a lot of guys, supposedly hard-working, good family men, who degrade their wives, cheat on them, treat 'em like dirt. You've never done that to me."

Comfort moved to elaborate on the surprisingly positive turn the conversation had taken.

"And I've been a good provider for you."

She looked at him strangely. "Where do you come up with something like that?" she asked.

"Haven't we always had enough money?" he asked defensively.

"Okay, so we've always had enough to eat, and enough clothes. But what I've never had is security. We never had investments or

295

insurance or anything like that. You can't live day by day. When you're younger you can, because you don't have responsibilities. It's different now with a family."

"You chose this life with me, Mill," he said. "You knew what kind of guy I was."

"I did. And in the beginning it was fun, it really was. All that excitement and night life and no concern about tomorrow. But I had to change. You said *you* would, but you haven't. You kept giving me the old con job that things would be different. The same old story. And I kept falling for it."

"It must mean you want to keep falling for it."

"Maybe I do," she said. "Maybe deep down there's too much love between us to ever make us separate. But then at times I think you're *not* thinking of me, and I hate you so much I want to tear your heart out."

"I know," he said, smiling weakly, "sometimes you've tried."

◆ 35 ◆

On December 14, 1972, arraignment for sentencing was held. Bobby Comfort and Sammy Nalo, their attorneys, and Assistant Attorney General Lowe stood before Judge Tyler's bench.

TYLER: Mr. Comfort, is Mr. Greenspan, standing beside you, your lawyer?

COMFORT: Yes, Your Honor.

TYLER: Did you hear him indicate to the court that you desired to withdraw your plea of not guilty?

COMFORT: Yes, Your Honor.

TYLER: Had anyone threatened you in order to induce you to change your plea?

COMFORT: No.

TYLER: Has anyone promised you what the sentence of the court would be in order to induce you to change your plea?

Bobby paused and thought, Well, this is the way the system works—he lies and I lie. "No, Your Honor," Comfort said.

Precisely the same routine was followed with Nalo.

Then the prosecution was permitted to make its statement. Lowe said that because of the seriousness of the crime, the fact that weapons had been used, that nineteen to twenty-one people were bound and gagged, and approximately $10 million in jewels and cash were taken, "The people ask that a maximum seven-year term of imprisonment be imposed."

Immediately, La Rossa and Greenspan objected. This was not the deal that had been set in July, they asserted. But Tyler had unexpectedly taken Lowe's position. He said Mr. Lowe had a right to represent his client, the people, just as the defense attorneys did. "Now, I think it comes with ill grace to suggest that the people can't make a recommendation with regard to what they feel is a proper punishment in this case."

"That wasn't in our prior agreement," said Greenspan.

Judge Tyler called for an adjournment to check the record. One week passed before the court reconvened.

Tyler then imposed his sentence: "Zero to seven years." Comfort shot a look at Greenspan. "What happened?" he asked. "I don't know," Greenspan replied, shocked. "I just don't know."

Comfort and Sammy immediately withdrew their guilty pleas. Tyler refused to accept.

Comfort was ordered to begin serving his prison term directly after New Year's, exactly one year after he had masterminded with Sammy the perfectly executed crime.*

"I'll beat it," he told Millie. "I'll get that four-year sentence he promised. I'm going to appeal, and I'll beat those bastards."

Millie listened, but like everyone else she was skeptical.

"There's nothing on paper to prove your case," she said.

"You're right, there isn't, but there were witnesses when Tyler made his deal with us."

For Millie the seven-year sentence was a tough blow. It meant that, even with "good time," her husband was facing five years away, and she was facing the same period of time alone.

As much as she sympathized with his plight, some of the bit-

---

* In separate proceedings Paulino and Fradkin received one-year probations for criminal possession of stolen property, and Bert Stern received a zero-to-three-year sentence for criminal possession of stolen property.

terness she felt for the life he had chosen welled up within her.

Conversely, she had no one to blame but herself. She certainly could have left him long ago if she had really wanted to.

On January 2, 1973, the last night before flying to New York to turn himself in to the authorities, Bobby and Millie went to their favorite restaurant. Bobby bought drinks and dinner for everyone in the place. The dinner check came to twelve hundred dollars. In the last few years, as his reputation had grown as a big-time jewel thief, Comfort had been made to feel like a celebrity in many of the places he frequented in Rochester. The more money he had, the more he spent, and the more he was catered to.

As the night wore on, Bobby drank heavily. Millie, watching him, was distressed. She wasn't sure why. Her feelings were confused. She couldn't decide whether Bobby was acting this way to ease the pain of leaving, or because he really didn't care about leaving her and Nicole. She was still in a quandary when they finally got back home at the crack of dawn. It had been a miserable party for her.

Bobby seemed oblivious, laughing and talking about the evening's great fun. Suddenly, something triggered all of Millie's pent-up emotions. She shouted and threw a chair at him.

"What the hell's this? What's wrong?" he cried.

"You don't give a damn about me. About me or the baby."

"Are you nuts?"

"Get out," she screamed. She picked up a lamp and smashed it over his upraised arm. "Get out. I hope you rot like a dog in that goddamn prison."

He grabbed her and wrestled her against the wall. She attempted to escape his grip and scratch him. He pinned her arms to her side. Helpless now, she began to sob, and as he released his hold, she remained against him.

Bobby raised her head and kissed her, tasting the salt of her tears. Then, gently, he led her to the bed.

Bobby Comfort flew to New York City the next day and surrendered himself at Lowe's office. From there he was taken to Sing

Sing for processing to Attica. After a few days he wrote Millie a long, loving letter. She did not answer.

He sent a second letter, and again no response.

After a couple of weeks he tried a third letter. It began: "Look, Mill, at least write me and tell me you're not going to write. This way I'm going crazy!"

A month later he received his first letter from his wife.

"Bob, you bastard, you left me pregnant. . . ."

She went on to chastise him for recklessly leaving her alone to care for one small daughter and, soon, a second child.

His reply was immediate. "You may be mad, but I'm excited that we'll be having another kid. Don't worry. Everything will be all right. I promise."

Meanwhile, he was researching the prison law books, preparing his petition to the New York Appellate Court to "vacate" his seven-year sentence, contending that Judge Tyler had erred in pronouncing a sentence that differed from oral agreement during the plea-bargaining process.

Comfort knew his appeal hinged on witnesses, particularly the attorneys who were present when Tyler had made his four-finger gesture. He wrote Greenspan, La Rossa, and DiRenzo, requesting affidavits from them attesting to the events in Tyler's chambers. Greenspan could not be a witness as well as a counselor for Comfort, so he now no longer represented him, and he did supply the desired affidavit. La Rossa did not respond immediately, nor did DiRenzo; but both eventually furnished their written statements.

The affidavits supported the position that Judge Andrew Tyler did agree that a four-year sentence would be imposed in exchange for the guilty pleas of the two men.

With these in hand Comfort sent a letter on March 19, 1974, to Judge Tyler. It read:

Dear Sir:

Enclosed please find a copy of Mr. La Rossa's, Mr. Di-Renzo's and Mr. Greenspan's affidavits, telling what really happened in your courtroom. If you are going to claim that

300

they are lying and that I am lying, <u>I demand that you charge us with perjury.</u> If we were lying to the court, there is a fraud against the court. <u>I dare you to charge us with any crime.</u>

If we are going by the court record, how come you said in the record that the D.A. does not dictate sentences to you? Does the D.A. usually dictate sentences to you? In this case you found it necessary to make a point that he would not dictate our sentence to you—or was this because that was one of the things you discussed with me off the record?

Why did you clear the courtroom before taking our plea? Is it because I told you, you could not ask me any question about missing money, or about partners that weren't caught—that the only thing you could ask was if we did commit the crime?

Now none of this appears in the court record, but you tell me why you cleared the courtroom. I watched you take pleas before; that's why I made that part of the deal in your chambers, because I have seen how you questioned other defendants before taking their pleas, and I made sure you did not question me in the same way. And you did keep this part of the deal.

Now Mr. DiRenzo, Mr. La Rossa, Mr. Greenspan, Mr. Stern, Mr. Nalo, and myself, who were all present, <u>will testify under oath to the truth about this deal.</u> Is all this really necessary, or will you admit to the fact that I was supposed to get a four-year sentence?

Now, while few of you judges have been honorable in your chosen profession, and you in particular are not an honorable man; <u>I am honorable in my chosen profession.</u> I am not like Mr. John Dean [counsel to President Nixon—and a federal informer] and other stalwart members of our country: I am sure glad a foreign power never got any of them or you; you would give up your mothers to save yourselves: I may be wrong, but I feel that I have been <u>honorable at all times in my line of work.</u>

No matter what promises were made to me, that I could

go free if I would talk, I leave that to people like you and Mr. Dean, and all the other leaders of our country. Few of you have any pride or principles, but I do, that's what makes me stronger than you even though I am a criminal.

I am sending you a copy of a magazine article, that came out of the book "*Target Blue*" by Robert Daley. That shows that Mr. Lowe committed perjury in your court when he said he didn't talk to any of the witnesses. Of course Robert Daley doesn't have much respect for your court or he wouldn't have exposed you in his book. Some lineup, wasn't it? Mr. Lowe telling Weathersby to help a brother, "to get Whitey," saying that you were playing poker with justice. Do I have any civil rights, or are they only for black people?

I claim that you, a black judge and a black D.A. and black witnesses, violated my civil rights. That you, because no one has any respect for your court or you, can brag in books and magazines, how they can have an illegal lineup, because you will not even recognize an insult when you read it.

Now I dare you again to charge me and the attorneys with any kind of a crime, or prove that we are lying. Unless you reply and correct the Dirty Rotten Trick you played on me, I am going to send this letter and everything else to every newspaper in New York State. One of them might help me, maybe even one of the black papers will. Why don't you do the right thing, and as Mr. Lowe said, stop playing poker with Justice.

> Robert Comfort #29108
> Box 149
> Attica, New York 14011

The appellate trial began in June 1974, in the New York Supreme Court Building in Manhattan. The defense lawyers and Comfort and Nalo were the first to appear on the stand.

Tyler was called as a witness but refused to come, explaining that he was in the middle of a trial.

Justice James J. Leff ordered Tyler to appear, threatening

him with contempt of court if he did not. Under this pressure Tyler finally did take the stand and said he did "not remember making any four-year promise."

At the conclusion of the hearing, Leff ruled that the "government's story was incredible as a matter of law, and incredible as a matter of fact."

Leff vacated the seven-year sentence and offered Comfort and Nalo the option of entering into a new trial or accepting the four years that Leff determined had been promised them. Comfort took the four years.

It was a resounding legal victory for Comfort and, with joy, he wrote Millie about it. Now he had less than a year to serve. But time passed more slowly during this prison sentence than any others he had served. For one thing, he was unable to get a release to be present at the birth of his second daughter, Stacy.

Six months after her birth Stacy fell from her crib and suffered a concussion. The baby was rushed to the hospital, where she was placed on the critical list. Millie was distraught. She needed Bobby desperately. She called Attica to ask for his temporary release in this emergency, but the Attica officials refused. She called Albany, the state capital, to learn that only Attica could issue a release. Another call to Attica was fruitless. All that time Comfort could do nothing but sit in his nine-by-six cell and wait for word. Meanwhile, Stacy recovered fully.

Comfort's father died a few months before Bobby's release. Bobby was offered the opportunity to attend the funeral but declined. He simply did not wish to stand up before the entire family in handcuffs, accompanied by prison guards. He figured his father would understand.

In recent years, even after the breakup of his parents' marriage—they were legally separated in 1949—Bobby Comfort had seen more of his father than at any time since boyhood. The old man hung around a gambling joint on North Street, which Bobby visited often. Old Joe Comfort had been critical of Bobby's decisions concerning the Pierre. He told his son that he had been stupid to trust Sammy; but nonetheless Bobby believed that his father admired him for his daring.

Indeed, among the effects found in the elder Comfort's YMCA

room at his death were several detective and news magazines which referred to Bobby as "Mastermind."

On June 23, 1975, Robert Anthony Comfort, Number 29108, age forty-two, walked out of the Attica Correctional Facility with his parole papers, having served two and a half years for hotel and private-home jewel thefts that collectively approximated a value of $20 million.

At the prison's front gate, seated behind the wheel of a metallic-gray Cadillac Coupe de Ville, was Millie, waiting for him as in all the times past.

Shortly after Comfort's release from Attica, he learned that Sammy Nalo had begun serving his prison sentence.

The reason for the delay was partially centered on Sammy's indecision about his guilty plea, changing it to not guilty, and reversing it again. Further information filtering down to Comfort indicated that Nalo, out on bail, had been targeted for death. Once, an attempt had been made on his life while driving out of the parking lot at the Market Diner in the company of his new wife. The gunman fired six rounds and missed.

A second attempt occurred one night as Sammy walked out of the Plaka restaurant on Broadway. A car with four gunmen sped by and pumped bullets into his stomach and chest. Sammy survived, but refused to identify his assailants to the police. The attempts at his murder remain unsolved, although police speculated that unpaid gambling debts were the reason for the attacks.

Finally, in the fall of 1975, after a period of hospital recuperation, Sammy was remanded to Attica to fulfill his four-year prison sentence.

After his release Sammy had called on occasion and Comfort had been cordial. "But," Comfort recalled, "I decided to lose his phone numbers."

304

Then on Saturday, December 8, 1979, Comfort heard on a news broadcast that Sammy and three other men had been seized by police while robbing Spritzer & Fuhrman, an exclusive midtown Manhattan jewelry firm, of $2 million in gems. Seventeen hostages were found handcuffed, with their mouths and eyes taped. It was noted by the police how similar the operation of this crime was to the Pierre heist. Coincidentally, another link between the two robberies was that Lieutenant Edward O'Connor, leading the police unit that burst into the jewelry firm, was also commander of the team that captured Nalo and Comfort after the Pierre robbery.

"I had surveillance on him for nine months," O'Connor recalled. "And we had good information on his activities. I caught him with his hand in the cookie jar. I yanked him right off the elevator with his black mask on." O'Connor also gave grudging respect to Nalo, whom he called "a master field general in crime." He added, "I always thought Sammy was the real brains behind those hotel robberies. But of course I knew less about Comfort because he lived upstate."

Sammy Nalo would nonetheless plead not guilty to the robbery. "I was just there to buy an engagement ring for my girlfriend," he said.

"With a mask and a gun?" someone replied.

Nalo shrugged.

He was found guilty and is now serving a 9½-to-19-year sentence for that attempted crime. When syndicated newspaper columnist Earl Wilson called Comfort for a reaction, Comfort said sincerely, "I like Sammy. I hate to see anybody get in trouble. I feel bad."

The last Comfort heard about Doc was that he was operating as a silent partner in a chain of dance studios/social clubs in the Midwest.

Country, meanwhile, had returned to his home in rural upstate New York, where in recent years he has substantially increased his farm acreage. He and Comfort would see each other occasionally in Rochester.

305

And City? Comfort said he never heard from him again.

As for the other principals in the Pierre case, Andrew Tyler remains a judge in Manhattan; Richard Lowe went from the district attorney's office to become deputy inspector general in the Department of Health and Human Services in Washington, D.C., and then in 1985 was appointed a judge in the Criminal Courts Division in Manhattan; Joe Holliday remains with the Federal Bureau of Investigation, and George Bermudez retired from the New York Police Department to become a private investigator.

For several years after his return from Attica in 1975, Bobby Comfort had no visible means of income. He had no job, though he spoke enthusiastically about opening a business with Millie. He liked the idea of an arts-and-crafts store in the nearby shopping mall, which would feature Millie's macramé plant holders. When Comfort mentioned this to an ex-con friend on the phone, the fellow burst out laughing and then called to his wife: "Hey, honey, did you hear the latest? The great rubber nose is opening up a hobby shop!" The project never got beyond the conversation stage. Periodically, Comfort took part in a card game for substantial stakes, and, as in days past, he never lost. As for stealing, he said never again. The chance of a prison sentence and loss of his family was too great a risk to take.

Every morning Comfort leisurely had a few cups of coffee, smoked several cigarettes, and tuned in to his favorite morning TV program, "The Phil Donahue Show."

In the afternoons he continued a habit ingrained after seventeen years of confinement in prison. With hands hooked in his waistband, he paced the width of his backyard, treading a path through the grass while listening to the birds chirping cheerfully in the trees. He enjoyed these periods of solitude in the peaceful setting. He said he liked being alone with his thoughts.

He did get a business for a brief period. He and a friend, a known fence, opened a gold-and-silver exchange in Rochester. "I deal in jewelry," said Comfort. "It's something I know about." But it wasn't a happy time for him. He complained of police harassment, and there were obviously other problems. One day, while he was away from the store, two men entered, went straight to his partner, and shot him in the face. Comfort's partner, and friend, was killed on the spot. After the negative publicity, Comfort found the problems of trying to operate the store insurmountable, and returned to retirement.

He was often the only father at the afternoon PTA meetings at the local grammar school. Friends often dropped by his home, including one who, from a long coat that had as many pockets as Harpo Marx's coat, withdrew steaks and sweaters and shoes and even household appliances.

One day a pal showed Comfort a copy of the *Guinness Book of World Records.* Under the heading "Jewels, Record Robbery," Comfort found the Pierre Hotel robbery listed. An unofficial estimate ran as high as $5 million, the entry read.

Comfort smiled when he read that line. A *New York Times* reference, made at the time of the robbery, had been more accurate. Comfort figured that the Pierre total, including cash, had come to more than $10 million.

As for the rest of the Pierre spoils, one can only speculate whether Bobby Comfort's ex-associate City ever called him again, as he had promised, and whether they ever met. Comfort continued to maintain that he never received the second phone call or saw the satchel again.

Of course, one of Comfort's more significant boyhood experiences had centered around a black satchel, just as a major event in his adult life focused on yet another.

When at age ten Bobby Comfort stole watches from his father's black satchel, he steadfastly denied the theft, even as his mother threatened him with a butcher knife at his throat.

Thirty-five years after that incident Comfort maintained a silence regarding the gleaming contents of the latter-day black leather satchel.

However one may assess the man Bobby Comfort, whether he is a "cold-blooded" thief or a "Robin Hood," a devoted friend and family man or a menace to society, a product of our culture or the practitioner of a twisted personal code—whatever the judgment, those two black leather satchels suggest that the life of Bobby Comfort had swung full cycle.

For several years Comfort, who smoked as many as two packs of cigarettes a day—though he might quit for a few weeks at a time, and then return to his habit—suffered from a shortness of breath. Sometimes he had coughing spells that made him bend over in pain. In 1985 he suffered two strokes and a heart attack. In the spring of 1986 he had a second heart attack; on Friday, June 6, 1986, in the Rochester General Hospital, Robert Anthony Comfort died. He was fifty-three years old.

EPILOGUE

A sunny May morning in 1978, and the plane that carried me to the Rochester, New York, airport swept down onto the gleaming tarmac right on schedule. I had been told that the man I was to meet and discuss doing a book about—the notorious jewel thief Bobby Comfort—would be waiting for me in the terminal. He would be wearing a red sweater so that I could readily identify him.

When I came off the plane, I walked through the small terminal and in and out of the coffee shop looking for a man in a red sweater, but I couldn't find him.

Fifteen minutes later, having grown increasingly restless, I looked up to see a man in a red sweater hurrying toward me. It was Bobby Comfort. He apologized for being tardy; and as we walked out of the terminal and into the car—where his wife Millie sat behind the wheel—Comfort explained why he was late.

It seemed that one of the first men off the plane fit my general description, as given to him by a New York publisher. This man had approached Comfort and asked, "Are you the one I'm supposed to meet?" Comfort replied that he was. They walked to the car, settled in, and Millie drove off.

Comfort observed how tightly the man held his valise, and thought it strange. Then he was surprised when the man referred to "going to the store" instead of to Comfort's home for the arranged talk. At this point Comfort and his wife exchanged glances, both wondering about the so-called writer in the back seat.

After a few polite questions the confusion was cleared up. Comfort learned that his passenger was not a writer at all, but a salesman.

The three laughed at the peculiar mix-up, and Millie turned the car around and headed back to the airport.

"By the way," Comfort said as they pulled up to the curbside of the terminal, "who were you supposed to be meeting?"

"Someone from Hershberg's," the salesman said.

"Hershberg's!" Comfort said. "Is that right?"

Comfort got out of the car and pushed the seat forward so his passenger could climb out. He jokingly advised him to be more careful about getting into cars with strangers. The man grinned sheepishly. They shook hands and the salesman departed.

When Comfort finished the story, I said, "I've never heard of Hershberg's. What is it?"

"Hershberg's," Comfort said with a smile, "is the largest jewelry store in Rochester."

"Oh?"

"And just before he left the man said, 'Lucky for me you're an honest citizen, because I'm a jewelry salesman'—he tapped his sample case—'and I'm carrying over half a million dollars in diamonds in this thing.'"

I.B.

310

Appendix

The following excerpt is an exact reproduction of records of the New York City Police Department's investigation.

HOTEL PIERRE ROBBERY

6 EAST 61ST STREET

NEW YORK CITY, N.Y.

SUNDAY–JANUARY 2nd, 1972

UF61#-55—19th PRECINCT

CASE #10—4TH DETECTIVE

DISTRICT ROBBERY SQUAD

INVESTIGATION

Persons Taken, Handcuffed and Blindfolded	Area in Hotel They Were Taken From
1. James Weeda Security Guard	1. Taken from Main Lobby
2. Benjamin O'Sullivan Assistant Night Manager	2. Taken from alcove-center of lobby-
3. Louis Rabon Bell boy	3. Taken from Main Lobby
4. Thomas Grady Security Guard	4. Taken in front of revolving door
5. Abraham Salib Room Clerk	5. Taken from behind front desk
6. Rufus Dash Cleaner	6. Taken from office behind front desk
7. Adolf Ross Night Auditor	7. Taken from vault room Located on side of front desk
8. Mr. & Mrs. Hilio Faraga Guests of Hotel	8. Taken on thirty-seventh floor
9. Mrs. Sylvia Barbosa Guest of Hotel	9. Taken from Room 3710
10. Charles Figueroa Delivering Magazines	10. Taken from front desk
11. William Irrzary Elevator Operator	11. Taken from in front of elevator
12. William Weeda Security Guard	12. Taken from center of lobby
13. Charles Robinson Security Guard	13. Taken from wash room-Located near elevators
14. Ralph Robinson Cleaner	14. Taken from entrance to Cafe Pierre-Foot of "La Foret Room"
15. William Parker Cleaner	15. Taken from main lobby
16. Elijah Cooper Cleaner	16. Taken from manager's area-Located behind alcove
17. Henry Hopkins Cleaner	17. Taken from Oval Room Located between ball-rooms-Before elevator.
18. Ignacio Unanue Elevator Operator	18. Taken from in front of elevators.

Persons Taken, Handcuffed and Blindfolded	Area in Hotel They Were Taken From
19. Francisco Velez Kitchen Help	19. Taken from center of lobby.
20. Victor Corbas Cook	20. Taken from center of lobby.
21. Elijah Weathersby cleaner	21.

SAFETY DEPOSIT BOXES BURGLARIZED

Name	Box Number	Cash Taken	Jewelry Taken	Total
Mrs. T. Yawkey Apt. 3601-04	44	$17,500	$17,000	$34,500
Mrs. Scurlock Apt. 1901	50	None	None	None
Mrs. Schulte Apt. 2711	105	None	None	None
Mrs. McLean Apt. 1602	137	None	Trinkets No Value	No Value
Mr. Biberman	148	No appraisal-Antique Gold-Jewelry		
Mrs. Lagerwall Apt. 3610	154 194	$2,000	$800,000	$802,000
Mrs. Nelson Apt. 2211	156	None	$19,000	$19,000
Mrs. Studner Apt. 1212	166	None	None	None
Mrs. Colt Apt. 2101-06	172	$7,500	$4,000 1-Ring Value Unknown	$11,500
Mr. Silverman Apt. 1516	173	Unknown	$3,100	$3,100
Mr. Akston Apt. 912	175	Unknown	$4,100	$4,100
Mrs. Uris Apt. 1407	178	None	None	None

Name	Box Number	Cash Taken	Jewelry Taken	Total
Mr. Rosenhaus Apt. 3011	180	Unknown	$103,920	$102,920.
Mr. Kulukundis Apt. 1107	184	None	$400,000.	$400,000.
Mrs. Levian Apt. 2304	185	$15,000	None	$15,000.
Mr. Gould Apt. 1702	186	$2,200.	$1,000	$3,200.
Mrs. Rogers Apt. 1802	190	$2,000	None	$2,000.
Mr. Mailman Apt. 2311	191	None	None	None
Mrs. Pearson Apt. 1007	192	None	None	None
Mrs. Hirsch Apt. 2204	193	None	$2,300	$2,300
Mrs. Friedman Apt. 2311	203	$6,724	Unknown	$6,724

The Above Persons Are Cooperative Tenants

Name	Box Number	Cash Taken	Jewelry Taken	Total
Mrs. Salabert Suite 1425	152	None	None	None
Mrs. Lea Caplan Suite 1308	155	None	$7,000	$7,000
Mr. Kravis Suite 1129-30	171	None	$375,000	$375,000
Mrs. Sherover Suite 1906-07	174	None	$100,500	$100,500
Mr. Crowley Suite 3506	40	$500	$500	$500.00

The Above Persons Are Transient Guests

Name	Box Number	Cash Taken	Jewelry Taken	Total
Dorothy Weinberg Nosegay Florist	9	$128.70	None	$128.70

314

Name	Box Number	Cash Taken	Jewelry Taken	Total
Florence Read Miller Ticket Agency	43	$1,991		$1,991.00
Helen Prestano Pierre Newstand	170	None	None	None
J. Ganecey Night Auditor	61	None	None	None
Michael Durcos Assistant Manager Hotel Pierre	157	$300.00	$400.00	$700.00
James Bennett Asst. to the President-Hotel Pierre	167	$2,800	$400.00	$3,200.00
Rudolph Honsch Asst. Manager Hotel Pierre	153	$1,500.	None	$1,500.00
Hotel	A B C 202 198 5	$12,075.11	None	$12,075.11

The Above Are Hotel Employees and Concessionaires

THE BELOW BOXES WERE BROKEN INTO; HOWEVER THEY WERE NOT ASSIGNED TO ANYONE AND WERE EMPTY

31	115	159
55	149	160
60	150	162
106	151	176
112	158	205

Recapitulate

Total Number of Boxes broken into:		55
	A. Cooperative Tenants	21
	B. Transient Guests	5
	C. Employees and Concessionaires	14
	D. Empty Boxes	15
Property Taken:		
	A. Cash Loss	$72,618.81
	B. Jewelry Loss	$1,877,720.00

SEARCH WARRANTS OBTAINED

No. 1 Search of 1967 Ford Galaxie
License VFM-559 N.J.
Car used by Soricho Nalo

No. 2 Premises 946 Anderson Avenue, Bronx, New York
Soricho Nalo's Residence

No. 3 Premises 534 West 50th Street
Apartment owned by Soricho Nalo

No. 4 Safe Deposit Box-Number 4834 & Number 1278
First National City Bank-86th Street & Broadway
Boxes in name of Sam Ballo-(Soricho Nalo)
and George Gogonis (Friend of Sam Nalo)

No. 5 Manufactures Hanover Trust Company
Box-953 and Box 979
Safe Deposit Box keys found on Soricho Nalo
at time of arrest.

No. 6 Chase Manhattan Bank
511 Gramstan Avenue, Mt. Vernon
Box 242
Safe Deposit Box key found on Soricho Nalo
at time of arrest

PROPERTY RECOVERED

Item	Quantity	Description
Diamonds	2	Round Diamond-Wt. 1.88 & 1.62 cts.
Diamonds	70	Round & Triangle-Total wt. 14.63 cts.
Diamonds	3	Pear Diamond-Wt. 2.36-2.41-3.21 cts.

316

Item	Quantity	Description
Diamonds	2	Emerald cut diamonds-Wt-12.09-6.65 cts.
Diamonds	3	Round diamonds 4.00-emeral cut diamond 11.86-Oval Cut 5.75
Diamonds	21	Round diamonts-Total Wt-22.39 cts.
Diamonds	173	Round and marquise-Total Wt-57.79 cts
Blue Star Sapphire	1	Cabb. Shape-32.90 cts.
Diamond bracelet	1	Plat. Containing 119 diamonds (Belongs to Kulakundas)
Necklace	1	Plat. containing 114 diamonds (Belongs to Rosenkaus)
Diamond Bracelet	1	Plat. containing 267 diamonds (Belongs to Rosenkaus)
Necklace	1	Plat. containing 214 diamonds (Belongs to Kravis)
Bracelet	1	Plat. containing 136 diamonds (Belongs to Kulakundas)
Necklace	1	Plat. containing 140 diamonds (Belongs to Rosenhaus)
Bracelet	1	Plat. containing 106 diamonds (Belongs to Kulakundas)

TOTAL VALUE OF PROPERTY RECOVERED $250,000.00

VOUCHER NO-45-19TH PRECINCT

72 M 0815

PROPERTY RECOVERED—JANUARY 8TH, 1972—948 ANDERSON AVENUE

Item	Quantity	Description
Curreny	$5,757.00	55 One Hundred Dollar Bills 6 Twenty Dollars Bills 3 Ten Dollar Bills 7 One Dollar Bills
Ring Setting	3	Three ring settings-No center stones in ring-Each ring with stones on side of center settings
Bracelet	1	One Yellow Metal Bracelet-Triple Loops in intertwined
Keys	24	Assorted keys

Item	Quantity	Description
Scale	1	One gold scale in wood box inside cardboard box
Hammer	1	One Hammer
Crowbar	1	One Crowbar
Wig	1	One Man's Black Wig

Currency	Voucher No. 51	19th Precinct
Jewelery	Voucher No. 52	19th Precinct
Wig	Voucher No. 60	19th Precinct
Hammer Crowbar	Voucher No. 110	19th Precinct

PROPERTY TURNED IN TO F.B.I. IN DETROIT

Louis C. Peppo
167-23 Comstock Street
Lavonia, Michigan

Turned in the below property to the Federal Bureau of Investigation in Detroit.

Jewelry valued at approximately $750,000.00

Property identified as that of Mrs. Gabrielle Lagerwall

Property in possession of F.B.I.

CAR RECOVERED—COLLSIUM GARAGE—59TH STREET

1967 Ford Galaxie

White

License No.	VFM-559 N.J.
Serial No.	7E55C146601
Recovered:	January 7th, 1972
Voucher No:	61- 20th Precinct
	72 M 0118V

318

Ira Berkow, sports columnist and feature writer for the *New York Times*, was born in Chicago in 1940 and was graduated from Miami University (Oxford, Ohio) and the Medill Graduate School of Journalism, Northwestern University. He is the author of eight books, including the best-selling *Red: A Biography of Red Smith*. He lives with his wife in New York City.